RECOMMENDATIONS FOR CHAT REPUBLIC

Chat Republic takes well-aimed (and well deserved) pot shots at cliché traders and mediocrity mongers. Read it and be enlightened. And reassured. And inspired.

—Johann Xavier, Chief Financial Officer, Saatchi & Saatchi Asia-Pacific & Greater China

Packed with anecdotes and stories about social media, this book can serve as a very useful introduction for those still sitting on the fence. Angelo Fernando correctly states that 'to refuse to chat is an invitation to others to take control.' Here he offers an accessible and engaging text to help more people participate in social media and have their voice heard.

—Emanuel Rosen, Author, The Anatomy of Buzz Revisited

Chat Republic is a must-read for anyone hoping to have a shadow of a chance at being heard through all of the chatter! This is the culture we are creating every day with every click, "like", post, and tweet...and Angelo does a brilliant job of making sense of how advancements in technologies are so intertwined with our daily lives in language and with stories that will catch you up to speed quickly if you thought keeping your head in the sand would make it all go away. Chat Republic will surely evoke your thinking.

—Cyndi Laurin, PhD. Founder of Guide to Greatness, LLC and author of bestselling *"Catch!"* and *"The Rudolph Factor"*

In the past it took men like Winston Churchill to use their gravitas and clout to stir the masses; today it takes 140 characters. Chat Republic is the lexicon of that social language used by today's digital Churchills. The book provides the origins, applications and parables of its emergence, power and influence. Read it, apply it and rule the world!

—Derrick Mains, President, Youchange

In a socially integrated era, this book is timely intervention for two types of people: those who express their conviction as a mere trend statement, and aren't fully committed to its potential, and for the antediluvians oblivious to the impact social media will have on their lives.

—Thayalan Bartlett, COO, JWT Indonesia

Throughout history, communication has often tried to give a voice to the voiceless. Angelo understands what makes these voices come together on social media. Chat Republic is a clarion call for the new revolution.

—Silvia Cambie, Expert on social media inside large organisations and author of International Communications Strategy

The unique power social media, of honing in to reach real human beings and build unique communities, has not been explored in depth until now. Communications expert Angelo Fernando provides the definitive look at how to get out of the "noise" and into real conversations.

—Pat Elliott, Journalist, Cancer Survivor, Patient Advocate

CHAT REPUBLIC

HOW SOCIAL MEDIA DRIVES US TO BE
HUMAN 1.0 IN A WEB 2.0 WORLD,
AND WHAT IT MEANS FOR BUSINESS,
POLITICS, AND THE REST OF US

ANGELO FERNANDO

Copyright © 2013 by Angelo Fernando

All rights reserved. No portion of this book may be reproduced, stored in a retrieval system, or transmitted in any form by any means – mechanical, electrical, photocopy, audio or video recording, scanning, photo-blogging etc. without prior written permission of the publisher and author. Brief quotations, however, may be used in articles, blogs, reviews, podcasts etc.

Portions of this work have appeared in CW Magazine, and LMD magazine.

Public Radius ISBN 978-0-9893380-0-4

Cover Illustration: Russell Miranda
www.chatrepublic.net

Please purchase only authorized electronic versions, and do not subscribe or promote electronic piracy. Your support of the author's rights is appreciated.

Printed in the United States of America
04 18 13

To Tanu, Aaron and Nadia who, unbeknownst to them, have shaped many of these ideas in this book.

To my mom and dad
who showed me the importance of being analog, first.

Mary

As the first person who knew about this, at SRE you can put this on your bookshelf - after you read it, that is.

Good Luck in your next phase

— Angelo

CONTENTS

Preface Zip It Up!   vii

Introduction Why Don't We Chat?   xi

Part I Push-2-Talk   1

  1. Talk On the Street   3
  2. Just Chatting   15
  3. Community as a Fire-pit   21
  4. News-speak 3.0   31
  5. Speaking Out of Turn   39
  6. Less Noise. More Curation   49
  7. Human Transponders   57
  8. Citizen Mo   63

Part II Link Love   73

  9. Talk Like a Wikipedian   75
  10. If These Press Releases Could Talk   85
  11. The Revolution Will Be Uploaded   93
  12. Voices On   103
  13. Bathed in Buzz   111

14.	Link Love	119
15.	Amateurs With Microphones	127
16.	Crowd-sourcing Ideas (Managers not Required)	135

Part III Chatter Boxes — 145

17.	Texting Under the Influence	147
18.	OMG! The State Department's On Facebook!	153
19.	Low-hanging Fruitcake	163
20.	Shut-up and Communicate	177
21.	Talking Like Humans	183
22.	Your Podcasting Voice	193
23.	Rethinking Digital Storytelling	201
24.	Can You Hear Me...Now?	209
25.	Your Chapter	223

Afterword — 225

Bonus Material — 229

1.	It takes a village (and a smart phone)	231
2.	You spoke. We listened	235
3.	A case for a Real-Time, 'Machine Readable' Democracy	239

Acknowledgements — 243

Notes — 245

Preface

ZIP IT UP!

It all began with a large FedEx envelope. It arrived at my door while I was toiling away at my day job in marketing,

I had ignored it for a few days, and when I opened it, it turned out to be a 'cease and desist' letter from a law firm representing Young and Rubicam (Y&R) advertising in New York. If you have never had the good fortune to receive one of these passive-aggressive pieces of correspondence, let me tell you it has the same effect as finding the severed head of a racehorse on the pillow next to you one morning. Ok, *The Godfather* comparison is a slight exaggeration. But you know the feeling, when you suddenly become aware that a huge unseen power has you in its sights. It makes the hair on the back of your neck do a weird break dance.

How had I landed in this mess?

My experience was not very different from that of tens of thousands of people at that time. We felt the mad rush of entrepreneurship, grabbed a shovel, and claimed our patch of land in this new frontier. In 1999, I was still finding my feet in the U.S., having migrated four years before that, leaving behind a career in advertising in Sri Lanka. The agency life at Ogilvy and Mather, and J. Walter Thompson was still tugging at my sleeve, my mind was still saturated with branding and marketing. Like many digital immigrants setting up 'homesteads' in cyberspace, I purchased my first domain name, www.brandbuzz.com, and posted my ideas about the advertising industry, adding some of my articles that were being published in a business magazine. A fun experiment! I didn't expect thousands of page hits. I didn't even know if I had an audience. I thought Brand Buzz had quite a nice ring to it. But I did get one big hit. It was more like one big headache!

Apparently Brand Buzz was the name of a relatively unknown digital arm of Y&R (which for some inexplicable reason had not laid claims to the domain). The godfathers had been quickly alerted that someone was squatting on their real estate. The two-page letter from the lawyers suggested that I pack up my shovels and leave. The basis for their cease-and-desist seemed ridiculous—that my content could seriously damage their client's brand. Y&R at that time had slick websites that comprised thousands of pages, probably put together by highly paid webmasters. Me? I was not even a registered company. I won't bore you with my exchanges with the law firm, but we eventually settled, with what seemed like a fair exchange for the domain and my time.[1]

FAN BOYS NOT INVITED!

So what did I do to ruffle the feathers of a mighty ad agency? According to them, I had been not just usurping the domain name (they didn't not use the term 'cyber-squatting' then), I was appropriating the language that only certain people were permitted to use. In other words, how could I, one guy with a funny accent, be qualified to talk about segmentation and positioning, brand voice and strategy, the stuff that Madison Avenue had laid claim to for decades? I was hacking into their space, a one-to-many communication business that had been humming along just fine. A fan boy from the hoi polloi was persona non grata in this new frontier of marketing and media. The World Wide Web was on a first-come, first-served basis; some saw it as a vast white space waiting to be filled with logos and taglines. Outsiders could go tell their stories somewhere else. I wasn't the only one being asked to get off the lawn.

In early 2011, a folk artist from Vermont decided to silk screen T-shirts in his garage. Bo Muller-Moore grew Kale, so he decided to promote it with the slogan 'Eat More Kale' on the t-shirts. No big deal, you'd think. There are many similar 'Eat More' promotions. 'Eat More Cheese' is a website hosted by some folks from Wisconsin, a state known for its cheese. There's a blog promoting trout fishing called (what else?) 'Eat More Trout' and so on. So it was a bit of a surprise when Bo received a cease-and-desist letter from a sandwich fast food chain known as Chick Fil-A. Its slogan: "Eat Mo Chikin." (The folksy spelling of chicken is everywhere on its marketing communication. The company also owns Eatmorechicken.com and Eatmorchikin.com.) Bo was as unhappy with this as I was, and his case is still being fought in a space where the most conversations take place today—on social networks.

This kind of 'scorched-earth policy'[2] by big brands toward fans, content creators, and 'curators' (a word that wouldn't be used for another decade) had to backfire, motivating a wide swath of those people on the edges who indulge in such things as mash-ups of *Star Wars* episodes,[3] parodies of television commercials,[4] unauthorized *Harry Potter* sequels,[5] music sites devoted to independent bands, music-sharing and online coupons. By putting up high walls, regulating, or criminalizing any nascent online creativity, Big Business has been having the opposite effect—fuelling our desire to resort to newer forms of storytelling. They told us to shut up or take our chatter outside, but were unwittingly giving us permission to enlarge the conversation.

And for that, we ought to thank them!

A LEVELED PLAYING FIELD

Today, we don't need authorization or domains to make ourselves heard. Not that the 'Chinese walls' have all crumbled. But while organizations and countries do continue to limit the chatter, we now have ways to pierce those walls, when needed. The playing field has been reasonably leveled.[6] As you will see, there are plenty of ways to connect with audiences through digital or analog means.

The ease of using social media has—heaven forbid!—turned everyone into a potential PR machine. The Web 1.0 experience, the 'text-only' Web that many people were used to, quickly turned into a many-to-many, interactive Web 2.0 world.[7] It has become what the original inventor of the Web, Tim Berners-Lee called the Read/Write Web. He noted that "the idea of the Web as interaction between people is really what the Web is…a collaborative space where people can interact."[8] A place where we all have a voice.

Forget the geeky, Web 1.0 and Web 2.0 stuff. If there has been a shift, I like to think of it as tilting the Web from a place where people who once said 'shut up and go away,' to a place where they beg us to 'send us a tweet.' From 'Buzz Off' to 'Like Us!'

Introduction

WHY DON'T WE CHAT?

Social media in this organization? Ha, ha ha!
You want me to approve employees using Facebook and Twitter?
Over my dead body!

You probably were part of a similar discussion. Perhaps you were broaching the subject, or were the one who alerted the boss that a few people in the organization were tweeting about its products, commenting on the poor customer service, or just bragging. So you wanted to initiate a social media strategy, and were asked, politely, to back off.

The pushback is typical. It comes from those who require employees to put their heads down, shut off all distracting communication devices, and focus on their work. The assumption is that only certain people ought to be communicating on behalf of the organization. That kind of skepticism is not unusual at the outset.[1]

Social media is not the only way to hold conversations in today's workplace, but it is certainly one that is broadening the conversation in a way that no other initiative or tool has done before. (Think newsletters, or company handbooks of old). Best of all, the use of social media does not depend on an expensive top-down initiative to gain adoption. Employees will take to it with or without management's blessing. It therefore poses some sort of threat, at least to those who once controlled the conversations that took place within and without the organization.

As study after study has revealed, the use of social media challenges traditional, ingrained ideas about marketing and brand management. This can be maddening as it is exciting since it also brings new opportunities for organizations to understand customers, and be able to forge strong, instant connections. Many organizations with a legacy of doing business the old way, face-to-face, are discovering how to update their peer-to-peer, B2B and B2C communications. Avon, for instance, a company founded by a travelling book salesman, stumbled on one of the earliest ways of using social networks to sell products via word-of-mouth—in 1886. The telephone had been invented a decade earlier, but was not commercially viable. The first Avon lady, Persis Foster Eames Albee travelled on horse and buggy, for heaven's sake! But today Avon is deeply engaging its customers and its Avon Ladies are using social media. [In Chapter 3, we will see how Avon, like modern research labs, is using social media-based communities to have rich conversations.]

Boeing, founded in 1916, dipped its toes into social media a few years back and quickly realized how social media could create a more intimate space for one-on-one communication. [More about Boeing's experience in Chapter 24.] Its communications director acknowledges that by engaging with social media, this "stodgy old company gets to be a little modern."

As one study by *The Harvard Business Review* put it, "Never before have companies had the opportunity to talk to millions of customers, send out messages, get fast feedback, and experiment with offers at relatively low costs." Companies that used to not chat with their customers, except through one-way advertising-based channels, are now realizing the big talk-back switch!

Of the sample, (the study was based on 2,100 subscribers of the *Review*) 54% of organizations were based in North America; 23% were in EMEA Countries (EMEA is the acronym for Europe, the Middle East and Africa); 19% were based in Asia. 25% were in marketing or strategy planning roles, 24% were in operational roles, 19% were in general management. Management and marketing are all talking, but the report also added that millions of *consumers* now have the ability to chat among each other; they are criticizing or recommending products—without the knowledge or input from a company."[2] Consumers? How dare they!

Scary? Indeed. I've heard some snickering, too. I've seen executives' eyes roll. Yet, many of these same executives are wading in. This book is for them.

I have grouped the chapters into three sections.

The first, **Push-2-Talk**, is about the friction we feel in our young Chat Republic that came into existence with the Internet's ability to amplify signals, and create both knowledge and noise.

The second, **Link Love**, is about being able to forge relationships with a few clicks, is so much a part of what we do. But it moves beyond chatter to the realms of crowd-sourcing, PR, customer service and even revolutions.

The third section, **Chatter Boxes**, focuses on what happens when we get carried away by our ability to have conversations and tell stories. We will see how listening in, or at least tuning in, to these conversations is such an important business practice, and why social media tools make it that much easier.

The good news is that organizations are turning the ship around, albeit very slowly. More than three-quarters of those surveyed in the *Review* study said they are either currently using social media channels (58%) or preparing to launch social media initiatives (21%). Most organizations recognize that whether it is for marketing, to elicit feedback to customer service, or for product development, they need to build and nurture communities, and see why/how social media could play a part. But among the biggest obstacles that companies face when trying to create a community, a Deloitte study found that 24 percent find that it is difficult to get people to join, 30 percent have trouble keeping them engaged.[3]

But how do you bring employees on board to become active participants? You could start by tearing down the firewall between internal and external communications. This includes locating groups within earshot of each other, and rewriting job descriptions so that (a) people don't come up with that twentieth century phrase "I'm not paid to do that" and (b) the new jobs don't ignite turf wars.

PepsiCo addresses just that problem in its internal newsletter. It essentially came to the conclusion, that thousands of employees who are not in PR or marketing could be brand ambassadors. [In Chapter 4, I discuss why archaic one-way information strategies backfire.]

NO MORE JARGON

Not every organization might be ready for this structural renovation, for an attitude adjustment to loosen up. Many I know of are still slowly coming around; they 'get' social media and see it as an integral part of their operations.

I have had the opportunity of working in the trenches of three industries that wrestle with how to improve communication: advertising, marketing, and education. I have interviewed hundreds of managers about audience perceptions, targeting, branding, and digital communications and they come across great chit-chatting in-between meetings, or over coffee. But no sooner than the meeting begins, when they are in 'presentation mode,' the jargon tumbles out.[4] Before you know it they are tripping over synergistic deliverables that circle back to bleeding edge strategic initiatives, striking out at core competencies that go after low-hanging fruit!

It never ceases to amaze me why some think it's cool to bludgeon us with language that no one but their inner circle gets—'BS in a ball gown' as someone aptly called it. On occasion (especially when I am not on their payroll), I would ask them "could you say that in English for someone who is not from your industry?"—an euphemism for "you're talking crap, dude!" Here's the funny thing. I never get pushback. No one throws my microphone out of the window. I've come to this conclusion: Professionals *yearn* for permission to speak like humans. Many communicators don't give them that space.

On the other side, most employees, even the ones *not officially* in communication, know spin and geek-speak when they encounter it. But they cannot slap their manager on her wrists and ask for a revised version. They simply snicker into their coffee and move on. The sad thing is that poor communication, apart from it offending us or losing our attention affects the bottom line.

Maybe, just maybe, we could return to those simple conversations we once had.

Maybe we could go outside and chat!

OUR NOISY REPUBLIC

What's the matter with us humans who can never stop chatting? Whereas we once kept our thoughts to ourselves, or if at all we shared an opinion we only mentioned it in one place, we now never seem to be able to keep our traps shut! What's more, we add commentary to other people's ideas, ranting about news stories and engaging in chatroom discussions on topics we are not even experts on. It's easy to dismiss all this as meaningless chatter, because some of it is.

But when you think about it, chatting is integral to our social fabric and a form of governance that is of the people, by the people—the very underpinnings of a republic.

A republic is indeed a noisy place, but therein lies its value. Absent the noise, if people did not generate ideas and talk back to each other, they would not be able to evaluate the best leaders, the best systems. Digital media and social media did not invent the mechanisms of feedback, even though some like to make it seem so. These many-to-many channels have taken us back to the banter and bustle of a bazaar; the friction and friendship of a schoolyard.

Our Republic of Chatter is a very young place with deep and diverse conversations; our constitution is a work in progress. Social media is the pervasive 'software' we use to hammer out the constitution.

In the chapters that follow, I will urge you to put your inhibitions (and your avatars) aside and dive in.

We move from public to private and back again in ways that weren't possible in an era when public and private media, like radio and the telephone, used different devices and different networks.*

—Clay Shirky

---

* *Cognitive Surplus: Creativity and Generosity in a Connected Age,* Penguin Press HC, June 2010.

1

TALK ON THE STREET

We must all move on the ground now and not talk to one another over Facebook.
History is made on the streets, not on the Internet.[1]

—Wael Ghonim

In 2011, the word 'Re-tweet' officially entered the lexicon, being one of the words included in the Concise Oxford Dictionary (OECD).[2] "What took it so long?" I hear you ask! Truth is, the speed of adoption by dictionaries always trails usage. It always causes a bit of an uproar. In 1911, when the OECD began publishing, its editors, two brothers, stated that "we admit colloquial, facetious, slang, and vulgar expressions with freedom, merely attaching a cautionary label."[3]

Whether you took the leap and registered your Twitter handle or not, you can't ignore the impact of people yapping away in 140-character bursts. Public chatter mixed with private conversations are now everywhere, thanks to social networks that serve as conduits for whatever happens, even something largely outside our network. It is the great babbling bazaar now empowered by a mash-up of media that is, by default, open, abundant, and free.[4]

Trouble is, conversations intended for one audience in this bazaar now spill over to another. It used to not be like that. The telephone was originally a point-to-point tool. Outsiders could only listen in by invitation. (The 'party line', also known as the multi-party line, enabled two or more families to share a phone line). Or spillover took place by accident, when there was a cross-connection. But with wider penetration of mobile phones, the telephone, is no longer an exclusive one-to-one device. Conference calling, email and texting, now core features of phones, have turned it into a quick broadcasting, or at least a one-to-many tool. More than 432 million people regularly log into Facebook from a mobile device.[5] In June 2011, people were sending out 200 million tweets a day![6] It is no surprise then that the mobile phone has contributed to so much of online conversations.

Conversations on the street don't always require a media platform, but having one helps. The organizers of Occupy Wall Street recognize that boundary-less, platform-agnostic environments are the potting soil of a vibrant grassroots community. As such they encourage broader, deeper dialog. "At the square (Zuccotti Park, New York), everyone is empowered to become mediators, to ask about each others' needs and boundaries, to communicate honestly, and to learn to accept conflict as possible points of community construction," notes Suzahn E, talking of the movement's chaos and interaction as a necessary experiment.[7]

Street talk is paradoxically vulgar and socially appropriate to its environment. If you happen to overhear a group of teenagers in a parking lot, the language sounds coarse. Gangs, at one end of the spectrum or a group of men, at the other, use language that is coded and sounds foreign. The reason? The language they use caters to their niche, so even if a person is barely outside that niche, it makes no sense. Graffiti, likewise, makes no sense to ordinary citizens who would never use a marker pen on a bathroom wall, but would happily send out a public tweet lacking etiquette, bracketed with hash-tags. That the cryptic 140-character message reads like a snippet of nonsense doesn't bother us, even if it shows up on our social media dashboard. We tune out graffiti the same way we tune out irrelevant noise on a Twitter stream. The point is, the lingua franca of the street is both private and public, and its crossover does connect us to the crowd.

NOMADIC MEDIA

Hobos during the Great Depression used their own hobo codes or 'hoboglyphs', which formed a secret language to communicate with other hobos about the availability of food, or water, and sometimes alert them about a hostile neighborhood or potential work. Oddly enough, the digital age has devised its own hobo-like signage for nomadic bands of urbanites. The Free Wi-Fi signs cropping up in small town coffee shops and restaurants are one part of it.[8] Yelp and Foursquare serve a similar purpose. Digital nomads spend a considerable amount of time advising other nomads with codified 'check-ins' on Foursquare, for instance. Yelp, founded in 2004, is a review and recommendation service that lets people in the United States, Canada, the UK, Ireland, the Netherlands, France, Germany and Austria share and access opinions, reviews and ratings of service providers in their local area. It had 50 million unique visitors in June 2011.[9] Because mobile-equipped nomads make good candidates for chatting with other citizens, Yelp taps into these mobile thumb tribes to speak out about good restaurants, bad products, and easy ways around airports. In 2010, the Yelp site recorded 27 percent of check-ins that came from an iPhone app.[10]

Then there are the actual analog signs people put up in the form of QR codes. This codified language may at first seem to have little value because encryption, by definition, serves to limit access. But smart phones can easily read these signs, and connect people to common interests.

Social activists have devised their own system of signs and spaces to hold conversations. During the anti-globalization movement of the 1990s, the so-called People's Global Action Network facilitated communication with its 'affinity groups' using information technology. These diverse groups did not know each other, but they were well informed and well-coordinated. (The mantra then was "membership

Hobo signs, used during the Great Depression of the 1930's, were left by migrants to communicate among each as they sought temporary work and food in new towns.

equals participation."[11])

'A PULSING INFOSPHERE OF ENORMOUS BANDWIDTH'

The babbling bazaar we left behind had something that we don't find in its replacement—the echo chamber. It was here that we engaged in debate or took collective action.

Paul de Armond describes how in 2004, the Direct Action Network, or DAN, improvised a network for street communication among anti-WTO activists. "Protesters in the street with wireless Palm Pilots were able to link into continuously updated Web pages giving reports from the streets. Police scanners monitored transmissions and provided some warning of changing police tactics. Cell phones were widely used."[12]

When this network was detected and brought down, they switched to Nextel-made cell phones. A Linux-based service known as TXTMob was used. The service worked both ways, enabling activists to register with message groups so as to receive updates, but also to be able to broadcast messages to members of their group via their cell phones. Journalists with Indymedia monitored TXTMobs as an information source, and used their own TXTMobs group as an additional way to distribute news.[13] Armond explains how they broke into talk groups of eight people in each subgroup. One of them overlapped with another talk group, helping one group communicate with the others, fast. He sums it up this way, describing how the hoi polloi find ways to route around obstacles to their communication on the street. "Floating above the tear gas was a pulsing infosphere of enormous bandwidth, reaching around the planet via the Internet."

To think that Twitter had not even been born!

GENERATION TXT

The anti-globalization movement relied on Meetups to inform and coordinate its actions. The Meetup site, which had been founded in 2001, made it dead easy for anyone to pull together a local group or set up face-to-face meetings. Meetups provided a backbone for people who felt compelled to show up on a street for a one-off event. It was a classic case of digital-to-analog community building, closing the gap of time and distance that often hobbles event planning. But it also provided a discussion space for what its members believed in, what they were in opposition to, and for clarification, etc. The World Wide Web was giving people a first taste of what people could accomplish when they were a few degrees of separation from each other.

No phenomenon of street coordination demonstrated this better than the Flash Mob. The use of the word 'mob' in social media might make some people wince, since it conjures up images of mindless crowd behavior. But there is no getting around the reality that it is something that happens spontaneously (or makes it seem that way) and it involves a crowd. Many streets and public spaces in metropolitan centers are magnets for crowds, so it's natural for this flash mob expression to manifest itself there.

Now that Facebook and Twitter have been around for more than five years, the ability to communicate with clusters of strangers and mobilize crowds seems an accepted feature of crowd communication. People seem to forget that Short Messaging Service, or SMS, filled this need not to long before. In September 2000, ordinary citizens staged a protest in London, communicating via SMS on mobile phones, and CB radios in taxicabs. They were protesting the sudden rise in the price of petrol. Throughout one week, a text messaging service was used for broadcasting news and media alerts, creating ad hoc mobile communication teams, growing subscribers, sending out event reminders, and sending 'strategic field alerts'. It also allowed flash mobbing.[14]

Soon after that, in January 2001, tens of thousands of Filipinos showed up on Epifanio de los Santos Avenue, a street known as Edsa. It was one of the earliest smart mobs on such a large scale, communicating in short cryptic text messages such as "Go 2EDSA, wear blk." Howard Rheingold describes these early 'swarms' as the emergence of thumb tribes—young people who are extremely good at texting, and using it to bypass slower, entrenched infrastructure such as postal service and railroads. The "legend of 'Generation Txt' was born" on the streets of Manila, he says.[15] Still, the Internet complements and reinforces, rather than replaces face-to-face interaction, as we have seen in the Occupy movement.

HASH-TAGS AND HISTORY

In the present Occupy Wall Street movement, the thought leaders realize the value of old media to communicate to its diverse community—a community that is semi-permanent (they live in tents and sleeping bags, after all) as well as transient (many arrived from other cities and stayed for a short while). There has been a lot of debate whether these communities would have come together without social media, or if social media was an add-on, not the cause. That's why, in commenting on the *Time* person of the year for 2011 being named as 'The Protestor,' Rick Engel noted that "this was not a wired revolution; it was a human one, of hearts and minds, the oldest technology of all."[16] Like the activists before them, they were organized around networks.[17]

There are more than 100 different hash-tags on Twitter in support of the Occupy Wall Street movement.[18] These include: #occupywallstreet #ows #occupywallst #occupy #occupyboston #takewallstreet #p2 #nypd. The movement is super-charged by people we might describe as being digitally savvy or digital natives. Being digital is part of their lives. So much so that providing an Internet connection in the Occupy sites is a big priority, with supporters creating mesh networks, and antennas powered by diesel generators.[19] But which medium do you think serves as a powerful way to keep incoming Occupiers and those already committed, on the same page? It is not YouTube. It is not a blog. It is something more 'old school'—a newspaper.

The effect of these voices cannot be overstated. "People who've experienced the power of having a voice will not easily go back to silence," notes Sarah Van Gelder, in the book on the Occupy movement. "People who've found self-respect will work hard to avoid a return to isolation and powerlessness…the 99% are no longer sitting on the sidelines of history—we are making history."[20]

The idea of a newspaper being published by a semi-permanent group of people underlines several interesting aspects of communicating on the street. First, it is a way of validating the space occupied by people who could, at any time by police action or a mayor's order, be evacuated. Second, it gives the semblance of a more structured organization, since people often assume that only legit, formal organizations have their own media.

STREET JOURNAL

Priscilla Grimm, a single mother who had taught herself HTML while nursing her infant daughter, is the editor of the newspaper known as the *Occupied Wall Street Journal*. (The irony is intentional, since the movement which started in Zuccoti Park in Manhattan, New

York, is just 15 minutes away from the address of the *Wall Street Journal*—a paper that often pokes fun at the movement.) Grimm is one of

Newspaper printed by the Occupy Wall Street movement

those so-called 'Occupiers' who understand the power of voice. She has a background of editing fanzines, and had previously been involved in online action to help people understand the FCC laws. She found herself drawn to the movement, and was soon recruited to edit and write for the newspaper, a broadsheet, which is now the flagship medium of the Occupy Wall Street movement. It is not however the 'official' newspaper of the movement.[21]

"At the beginning, it was a cross between a fanzine, flyer and a magazine," she said. She says that the broadsheet idea was conceived because the publishers thought that it was important to hand out a paper during marches to make it a better experience. The paper contextualizes what's happening on the street. If someone was new to the place or the movement, and was to hear chants and could not make sense of what was going on, the paper would outline the ideas of the march.

Was it ironic that a digital media person was working in old media? Not really, said Grimm. I asked her how they could go on publishing this paper, and distribute it free. Is there a sustainable model for it? How does the press get paid? Who's doing it for them? She laughed, trying not to answer the question. "They get paid. They are getting paid," she said. (The paper is printed at a press in nearby Queens, New York.) It is sustained by payments that came via donations via a Kickstarter campaign, online. Interestingly, it publishes *Occupy Gazette* through a sister movement called N+1. It is a magazine about politics, literature, and culture. It also publishes *Indig-Nación*, a Spanish-language paper of the 'affinity group' associated with the movement.[22]

As for people like Grimm who amplify the voices on the street, they are working pro bono. "We are not getting paid," she says speaking of the handful of editors, designers and copy editors. "I just paid four months of rent by way of my tax return. I'm a single parent. We are bringing in enough money to take care of printing costs, but it is an all-volunteer effort by individuals who give of their time for this messaging and communications."

Is she optimistic? "I am very hopeful," she says. "What's going to make a sea change is when we have more people on the street than cops. You don't get to change the world that often. The way you do that is that you need to educate people as to what needs to be changed and why."[23]

BULL HORNS VS HUMANS

Bull horns and electronic speakers are typically prohibited in public spaces, such as in Zucotti Park, in New York. They require special permits, which are rarely given. So the Occupiers didn't miss a step, and mobilized a great device to keep the dialog on the street, and indeed the vociferous debates, from being muzzled. It was a creative way to not just get around the ban, but amplify and transmit their voices that resonated (literally) with those joining the movement. We will return to this in Chapter 15, where we will see how the Occupy Wall Street movement taps into the ultimate gadget—the human voice.

2

JUST CHATTING

Life is visceral. Get off the computer and connect with real people.[1]
—JOHN JAY

Voices Off! It's a common exhortation of teachers in school. The urge for young people to chat with and engage the person next to them is so prevalent that it sometimes seems like a problem. Yet, in a different realm, in universities, for instance, discussion with a classmate is vigorously encouraged. Double standards? Or are we as a society not sure of our stand in the world of conversations.

It gets more complicated. In many businesses that have some sort of online presence, the terms 'join the conversation' and 'start a conversation' have become a *de facto* tagline. This is probably in recognition of the fact that corporate communications has always been asymmetric—there is no talk-back button when you are spoken to via an advertisement. It's always been hard to speak to a flesh-and-blood person. Suddenly they all want us to chime in, whether it is by way of leaving comments on a blog, punching a 'like' button, or talking up a brand experience via a handful of social networks. Evidently they want our voices on!

In marketing, sensing the imbalance of power that has been shifting from the marketer to individual, brands are getting their hands dirty, engaging in rich, deep and meaningful conversations—which one might add are conversations *already* in progress.[2]

The urge to chat is a built-in feature of Homo sapiens, not some bolted-on widget we acquired with the swirl of new media. Early experiments in why we chat online, even with strangers, reveal that we are often spurred on because participation is both anonymous and disembodied.[3] Chatting is an involuntary act of humans driven to share information that stems from our survival instincts, says Emanuel Rosen. "We no longer trade information about bison hunting, but we're still programmed to do so."[4]

Chatting, and holding conversations, even between unequal partners, has been widely experimented with. Franklin D. Roosevelt began his 'Fireside Chats' in the 1930s as a means to engage citizens who had very few ways with which to know their president. They weren't chats in the true sense—they were speeches.[5] But they had a conversational quality to them. The radio, a fixture in people's living rooms, was a one-way, one-to-many medium. But the tenor of these radio communiques in which Roosevelt candidly spoke to Americans during terrible times of war, strikes, a banking crisis and the Great Depression, turned their living rooms into early chat rooms.[6] Roosevelt used these moments to keep people informed, with no holds barred.[7] It may now seem like a one-way conversation, but given the medium's limitations, it became more than that.

After his first fireside chat, which took place a few days after he got into office, Roosevelt made a request urging people, to share their views with him. The White House received thousands of letters from ordinary people who related to this conversation hub and were convinced that the president was willing to listen to them. And he did.[8]

Citizens would 'talk back' to him sending him telegrams. FRD didn't use radio to deliver a speech, but to talk.

EARLY CHAT ROOMS

With the birth of the Internet, there was an explosion of interest in two-way communication as synchronicity suddenly became possible. In the late 1980s, as people signed up to online worlds such as America Online and CompuServe, there arose something called Internet Relay Chat (IRC), a way for people who had access to computers to conduct group discussions, or one-on-one chats. IRC Networks had names such as ExpertNet, IRCGate.it, and GeekNode. These patently geeky hangouts, enabled by patching together servers, were the early digital chat rooms for people who were finding their voice. However they were chatting in text mode. Chat rooms have since evolved to include graphical user interfaces, moderated (virtual) rooms, and the ability to chat on dozens of public online sites. A company called Meebo provided a chat application that allowed employees to chat behind a company firewall.[9]

Then there was Second Life, the 3D virtual world which was all the rage around 2007. Cyber-geeks signed up as 'residents,' and clamored about the immersive experience they found, 'inworld'. Major corporations like IBM, Reuters, and Toyota used it to conduct training, product simulation, and one-on-one marketing. The bloom is off the rose in Second Life, but it is still in existence. Engaging in one-on-one means going avatar-to-avatar, with people in real life taking on proxies and persona. There is even software for residents who are visually impaired to communicate using a screen reader, or through self-voicing with built-in speech synthesis. This rich conversation space, while it may have been great then, has been sometimes described as a glorified chat room. With the rise of Twitter and Sina Weibo (the Twitter equivalent in China), it's easy to see what makes online chat zones successful: they need to be open (as far as API's are concerned) so as to be accessible from any platform, through any hack; they also should not be process-heavy.[10] Chat rooms since then have been simplified, and we now take video chats and chatting via text messaging for granted. There is even a 'disposable multimedia chat room' known as TinyChat, where someone could sign on with a Twitter username. These tiny chat rooms could be embedded in blogs or regular websites. The point is, chatting is now a common online feature; to join the conversation requires very little urging.

While there is a definite upside of chatting as the new 'social' virtue, the media that enable these conversations don't automatically deepen the engagement. Sometimes, as Roman Krznaric observes, the "quick-fire and efficient online talk—which is more about exchanging information than emotions—threatens to send the quality of conversation back to the Middle Ages."[11]

Talk shows or chat shows on television and radio were also pioneered as a way for the audience—a guest invited into the studio, say—to talk back. The coupling of the telephone and the radio refined this relationship between speaker and listener.

For a few months in 2010, I co-hosted a radio talk show in the Phoenix area, a show focused on entrepreneurship, sustainability, and social media. (More about this in Chapter 24.) It was called *Your Triple Bottom Line* (www.your3bl.com). The chat format can be complicated. The host needs to be able to do more than keep a conversation going. He needs to encourage disagreement, listen to what callers and guests are saying—and not saying—and be prepared to wander into topics not planned for. But today, radio is able to combine much more than a transmission tower and a telephone to start a chat. In our show,

Derrick Mains (my co-host) and I used a variety of social media channels in real-time. We could, for instance, hold multiple conversations with online and on-air listeners via Twitter, Facebook, and a blog. Mains could juggle these sidebar conversations effortlessly.[12] There is nothing worse than a talk show where the host is doing nothing more than ranting—which is a technique many political talk shows employ. The 'conversation' is more lecture and rant in the guise of a dialog.

The rise of activism, and its use of bottom-up, de-centralized communication, has begun to reveal new developments in how to hold conversations.

Today social media provides several channels for the audience to talk back. The number of talk-back channels will continue to increase and mature. But apart from providing new ways to entertain more voices, the real value will be in how the conversation can shift between online and offline, not just for radio shows but for 'boring' exchanges between a government and its citizens, between a school board and parents. These communicators will need to closely monitor a suite of chat venues as one government department in Australia has realized.[13]

Indeed chatting has changed. There are newer tools with which to hold our modern day fireside chats. In January 2012, Google announced a Fireside Hangout with President Obama. "Here is your chance to ask President Obama a question about the issues that are on your mind," said the White House YouTube channel about this. It promised that President Obama would answer top-voted questions, live from the West Wing.[14] Just broadcasting? Or just chatting? There are powerful ways to understand what our audiences have to say. If we only tune in.

3

COMMUNITY AS A FIRE-PIT

We now host conversations and get the hell out of the way.[1]
—Tyler Fonda

The word 'community' gets slung around a lot in our online and offline worlds, doesn't it? (Google it and you'll get more than five million results.) Podcasters don't have listeners; they have communities. Non-profit organizations don't aspire to have thousands of followers on Twitter; they reach out to 'peeps' like you and me who act individually, or in consort, as a community of advisers or evangelists. Media organizations, book stores and political organizations have similar needs. They want us to bond, and speak out as a *community*.

I get that. I'm sure you do too.

While social media could sometimes feel like a fire hose, online communities powered by social media could be a fire pit. Social media has been fawning over the word community. New job titles such as 'Social Media Community Manager' quickly appeared. It was one of Kiplinger's (a publisher of financial advice and business forecasts) 'ten jobs that didn't exist ten years ago.' On Quora, the popular site for answers, the question was posed about how much should a Social Media Community Manager make. The answer was between $35,000 and $40,000 a year at minimum. Here's how someone put it:

> For larger brands with established social profiles where their social strategy is part of their brand identity (I would *think we are moving from social media manager role to a brand manager or curator*) - a role that is more about defining a brand, I could see a salary range north of $80,000.²

But the word 'community' is fraught with problems. It is overused, in the same way the word 'strategy' was abused in the 1990s. In a lot of discussions, you could substitute 'communities' for 'audiences.'

I like to think of a community as a group of people gathered around a fire pit, swapping stories and building strong relationships, without ever needing to reach for an iPhone. Or a group of people sitting around the village water pump, informing a newcomer about where he could go to get supplies, probing him for 'news' about the town he came from, and checking out his credentials in a friendly way. The visitor picks up a twig and sketches on the sand a map of his village, and his family tree. His simple 'infographic' draws them closer. His 'stylus' does not need a tablet to enable knowledge sharing. The people around get it. They thank the fellow, give him a bag of corn for his insight, and for 'checking in' at the pump, and go on their way. This is not to dismiss the value of technologies that give us a new kind of connective tissue, but rather to consider communities in terms of *what* gets shared, not *how*.

Building a community takes a lot more than automated invites to a Facebook fan page that takes about eight minutes to set up. I've joined, set up, and been invited to a few dozen of them over the past few years. Each one has a different dynamic. Some are clunky and badly designed, but have surprisingly great participation. So what is a community?

If you reach back to early academic discussions on something known as *asynchronous group interaction*,[3] you'll recognize that what we have today are ongoing experiments on how people gather around different fire pits and water pumps to share ideas, argue and work out solutions. We may use technology, but we are "transitive" to the Internet's communication flow. It is another way of saying that our online engagement and participation in social good is as important to the healthy workings of the Internet as it is to us.[4] We still meet strangers at the local gathering place, but the heat source and refreshment happens to be online.

CROWD-SOURCING A CURE

Pat Elliott came across one the hard way. Interpersonal communication studies explore how humans are hardwired to function as nodes through which our communication flows, and I would consider her one of these nodes. A Phoenix, Arizona-based communication professional, Elliott joined several—70 and counting, she says —online communities. As a communicator, she had run into CaringBridge, a nonprofit Web-based service that builds a community around someone facing a critical illness or undergoing treatment. But it wasn't until she was diagnosed with chronic myelogenous leukemia (CML), a rare form of cancer, that she signed on.[5] More than half a million people connect through CaringBridge every day.

These online communities are not just places where patients share small talk, and provide virtual shoulders to cry on. They are deep in conversations that are proving to be valuable to more than patients. Researchers, for instance. MIT Media Lab set up a unit called MIT Media Medicine for just this kind of knowledge sharing. It believes that patients are the most underutilized resource within the entire healthcare system. Patients! Few people think of patients as communities. It's easy to see why Six Sigma users, recruiters, or project managers, might form online communities, but there has been a recent explosion of patient communities.

In one instance, in studying Lymphangioleiomyomatosis (known as LAM), a fatal disease affecting the lungs, kidneys and lymphatics of women in their child-bearing years, MIT began looking into how these patients could connect via chat rooms and social networks. The idea was to see how these conversations could be mined for potential therapies and a cure.[6] The community site it set up, LAMsight (www.lamsight.org) enables patients to teach investigators about what researchers might be overlooking. They can ask questions of their peers and see various trends in data through pictures, graphs, and charts.

> "Social media and communities are expected to continue to play a significant role in the way in which companies are interacting with employees, customers, partners and the larger business ecosystem, thereby redefining the very edge of the corporation."
> —Ed Moran, *director of product innovation, Deloitte Services LPP*

Another group, known as the Patient Safety, Pharmacovigilance and Risk Benefit Management Group, founded in 2008 on LinkedIn, has 1,850 members. A snapshot of its activity shows that discussions on drug safety are high.[7] Even doctors and radiologists huddle together in similar communities to share knowledge. MIT believes that these unlikely communities forged between non-clinical "experts"—anthropologists and computer scientists—would pose the unconventional questions, and elicit breakthrough answers. These questions would spur innovation in medicine.[8]

More organizations will move into this kind of engagement online toward finding cures. But beyond being another "family and friends" social network, CaringBridge has given Elliott an easy way to stay in touch and form bonds with doctors, researchers, and strangers from many parts of the world. It also lets members maintain a journal and invite people in their network to visit and stay informed. By tracking back-and-forth communication, it eliminates the need to send or respond to dozens of individual e-mails or Facebook, LinkedIn, text and Twitter messages every day. "If you suddenly find yourself having to deal with something you know nothing about—like a very rare illness—it's highly likely that there's support literally at your fingertips from others who've walked in your same shoes and will share what they've learned with you," Elliott says. These people are from diverse backgrounds, with completely different world views.

COMMUNITIES OF PRACTICE

SUPPORT FOR CANCER PATIENT

Pat Elliott's illness came during the healthcare reform debate and was a topic on several blogs. The passion shown by the bloggers led her to make her own illness public. She discovered the power of community.

"The books available from my local library are out of date. The data available from the nonprofit charitable organization for my illness is out of date. The local cancer organizations don't provide extensive information on the rare forms of cancer. Through social media I've connected with fellow CML survivors and healthcare professionals who specialize in treating CML and gained access to cutting edge, real time information on how CML is treated around the world."

Social communities have another benefit, says Elliott. "My co-survivors use online groups to bring us the latest 'news' about CML before it even hits the healthcare professional media—and this is information that the mainstream media does not cover."

Online communities come in various flavors. Digg is a community for sharing and discovering content. Members of the American Society for the Prevention of Cruelty to Animals (ASPCA) community share ideas on topics ranging from pet care to animal cruelty. Or consider Freecycle.org, a global community built around sharing and re-using items. Teachers and Wikipedians form communities. As for teachers, in the U.S., their fire pit is what's known as "communities of practice" or 'CoP,' in which peer-to-peer learning opportunities are encouraged.

The Wikipedia entry for 'communities of practice,' states clearly that this is not just some online phenomenon, populating the usual

> **MIT'S NEW MEDIA MEDICINE MANIFESTO**
>
> MIT's Media Medicine lab asks the bold questions central to its knowledge sharing goals, which are also pertinent to the collaboration and knowledge in online communities.
>
> What if we could make the doctor a persistent educational presence in the patient's life, using avatars, intelligent agents and awareness systems instead of a few rushed office visits? What if we could empower ordinary people to report on outbreaks or health events in their communities, with timely information not captured by traditional health establishments?
>
> In its New Media Medicine Manifesto it sets out three principles.
> - Principle # 1: Patients are the most underutilized resource in healthcare.
> - Principle # 2: The revolution must take place in our everyday lives, not in the doctor's office or the lab.
> - Principle # 3: Information transparency, not information is the solution.

places such as discussion boards and newsgroups. But they are also found "in real life, such as in a lunch room at work, in a field setting, on a factory floor, or elsewhere in the environment."[9]

If you should venture into building a community of practice, keep in mind that communities are all about empowering people through interactions, not commerce. Social Media Community Manager positions often involve shades of brand management. When this role is engaged, there is a temptation to steer conversations by starting 'brand conversations,' because, after all, most organizations want to check the pulse of how its community is connecting with its external communication and branding. There are terrible ways to do this, and there are smart ways. The more egregious are when an organization starts a Facebook community just to create happy talk about its marketing. It goes well until, well, someone throws a grenade into the crowd after finding out the organization is engaging in double standards.

Unilever's Dove commercial came under attack on Facebook when someone noted that the same company that promoted 'beauty from within', was creating crass, misogynist advertising for its Axe brand. The community it didn't know existed came out of the woodwork to engage with the brand. Avon, on the other hand, no stranger to social marketing, lets brand talk evolve organically. At Avon Connects, (www.avonconnects.co.uk) one of its 10 online communities for its 6.4 million independent sales reps, someone asked about "Avon Branded Trolleys—Yes or No?" It received 246 replies and suggestions.[10]

PEOPLE SEEK PEOPLE, NOT PLATFORMS!

Where do you start if you want to build an online community? There are a number of online venues—also known as 'platforms'. Ning, which is the platform behind the ASPCA community, does not require Web design experience. In fact, Ning is also the platform behind a diabetes site, Tu Diabetes (www.tudiabetes.org), run by the Diabetes Hands Foundation. One of the features on this community is TuAnalyze, an application through which patients could track, analyze, and compare their Hemoglobin A1C levels.[11] Big Tent, another free community building platform, is easy to set up as well, attracting groups such as nonprofits and homeschoolers.

It is important to pick a platform that suits your organization's long-term needs, and not just be tempted to go with the look and feel of a flashy interface. I was able to set up a Ning community in less than fifteen minutes. It did not require any design or coding skills to include apps for photo sharing, a polling feature and being able to set it up for live streaming of video.

Also consider how much moderation you will need. Unlike traditional, static websites, community sites let a non-technical user take charge. But there's a flip side to this. Someone should maintain updates, and keep the site dynamic. A 2009 study by Deloitte, LLP., of more than 140 organizations involved in building online communities recommended against adopting an "if you build it, they will come" attitude.[12] Why? It needs constant maintenance and human input. Some things—human passion included—can't be fully automated.

A community after all, is more than the sum of the social media technologies you throw into the back end. In communities, as in communication (as the Deloitte report wisely noted), it's important to tap into Human 1.0. We are so enamored with the technical bells and whistles of social media that we forget that communities come together in spite of these, not because of them. The app or the device may be the onramp, but it isn't the glue that holds people together. Learning the technology of community building is a lot easier than learning people, observes Richard Millington. "Technology is an inputs-outputs process. It's easy once you know how. People aren't so robotic."[13]

It is easy to be seduced by the idea of 'instant communities.' Sometimes, as in the case of disasters or controversial issues, a spontaneous community may come together. But building a community and benefitting from a sense of community are two different things. It takes time, not apps.

In the next chapter, we will see how supplanting passion with automation is not enough.

> **WHAT DOES IT TAKE TO BUILD AND NURTURE A COMMUNITY?**
>
> - **Think micro, not mass.** Mass media went after big audiences. Social media work best with niche groups. Online communities are best when they have a personal look and feel to them.
> - **Empower users.** Provide the tools to let everyone—not just the admin person—steer the boat. Lay down some basic guidelines, but let users manage the service on their terms. They are up to the task, and want to chat to each other. About 32 percent of members in online communities post comments.[14]
> - **Don't build a silo.** It's easy to turn a community into a content dump. Ning (Ning.com) and Big Tent (Bigtent.com) let you connect the dots to other areas where people interact and engage with complementary communities. CaringBridge, for example, partners with healthcare organizations, professional groups such as the National Alliance for Caregiving and several foundations.
> - **Be social, not commercial.** It's tempting to promote products or an agenda, or to "monetize" the site with floating ads and pop-ups. Don't! Many community managers make the mistake of forcing 'brand conversations.' Focus on bonding, not branding.[15]
> - **Be open to ideas.** The community will let you know what works and what doesn't. Be open to feedback. Be prepared to re-arrange the furniture as new members with new ideas sign up. A community is always a work in progress.
> - **Assign someone to the care and feeding of the community.** 32 percent of online communities have no full-time employees assigned to them. Be part of the 68 percent!

4

NEWS-SPEAK 3.0

Woolly minded people write woolly memos, woolly letters and woolly speeches.[1]

—DAVID OGILVY

Is the marriage between newsletters and readers on the rocks? Has your external communication lost its voice? Should you kill that eNewsletter? Or reinvent it?

This is a wake-up call for a fresh voice and a new language of newsletters—something I like to call News-speak 3.0. George Orwell coined the word 'newspeak' to refer to the language of a totalitarian regime in *Nineteen Eighty-four,* a language that suppressed thought. He called this language "a tour de force which could only be carried out by a specialist," and one that would get rid of 'Oldspeak' or at least make it obsolete. Newsletter writers and publishers in a Web 2.0 environment, the new *specialists,* need to rethink newsletters as embedding the real-time voices, rather than the frozen ones, of an organization; as devices that invite thought, not leave it out.

Let me preface what I am about to say with this: I've always liked newsletters. Next to blogs, newsletters feed my writer's appetite for 'trade' information, especially those trades that don't get covered in newspapers: business, banking, advertising, education, PR and a host of others. They used to have a handmade feel to them; they felt like they were penned by real people, but they've got all dressed up now, and some of them have lost their charm.

Then there is TMI—too much information. Earlier this year, I felt I just could not cope with the torrent. It was compounded by another problem. Many newsletters were thinly veiled sales pitches. Also, it began to feel there was too much overlap, with editors mixing original content with the same stories grabbed off other sources. The invasions of cut-and-paste culture of lazy publishers. Have you had a similar experience, or is it just me? Soon I began to hit the unsubscribe button pretty hard. For those that are slow to purge me from their databases, a Google email filter does the trick!

But this is not so much about too much information, but too little relevancy. If we have embraced, or unwittingly adopted news-speak 1.0, it's time for an upgrade. Version 1.0, the *lingua franca* of corporate newsletters, employed well-crafted, jargon-infested language. Its primary goal was to push information out. It made a big—flawed—assumption that its audience was all ears; a push-to-talk experiment where one side did all the talking. Listening was optional. It quickly migrated to version 2.0 that built automatons into the delivery process: auto-responders that made it seem like someone cared. Fake humans! The reader clicked on a link and commented or checked a box indicating interest, and the pre-set software generated a message. Impressive but disgusting. In Chapter 19 we will discuss how machine language tends to creep into other forms of communications, from speeches to press releases.

You have to imagine that publishers are acutely aware of the rising 'Unsubscribes' and are working on ways to retain us. "Once you register with Knowledge@Australian School of Business you will automatically receive a fortnightly newsletter via email," says the University of New South Wales. Automatically! This used to be considered a good thing many years ago, since it showed that an organization you connected with had a system in place to stay in touch. Today, that degree of automation is not always helpful. An auto-responder cannot convey the same feeling you get when someone shoots you a thank you note after you 'follow' an organization on Twitter. We'd rather have humans not templates send us stuff.

So what does News-speak 3.0 look like? What's the secret sauce for getting people to subscribe to an e-newsletter? "The trick to building subscribers is having great content and excellent search engine optimization," says Marc Wright, of Simply Communicate, a British-based internal communications community with 18,000 registered members.[2] (I am certain Marc used 'trick' as a synonym of 'secret.') "We spend a lot of time working on the subject line to encourage readers to open us up rather than hit the delete button." Aha! Subject lines.

It's not as simple as amping up the keyword density and getting creative. The worst subject lines, cautions MailChimp, an eNewsletter company "read like headlines from advertisements you'd see in the Sunday paper. They might look more 'creative,' but their open rates are horrible." Hear! Hear! MailChimp—though I get a bit queasy about a robotic chimpanzee in charge of a database. (It dredges up that snide observation about how 'any monkey can be trained to use a word processor.') An 'Open Rate' for the un-initiated, refers to the number of emails that get clicked on, divided by how many people on the database it was sent to. It is usually tracked by a transparent image tag that tells a server each time the image loads.

In our chat republic, newsletters that adopt News-speak 3.0 are not finished products but on-ramps to broader, deeper conversations.

They are the start of back-and-forth dialogue that lets writers and editors shed their machine language persona and speak as they are. Their ideas are embedded with (and hyperlinked to) conversations with others—those readers who may even question and snipe. Newsspeak 3.0 makes a newsletter a living, breathing engagement tool, not some product to be archived. We may have a long way to go to get to this point, but it's within our reach.

YOU WIN SOME, YOU LOSE SOME

Organizations know that readers today arrive through many channels, and not just via email solicitations, as was the case a decade ago. It is easy to keep niche networks informed about what they do, which means better targeting through 'pull' practices mixed with some 'push.' Targeting improves feedback, which in turn improves the quality of the content. To refine its subscriber database, a newsletter publisher could send one link (a controversial story) to friends on Facebook, another link (a case study) could be sent out to a special-interest group on LinkedIn, and a third link (a discussion about a video) sent to a FriendFeed room. This kind of approach helps build a newsletter around the different interests of each segment, not the organization's latest award! You may lose the odd reader who reads a newsletter from front to back and sideways, but you gain better quality subscribers.

Most organizations agree that a newsletter is a great marketing tool. It is great "for soft-selling (to) build relationships with your customers, and they're great if your products have a very long sales cycle," says MailChimp. They recommend using it to 'slowly soften' customers or to make them empathize with a brand. I don't know about you, but the suggestion that one could 'soften' a customer raises my hackles. A newsletter is more than a marinade—it's a conversation starter. But using it as a marketing tool has its downsides.

For Simply, this means operating with a 'you win some, you lose some' mindset. New readers come in, and some head for the exits.

> **FIGHTING CLUTTER WITH CLUTTER?**
> Here's what this might mean to us communicators. Let's start fighting clutter with relevance. This means:
> - **Clean up your database.** Do some serious database hygiene; purge, segment, and double-check who's on your lists. Maybe people have changed jobs, moved laterally, or just assign the provided email address for 'junk' mail when forced to subscribe.
> - **Stop automating.** Don't just fill up a template with 'stuff' because you don't like to break the cycle. (Skipping one issue might give your audience a breather!)
> - Write better stories. This shouldn't be hard because it requires some real storytelling.
> - **Link to relevance.** Point the story and newsletter to something more satisfying than the bland website. Too many e-newsletter stories are nothing but traffic drivers because someone likes to see a spike in page hits.
> - **Use analytics.** Track how many 'opens' are truly engaged people. Many maybe stashing your newsletter (and dozens of others) to be read over the weekend. Maybe that group could become a secondary segment for less frequent mailings, or a shorter version.
> - **Make it Interactive.** If readers have access to other social media venues, asking them what they like most (or what they hate most) is a great way to start a conversation.

"The biggest reason for 'unsubscribes' is when we send out an email selling one of our courses or conferences. For every sale you make you have to expect around 5 unsubscribes." That's ok, because, as Wright notes, Google analytics tells them that there's a direct correlation between e-newsletters and readership and sales. In one version, Simply lost 175, but knows it will make up for that loss by gains they make by others opting in—those who find them via search. They also make the calculation that those who unsubscribe "are probably no longer as interested in our content as those who join"—in other words, the database is really getting refined over time.

Refining a database helps better targeting, and they often integrate well with CRM software such as Salesforce.com. For a newsletter targeting different segments, service providers offer a choice of templates that dynamically matches content to each segment's preferences.

But the content needs to be customized, too. "Admittedly, writing different content for different groups of your audience is more time consuming, but it's also more effective," notes Kevin Gibbons, Director of SEOptimise.[4] You might even integrate a social channel with your newsletter. Joe Manna says he uses a blog to complement a newsletter. "What I like to do is to publish an article on the blog and

> **HOW TO RETAIN SUBSCRIBERS**
>
> **Manage Expectations.** "If your recipients signed up for these kinds of emails, don't expect them to be very enthusiastic when, out of the blue, you send an email with a subject line like, "10% Discount! Open Now!" MailChimp
>
> **Ask For Readers Opinion.** Ask your readers to comment on the newsletter. They will tell you what they liked, disliked, or want to see more of. Additionally, the interaction with your readers draws you closer to a sale. Joe Manna, Infusionsoft
>
> **Reward Attention.** The nineties was the decade that people rewarded us with insights. Today, people are looking for relevant 'data' to solve their problem. Seek to deliver smart incentives.[3] Andreas Weigend, Amazon
>
> **Segment, Segment, Segment.** While you may be 'emailing by consent,' don't treat all opt-ins alike. It may be a good idea to send new subscribers different version of the newsletter than long-term subscribers.
>
> **Respect Your Readers.** Minimize spam complaints and unsubscribes by meeting and exceed their expectations. Send only valuable information. Believe it or not, but asking people to unsubscribe on the top of the message greatly reduces unsubscribes by at least 40 percent! It's all about trust. Joe Manna

point to it from the newsletter with a crafty headline and a one-liner summary driving people to it." Manna is Community Manager at Infusionsoft, a marketing automation company, and is editor of a customer-focused newsletter. Like Wright, he too thinks of unsubscribes as a "healthy component of the cycle." He would rather have someone unsubscribe instead of submitting an ISP spam complaint.

Recently, there has been a lot of discussion around relevance. Manna approaches relevance by saying that editors ought to first figure out what their readers want. Sounds obvious? Trouble is, he says, "too many newsletters are used simply to boast"—perhaps built around what the boss wants. News-speak 1.0! In the effort to use the newsletter to promote a business, many forget that people subscribe to one because the topics appear to have immediate relevance to them. Brevity is important, too. Infusionsoft recommends sharing no more than four key articles, and using a simple paragraph summarizing them, including a YouTube video or images. "It gives it more life and expands the spectrum of engagement," says Manna.[5]

One of the best written and well laid out newsletters that I subscribe to is from Trader Joe's, a grocery chain in Arizona. There's nothing automatic about it—it's in print! I opt-in by visiting the store and picking one up from the rack outside. It is well written, and has a stunning format. Its platform is 1.0 (print), but its language is News-speak 3.0. E-newsletter publishers could learn something from this. Manna also advises to "make it look good" because the visual impact of your newsletter can make all the difference. "Make it brief (you only have the reader's attention for a few minutes), use bullets, appealing headlines, and include graphics."

So, the next time you or your editor is on deadline, and are tempted to cut and paste story ideas from other sources, it may be time to rethink the push-to-talk strategy. Please don't send it to me, either. I may not be ready to dive into your marinade.

We have all been duped by salesy invitations claiming to do no harm. This Monty Python skit captures this best.

Encyclopedia Salesman: Burglar! [rings again] Burglar!
[woman appears at other side of door]

Woman: Yes?

Encyclopedia Salesman: Burglar, madam.

Woman: What do you want?

Encyclopedia Salesman: I want to come in and steal a few things, madam.

Woman: Are you an encyclopaedia salesman?

Encyclopedia Salesman: No madam, I'm a burglar, I burgle people.

Woman: I think you're an encyclopaedia salesman.

Encyclopedia Salesman: Oh I'm not, open the door, let me in please.

Woman: If I let you in you'll sell me encyclopaedias.

Encyclopedia Salesman: I won't, madam. I just want to come in and ransack the flat. Honestly.

Woman: Promise? No encyclopaedias?

Encyclopedia Salesman: None at all.

Woman: All right. [she opens door] You'd better come in then.

Encyclopedia Salesman: Mind you, I don't know whether you've really considered the advantages of owning a really fine set of modern encyclopaedias... You know, they can really do you wonders.

5

SPEAKING OUT OF TURN

Intelligible speech is often the most distracting sound in the workplace. ChatterBlocker lowers the intelligibility and reduces the distraction.

—Chatterblocker.com

Being outspoken, and speaking out of turn has become the new normal. To create 'media,' even those raw, random acts of journalism, may involve jumping in and out of a conversation, speaking not only when we are being spoken to. It may be messy, but so is a republic.

We grew up in a world of 'he-said, she-said' media. It was founded on the principle that stories told by the journalist needed to be fair, and this meant giving equal weight to both sides of the story. As such, we were given a narrator who gently introduced us to two conversations taking place in the formative story. The employee said this, the manager said that. The United Nations' spokesperson said this, the warlord said that. You can easily spot the problem here. The journalist became some sort of referee, making sure the ball went into each other's court, with no player overstepping a boundary. No foot faults.

This journalistic practice—nay, the journalistic 'canon'—of balanced viewpoints dates back to 1922, when newspaper editors got together and formed the American Society of Newspaper Editors, and crafted a Code of Ethics that included principles of accuracy and impartiality. Later, in 1949 after the Federal Communications Commission (the FCC) ruled that since the airwaves constituted "public property," it required broadcasters to make their channels accessible to differing viewpoints, so that all sides of a controversial topic being covered would be represented. The so-called "Fairness Doctrine" was even extended to candidates running for political office.[1] But before that, early newspapers in America were partisan, with the Whigs and the Tories using the press to attack each other. In other words, balance was a new phenomenon, not a given.

> There's an inherent pomposity in much of what passes for corporate communication today. Missing are the voice, humor, and simple sense of worth and honesty that characterize person-to-person conversation.
>
> —Rick Levine, *The Cluetrain Manifesto*

All this sits uncomfortably with those who generally assume that fairness and objectivity were part of the DNA of early media in America.[2]

Nowhere is this friction over balanced journalism more prevalent than in politics and war, or more precisely the politics of war. The media bias, which conservatives and liberals accuse each other of, is often nuanced, but screams out. Steven Poole, in his book *Unspeak*, makes an interesting case of how the media becomes an accomplice in reporting the war.[3] Euphemisms and words are 'smuggled in' to the language of the media to convey a subtle bias, he claims. Poole ought to know. He's a writer for the *Guardian* newspaper. Unlike in the Orwellian totalitarian society where words were forcefully purged, and books burned, language is now manipulated so as to saturate our discourse, and tilt the balance.

Then along came the Web—which is twenty years old, if you need a reality check—which shook things up. In becoming a democratic medium practically overnight, it allowed some young, loud-mouthed 'new media' upstarts to play this storied game, too. They treat the he-said, she-said model as more the exception than the rule. They ignore the umpire and mess with the chalk lines on Center Court. Citizens are generally partial, so expecting them to uphold impartiality in the stories and the conversations they generate online would be foolhardy.

NOISY HYBRID MEDIA

Prior to the last few years of the 20th century, citizens had to wait their turn to speak, if they expected to be heard. The letter to the editor had a slim chance of being published. The idea dropped into the suggestion box at work didn't always get a response from the chief executive. The *Cluetrain Manifesto,* an online screed that was subsequently published as a book, railed against this and urged people to speak out. The value of our voices is immense, they claimed. What passes for communication between companies and customers is too "washed" noted Rick Levine, one of the authors. "We of genus Homo are wired to respond to each other's noise and commotion, to the rich, multi-modal deluge of data each of us broadcasts as we wade through life."[4] In other words, we have it in us to speak up, speak out of turn, and add to the conversation, outside the hard boundaries set by broadcast media.

Media for the most part of the nineteenth and twentieth century was largely defined as (and by) Big Media. It did not seem to include anything that the *hoi polloi* might be engaged in. Private opinions and ideas remained outside the public domain, because the means of public-*ity* remained in the hands of a few. "If you had something you needed to say in public, you couldn't. Movie reviews came from movie reviewers. Public opinions came from opinion columnists. Reporting only came from reporters," noted Clay Shirky.[5] "The conversational space available to mere mortals," observed Shirky, "consisted of the kitchen table, the water cooler, and occasionally letter writing."

THE UN-ASKED 'SPOKESPERSON'

Did you hear how 'Janet' started tweeting about Exxon Mobil? In July 2008, during the early part of the BP oil leak in the United States, a persona who went by the name of Janet took to Twitter, using Twitter.com/ExxonMobilCorp to speak on behalf of the company that maintained a very tight control of its external communications. (This Twitter handle is now a 'protected' account, for confirmed followers.)

> **ExxonMobilCorp**
>
> **@AndrewDavies**, I am an employee of ExxonMobil, who has decided to put forward her pride in her own company.

Janet, who branded the site with corporate logos, and started communicating to the world on July 28, 2010, took everyone by surprise because 'she' was speaking so freely about the crisis. Was this communicator sanctioned by Exxon-Mobil's corporate PR? Was it a lone wolf out to embarrass the oil giant? It turned out that this rogue communicator was only trying to do in the digital space what most employees do in the analog world—tell others about their company. She was not critical of her company. In fact, her tweets seemed a lot like spin. They included *"We are not an earth hating organization, and we're working hard to improve how we drill for oil, these are difficult times,"* and *"Did You Know? ExxonMobil reduced its Greenhouse Gas Emissions by 5 million metric tons from 2006 to 2007!"*

Very quickly 'Janet' was escorted off the social media property. "She is not an authorized person to speak on behalf of the company," a spokesperson said. Subsequent statements such as "We want to make sure anyone who is speaking for the company is doing so accurately," and "We're happy to provide our positions via our web sites," made by ExxonMobil, made it clear that that its employees could only use orthodox—meaning corporate sanctioned—channels to communicate with the outside world.[6] Social media may be what most organizations say they love to embrace, but even within its perimeter, no one is supposed to speak out of turn!

The company now uses a Twitter handle @exxonmobil as its official account. Its VP of Public and Government Affairs has his own Twitter account. His blog, begun on 14 June, 2010 (just two days before BP's chairman and chief executive agreed to create a $20 billion fund for damage claims from the spill) now promotes dialogue. Comments on the blog are moderated.

In 1999, before many of us began thinking deeply about the role of the Internet in the future of media, USAID (The United States Agency for International Development) foresaw the need for citizens to be able to "make informed decisions and counter state-controlled media."[7] It talked of encouraging diverse and plural voices, to let citizens have access to government and corporate information, and called for nurturing alternative media.[8] This kind of talk may have made many people uncomfortable. Mainstream media journalists thought that this might lead to erosion in trust.[9]

Organizations then, may have never dreamt that social media would deliver this alternative into our laps—and phones, and tablets and media players. It seems like the model of media is being overturned on a weekly, if not daily basis. Instead of media being the filter, media could be an ecosystem; whereas media once thrived on scarcity, media today is based on abundance; rather than striving for balance, media today strives for trust. This off-balance media is well suited for something we are all good at—conversations. These "communities of geography and interest" create deeper, more nuanced understanding of what information is valuable to our communities, says Dan Gillmor.[10] It is as if the whole population of media consumers has begun talking out of turn!

The Net has been grooming a young generation to believe that they have a voice, no matter what country they come from. The events in Tunisia, Egypt and many other nations where speech was curtailed have proven that voices will surface, despite brutal censorship. "The Internet is the First Amendment brought to life," noted Jeff Jarvis writing years before the revolutions swept out governments in the Middle East.[11] "It abhors and subverts censorship—for whatever speech is trampled down in one place can and will arise somewhere else."[12]

NOT QUIET ANYMORE

If you've watched a Wimbledon game, you would have not missed moments of the game when the umpire intones "quiet, please!" and everything stops. In certain environments, governed by broadcast models of who might be allowed to speak, we observed these court rules. We were spectators, after all.

It's not quiet anymore.

Consumers don't even seem to want the quiet. In 2005, the Pew Research Center which tracks newspaper reading habits, recorded a curious shift. It observed that people were turning away from traditional news outlets, particularly those "with their decorous, just-the-facts aspirations to objectivity." And what were they gravitating toward? They were turning toward "noisier hybrid formats that aggressively fuse news with opinion or entertainment, or both."[13] Yes, you read that right—noisier formats.

Look around you. There appears to be something quite invigorating about the noise coming from the stands. Even mainstream media appear to be sensing this shift, creating 'noisy' environments for their stories. The front pages of online newspapers are well stocked with videos and podcasts, slide shows and infographics. Today, some journalists have spoken out about abandoning the convention of giving 'both sides' their space. "We need to do this more often. We have no real choice (abandon the 'two sides fallacy')" says Dan Gillmor, in a recent book, *Mediactive*.[14] Gillmor teaches media entrepreneurship at the Walter Cronkite School, Arizona State University.

If he-said, she-said journalism is on its way out, where are we headed?

Citizen journalism is one place where media is heading toward. The door to a broad swath of channels has been left slightly ajar, letting in new voices to fill the void. They are making their own journalistic 'rules', speaking out of turn. When I interviewed Gillmor in 2009, he commented on the learning curve within the media as it grappled with digital formats. "I think the traditional media are still in a transition period of getting it and learning what it means to their communities, but (digital media) was clearly an unstoppable force at the time." He went further, to say that readers and viewers know more than media professionals do, implying that there are many more sides and voices to a story piped through former mainstream media. Isn't that a rather unpopular position for a mainstream journalist like him to take? "If anyone thinks about it for more than ten seconds, they realize it's true by definition."[15] There is no proper definition as to what citizen journalism is, but it's certainly not he-said, she-said journalism.

What seems to be happening here is that there is a growing recognition that media is the product of not just media people, but 'mediactive' people. Anyone of us, indeed, many of us will never be journalists, says Gillmor. But we could commit 'acts of journalism' now and then.[16] Jay Rosen, a journalism professor at New York University, talks of the upheaval in media as a result of five stresses, all from bloggers. "The first is a collapsing economic model in mainstream media, with print and broadcast dollars being exchanged for digital dimes. The second is from new competition thanks to the disruptive Internet. The third stress comes from a shift in power, and the loss in control as the *hoi polloi*, the 'people formerly known as the audience' become producers and consumers. The fourth stress is being felt because of the new information flow; it happens when "stuff" moves horizontally, peer to peer, from producer to consumer, just as effectively as it does vertically. Finally the fifth stress comes from the erosion of trust in Big Media, and the consequent loss of authority."[17]

These new media pressures will 're-imagine' journalism even further. It is not the same thing as saying that new media will *replace* old media. It may involve some renovating, re-placing of broken or missing parts, even inventing a brand new operating system. To occupy the media ecosystem is to participate in it. To create 'media,' even

> **MEDIA AS EMPOWERER**
>
> Consider three news organizations that have been experimenting with news as conversations.
>
> **Internews,** an international media development organization, empowers local media worldwide. It is not only a distribution channel for global voices, but it gives people the tools to connect, and thereby be heard. The organization has helped countries it operates in move towards a more democratic model.[18] It helped develop radio in Afghanistan. In 2001, Afghanistan had just one government-operated Voice of Sharia, station. Today there are 100 radio stations, and more than 30 television outlets.[19]
>
> **Global Voices,** is a nonprofit foundation comprising an international team of volunteer authors, and others who are active in the blogosphere. In fact, one of its divisions, Lingua, amplifies Global Voices' stories in languages other than English with the help of volunteer translators. It translates content into more than 15 languages.[20]
>
> **Witness,** an international human rights organization provides video training (and equipment) for local groups involved in human rights advocacy campaigns. Its role is to be a "broker (of) relationships with international media outlets, government officials, policymakers, activists, and the general public."[21]

those raw, random acts of journalism, may involve jumping in and out of a conversation, speaking not only when we are being spoken to (when one is interviewed, asked for a video response, or a comment on a blog) but speaking out of turn. The process of permitting people to speak when they are *not* being spoken to will be messy. But in any young democracy, it always is.

Welcome to the noisy, brave new world of hybrid media!

Sanjana Hattotuwa knows a lot about 'Mediactive' people. He founded the first citizen journalism organization in Sri Lanka, *Groundviews* that has been in operation since 2006. While many in the media complain bitterly about the quality of citizen participation in online communities and the prevalence of 'trolls'—the term used to describe people who incite a controversy among members, by posting inflammatory or even off-topic remarks—Hattotuwa takes a contrarian view. Indeed, he says, online anonymity and pseudonymity does sometimes encourage violent types of social engagement, but we should not damn the Web for this. "We don't damn mainstream print media because of tabloids, or television writ large because of Fox." The secret is to have "clearly established markers and guidelines for content, including comments."

One of the reasons his site has seen a qualitatively higher standard of debate and zero abusive trolling, is that *Groundviews* has established strong community guidelines that sets the tone for constructive debate. This kind of built-in moderation requires careful design, dedication and careful curation.

Sanjana Hattotuwa teaches citizen journalism production team
to use WordPress for content distribution.

"If you don't create a safe space for debating highly emotional issues, the noisiest will overwhelm the most insightful. It's not the default, it's not easy, it's thankless, it's exhausting," says Hattotuwa.[22]

In the end, Hattotuwa is optimistic that new media's imperfect recipe for democratic discourse will work for any community.

6

LESS NOISE, MORE CURATION

Where is the wisdom we have lost in knowledge? Where is the knowledge we have lost in information?[1]

—T.S. Eliot

Content creators bring a newfound order to the messy, chaotic Web. It brings about a new intimacy between creators and consumers. While early content was organized around knowledge 'faculties', today's content is being organized around conversations.

The 'echo chamber' is full of content creators. The trouble is they produce the wrong sort of content. Like machine-gun fire into the night sky, the echo-chamber doesn't care about targeting. Much of it adds little useful information—just noise.[2]

You and I may have even indulged in some of this. A photo on Facebook gets tagged by three people with semi-useful information, only to be pounced on by 64 others who throw in their inane comments, just because they could. Indeed the tools that enable us to communicate better can exacerbate the problem, where content lands all over the place like spent cartridges. The problem is amplified by social media. If you are at the receiving end of it, that is to say if you subscribe to the RSS feeds, you have experienced it first-hand.

There are many ways to deal with TMI. You could block it. You could ignore it. Or you could distill it. Blocking information is a fool's errand. Ignoring content on an *ad hoc* basis is not realistic. Besides, as anyone in PR or marketing will tell you, the surest way to invite a crisis is to create a blind spot. Which leaves you the CMO or the CIO (Chief Insight Officer) with the option of distilling content. But how? This is where the value of a Content Curator comes in.

CURATION VS THE FIREHOSE

What exactly is content curation? There are several definitions. (It is sometimes referred to as digital curation.) I prefer this one that lays out three important tasks: *Content curation is the selection, maintenance, and archiving of digital assets*. It sounds very simple, but each discipline involves a lot of subskills, such as due diligence, an editorial eye for objectivity, and an inside knowledge of the architecture of the tools being used.

Selecting and archiving knowledge in and of itself is a noble calling. The earliest example of vast knowledge curation was the ancient Library of Alexandria. It was more or less the collective works of humankind up to the third century BC. Content was organized around 'faculties' of knowledge by scholars, and the library had rooms for discussion. Its curators and editors were eminent scholars such as Apollonius of Rhodes (who was also a poet).

In a multi-channel, rapidly updated media environment today, that task of organizing the collected works of humankind today is daunting. Consider Twitter, the great fire hose of all communication channels. It lets people throw out little nuggets of information, but when millions of people begin sharing information this way, it swells the global knowledge pool at the rate of 250 million tweets a day.[3] People have used Twitter and YouTube to answer questions, report on events, fact-check stories and provide rebuttals, making it a trove of knowledge that gets continually refreshed and archived. Twitter, and its ability to create intimacy between strangers, may have content value beyond the 'noise' that rises to the surface, as Leisa Reichelt observes.[4]

The trouble is that potentially useful content gets submerged by bad content—such as when people use it for status updates. There is another problem with the tool—the re-tweet function. Some consider it Twitter's big flaw. "Deep down, however, I wonder if a no re-tweet diet would make for better blogging and content curation," ponders Stanford Smith, a curator at PushingSocial.com.[5] Could a re-tweet (just like the forward button in email) inadvertently dilute a discussion rather than adding to it? "A missing re-tweet button would compel the curator to visit the site and physically view the post they are sharing. Without a re-tweet button, I would visit less sites but the quality of my interaction would increase."

> **TWITTER'S 'AMBIENT INTIMACY'**
>
> "Ambient intimacy is about being able to keep in touch with people with a level of regularity and intimacy that you wouldn't usually have access to, because time and space conspire to make it impossible."
>
> —Leisa Reichelt

Smith's assertion is important. Curation, when it involves re-publishing (re-tweeting) the curated content, glosses over the knowledge value of what is being pointed to. The reader seldom sees a new perspective, especially if a hundred people re-tweet, verbatim, what has appeared in their feed. If this new job in content curation seeks to justify its value by alluding to that of an art curator, then it comes with certain responsibilities.[6] An Art Curator's job involves collection and management related tasks such as acquisitioning, accessioning, cataloging, etc. But while it might involve collaborating with researchers, and publications, it doesn't involve publishing as a job requirement.

But let's not make Twitter the culprit. TMI is not a by-product of tools themselves, but of people and organizations. We don't complain too loudly when news organizations continue to pour content out of their content buckets at an increasing pace. We welcome more information during a catastrophe or scandal because more photos, an abundance of links, multiple or slightly redundant videos and tweets give us more context and deeper perspective. But as citizen journalists, bloggers and podcasters keep adding to the torrent of information, as do teachers, preachers, politicians, and PR professionals, it begins to feel overwhelming.

It's not just 'them' who are capable of doing this. Every one of us, even those who do not have copywriter, communicator or editor in our title, is adding to the torrent. "We used to live in a content world that was curated for us, but that's all changed because we have become the editors, curators, sharers and distributors of a lot of content," says Adam Shlachter, Managing Director of MEC Interaction, a media agency. With so much content in so many channels, the difference between premium content versus niche content, what's user-generated versus professional, has blurred, he says. Consumers and brands are curating content for others and for themselves. "These (content) experiences are more accessible, portable and liquid because they just go with you, and you can choose to interact with them when, where and how you want."[7] All this poses a problem. You could boil it down to one word: Attention.

Does more information make us more knowledgeable? To update T. S. Eliot's question about wisdom and information it would be good to ask: Where is the attention we have lost in the knowledge? Where is the context we have lost in the sea of content?

CURATION, A FULL-TIME JOB?

Hence the role of the content curator has gained currency. Some believe it will soon be a coveted job in most organizations. This becomes more a reality with the prospect of a modern Alexandria being created by Google, attempting to digitize and archive the world's knowledge through the Google Book Search Library Project. Amazon recently announced that it was making available e-Books books from more than 11,000 public libraries, downloadable to its book reader, the Kindle. All this content quietly becoming available online, in some ways will make it more difficult to dig up that nugget of information, buried in the digital haystack.

When the new 'virtual Library of Alexandria' comes about, who would be its curators? And what would a content creator do in an organization? Shel Holtz, who has written extensively on the topic, recommends five categories of content that an employee could be assigned to curate.[8]

> In the Library of Alexandria, content was organized around faculties of knowledge. Apollonius of Rhodes was one of its content curators.

- **Training Material** – Why reinvent the wheel and come up with original material? If the resources already exist, you could link to with consent from the original source.
- **Company positions and statements** – Employees who are constantly required to respond to customer inquiries about company positions on CSR or other workplace issues could find a single repository convenient to get to.
- **Employee blogs** – With more employees blogging, a curat-

ed blog site could help them discover each other, and share knowledge in their work.
- **Projects** – Keep different project groups up to speed on developments in the field by grouping them on one content site.
- **Initiatives** – As companies launch new initiatives (such as wellness or sustainability) curated content could help employees stay on top of the new ideas and the new initiatives.

Would you be that kind of communicator? Someone who harvests collective intelligence? Adding software filters isn't enough. There are plenty of them—often referred to as 'consensus filters'—which enable sites such as Digg and Reddit[9] to aggregate knowledge. But that's really not curation. Aggregation and filtering is automated. Curation requires humans, who vet content on an ongoing basis.[10]

It is important to distinguish the role of the content curator from other roles in communication. Whereas a director of marketing communications is like the conductor of an orchestra, waving her baton at different players, the director of Content Curation is the one who samples the music before it reaches the audience.

The human curator will be an asset for both internal and external organizations of an organization, and for an organization's external audiences. If you have ever called a company for help logging into its website, and been confused as to where the link or drop-down is even while a live human is pointing you to it, you would have had a glimpse of why a curator is sorely needed. There is another side-benefit that would make the marketing side of the organization very pleased. Pawan Deshpande, a go-to person on the topic of content curation (writing for *Forbes* magazine) noted that "Content curation is a game changer when it comes to SEO performance."[11] He believes the process of finding, organizing and sharing content practically guarantees placement on page one of the search results. Guarantees? This sounds a bit too much of an over-reach. There are plenty of fly-by-night operators who guarantee keyword rankings within the first 10 entries on a Google search.[12]

Nevertheless, the idea of content curation seems to have caught on. Rohit Bhargava, a marketing strategist, thinks this new job will not be limited to one of creating more content, but to also 'make sense' of other's content. Content curators, he says, "will bring more utility and order to the Web, which after all is the 'social Web.' They will enable "a new dialogue" based on the new content they bring about.

Hard to disagree with that. The Web isn't lacking good content. But it sorely needs one thing: humans who can reduce the cacophony and chaos.

The Web needs humans who write like humans rather than bots who stand for human thought; humans who condense the core of multilayered, conflicting conversations. I am convinced that the blogosphere, the twitterverse and the billions of people popping in and out of chat rooms and comment threads would soon be drowning in noise without curators. It is, for now, an unpaid job, but I am optimistic that it will someday earn more recognition in our young Chat Republic.

7

HUMAN TRANSPONDERS

Pssst! Who's telling and retransmitting your story? If you're only tapping into the usual marketing, media and Internet channels, it may be time to start tapping into humans again!

Forget your professional role for a second. How many messages that you encounter—advertising, email, word-of-mouth, or a story you overhear on a train—do you forward or repeat to others every day? You probably never think about it, but many aspects of your interaction with others are loaded with nuggets of information that then get passed along by others. Americans talk about 70 brands a week. We could assume that this refers to human brands (celebrities, leaders), events and companies. Not uncommon to hear: "so my girlfriend told me this funny story about her professor..." Or: "I'm so mad at Denny's this morning—they've stopped giving away free Grand Slams to everyone. How crazy is that?" Branded or not, punctuated with angst, our stories, email forwards, tweets, text and phone conversations are all part of the world of Buzz.

Buzz, however, has evolved from a nascent, hyped-up tactic to an activity that takes on a definite form so as to deliver measureable results.

Why is Buzz so important? To get some clarity I went to two sources. First, I talked to someone who's an authority on buzz—he wrote the book, and updated it!—Emanuel Rosen. Then I checked back with the Word-of-mouth Marketing Association (WOMMA), the organization that came into being in 2004.[1] More specifically I wanted to know what exactly do we mean by buzz in the digital age?

> "Most new information comes from weak ties—from people who belong to other social clusters and are exposed to different sources of information."
>
> —Emanuel Rosen, *The Anatomy of Buzz*

In the year 2000, before anything like Stumble Upon, Friend Feed, or Twitter had been conceived, Rosen came out with an exploration of the notion of Buzz that stoked the debate. This was the height of the dot-com era, when people imagined we had reinvented communications. But Rosen, in *The Anatomy of Buzz* was saying that all lifeforms were pre-wired to communicate and pass along information, consciously or not.[2] Or in other words: We human transponders were inherently buzzy. We are hard-wired to chat from the get go. We can't stop sharing our thoughts, even when we are untethered to the grid!

POSITIVE BUZZ GOES FURTHER

Many of you are nodding your heads in agreement. You probably know people who are inherently gossips—industrial strength buzz machines. Rosen looked beyond people and discovered ravens. (Yes ravens!) The case involved a University of Vermont study that did experiments placing a carcass of a cow to see how a raven would respond to it. When a single bird flew by and stumbled upon the food source, it did not swoop down to take a bite. It flew away! But a few days later it returned with dozens of other ravens. This experiment was repeated many times, and every time they returned with a group, having apparently spread the word to the community. "Sharing information," says Rosen, "is an effective survival mechanism for ravens, bees, ants and people." And you thought learning to use SlideShare[3] and being able to re-tweet (the ability to forward a Twitter post from someone you are following to your network of followers) made you super cool!

Maybe buzz as a 'survival' instinct means we trade tidbits of buzz to help us function better in a competitive environment. The odd things, says Rosen is that while people do spread negative buzz about bad experiences, conversations about brands are largely positive, in the ratio of eight to one. Why is that? "Because negative word-of-mouth tends to suffocate itself." This seems counter-intuitive, since we have all come across examples of bad experiences spreading fast by the sheer force of Word-of-Mouth. But there are numerous examples of positive buzz too. WOMMA differentiates between *Amplified* buzz and *Organic* buzz. The amplified kind includes building communities, developing sharing tools, reaching out to influentials and monitoring online conversations. But it is the organic kind of Word-Of-Mouth that looks more interesting because it involves focusing on positive elements—such as customer satisfaction, and responding to concerns and criticism—just as Rosen maintains.

RESPECT FOR THE WEAKEST LINK

Another interesting revelation is the power of links. In the digital age, we tend to think that social networks are a great transportation system for Word-of-Mouth, but here's something to consider before going after your A-list of contacts in your networks. Between the strong links and the weak, the weak links offer the most potential says Rosen. "The people with whom we maintain strong ties—the people who we see everyday—are often exposed to very similar sources of information as we are." Translated, what you think is important is not as buzz-worthy to them, since they already know about it. "Most new information comes from weak ties—from people who belong to other social clusters and are exposed to different sources of information."[4]

So if we human transponders are so good in creating buzz about things we care about, could individuals be tapped to be agents of buzz —like one-man or one-woman agencies? In December 2008, a word-of-mouth controversy erupted when one such human agent decided to spread the word about a brand. The person was Chris Brogan, a well-known promoter of all things connected to social media. Brogan, who has two prominent blogs, decided to use one of them to conduct an experiment for a client of a friend. The client was K-Mart, and he was paid a small stipend for his services.

To some, the very idea of a well-respected social media evangelist accepting payment for being a transponder of a marketer's message seemed like a sell-out. Brogan responded by reminding critics that he had been quite transparent about the exercise, so what was the big deal? The incident illustrated the conflicting positions many people seem to have with buzz agents. It's OK when someone talks up Starbucks, becomes a fan of the brand on Facebook, and asks others in his network to join the fan club, but it's a sell-out to be doing it as a free agent! As Brogan fired back (in his blog), we should face the reality that buzz marketing is ingrained in our social connections. "Marketing and advertising is part of the social Web. You don't have to like it, but if you're ignoring that businesses are trying every day to figure out their place in this world, you're drinking a whole different kind of Kool-Aid."[5]

> **HUMAN BUZZ AGENTS**
> BzzAgent White Paper: "Measuring the value of a WOM program in a test and control market." http://tinyurl.com/dgq5hf

An extra dose of transparency won't hurt a buzz campaign. The organization **BzzAgent** (Bzzagent.com) which preceded WOMMA by three years, faced criticism early on about agents disclosing their identity. The company recruits about 4,000 agents a week for hundreds of clients. It claimed that Word-of-Mouth is a legitimate program with measurable results. Likewise Tremor, the word-of-mouth division of Proctor and Gamble, describes what it does in marketing as having scientific rigor. It recruits 'connectors' whom it says "are not your average consumer," because they have social networks 5 to 6 times larger than normal. "Connectors have a propensity to talk, are highly influential, and amplify YOUR product's message across their networks of friends, family, co-workers and acquaintances."[6]

So what are the takeaways for communicators attempting to harness the power of buzz? Six things worth keeping in mind:

1. **Think Positive!** Buzz works when people share positive experiences as consumers. Notes Rosen: You never ask a friend: "Have you read anything bad lately?"
2. **Show, don't tell.** Social networks amplify buzz, but the differentiator is that in these spaces the emphasis is not on the *telling*, but more about the *showing*. Even Email works better when you show, not tell. Check out how a disgruntled Virgin Atlantic passenger complained to Richard Branson by sending him an email with pictures of the in-flight meal that he found offensive. (tinyurl.com/amk7tx)
3. **Nurture your weak links.** We spend far too much time providing care and feeding of our strong links. To spread the word, says Rosen, go beyond the comfort zone and diversify your connections.
4. **Buzz should solve problems.** Buzz works when it helps peo-

ple make sense of information. "Microsoft has a new operating system" is just data, not buzz says Rosen. Communication that answers the questions "Is the operating system stable?" is more buzz-worthy.
5. **Organic Buzz beats amplified.** There is a whole sordid industry that has sprung up hiring people to amplify a discussion. They have earned the name 'sock puppets' because they are hired, like puppets, posing to be independent, but are fed by a puppet master.[7] True buzz grows organically.
6. **Don't try to create buzz in stealth mode.** Be transparent. Be honest. Be clear.

8

CITIZEN MO

Pixels talk.[1]

—Joey Flynn

A dead battery could really jinx things up for someone communicating via social media. But it holds true for old media as well. Imagine for a moment what history would have recorded—or not—if Abraham Zapruder's Bell and Howell camera ran out of juice as John F. Kennedy's black limousine rolled by. The 'Zapruder film' shot on Kodachrome is one of the most reliable—and debatable—pieces of accidental citizen journalism from an era when citizens typically did not create media for public consumption.

"This is not good anymore…Once the battery charges, I'm going to download it from the camera and stream it to you live. I mean I don't believe this is happening. Seriously I don't believe this is happening…" These were the last words of one of the bravest 'citizen journalists' in our time, Mohammed Nabbous, who was killed in Benghazi, Libya, in March 2011. (Find it at bit.ly/LMD0811)

When we typically talk of citizen journalism, we think of accidental reporters, who in the face of a catastrophic event, grab a cell phone, and capture a story that would have otherwise never been recorded. Many in the West recall the first heartbreaking reports of the 2004 tsunami, captured by citizens in Sri Lanka. Commuters, not trained reporters, provided the first grainy videos when terrorist bombed subways and buses in London in 2005. Likewise, the first images of the dramatic 'splash landing' of an U.S. Airways flight into the Hudson River in Manhattan, New York, were captured by a citizen journalist.

But just as mainstream media journalists put themselves in harm's way (those like Daniel Pearl of The *Wall Street Journal* killed in 2002, Tim Hetherington, killed in Misrata, Libya), citizen journalists today are following in their footsteps. As large media organizations downsize, citizens are often filling the gaps. Whether we approve of them or not, they are often the first responders, covering a broad range of events—the wars, hurricanes, earthquakes, elections, civil unrest, famines, and terrorism—that seem to take place with greater frequency. They come in all shades, from the daring, to the thoughtful. These are often 'accidental journalists.'

George Holliday, a plumber, was one night awoken by police sirens outside his home in Los Angeles. He grabbed his clunky Sony Handycam and stepped out on his balcony and began to videotape nine minutes that would make citizen journalism history. That video segment, shot on March 3, 1991, which he offered a TV station, lead to the trial of four police officers. We today know it for the name of its victim who was brutally beaten by police officers: the Rodney King video. The officers were subsequently acquitted, but the rioting that ensued resulted in 53 deaths and many injuries.[2]

So what's a good definition of Citizen Journalism? "I like to compare the bloggers here and elsewhere to the underground writers and partisan reporters of France during the World War II," wrote Stephen

Franklin, a Knight International Journalism Fellow in Egypt. "They were hardly perfect or well-trained. They were not observers but activists, because they rightly felt that their lives and their futures were on the line. They wrote snippets of truth, not whole truths and hoped that alone would help ... A handful of today's bloggers in various parts of the world have inherited their proud legacy and costly responsibilities."[3]

MEDIA TEST KITCHEN

There are many questions as this accidental profession shows signs of turning more professional ('Pro') than amateur ('Am'). How will established news media organizations deal with this? Or, the more important question is, how will governments adapt to this reality? First the relationship between the 'Pros' and the 'Ams'.

In the early years, the Pros were skeptical. Yet, more recently across the world, as mainstream media organizations began cutting back on staff, it gave rise to newsrooms where Pros could be sought after—'outsourced'—like Ams. Steve Outing, director of the Digital Media Test Kitchen, once observed that "few news organizations have the staff manpower to cover everything that their readers are interested in, but by tapping the volunteer (or cheap) resources of the citizenry, a news organization can potentially provide coverage down to the Little League team and church-group level, as well as offer better and more diverse coverage of larger issues by bringing in more voices and perspectives."

In 2006, probably the turning point of citizen journalism, the BBC announced that it would actually pay Ams for their contributions that could include video taken on cell phones. The BBC's director of Global News, Richard Sambrook, observed how invaluable citizens' input had been in reporting the London bombings the previous year: "Within six hours we received more than 1,000 photographs, 20 pieces of amateur video, 4,000 text messages, and 20,000 emails. People were participating in our coverage in a way we had never seen before."[4] Sambrook called this phenomenon 'open source journalism' where there was collaboration between a Pro and his/her readers on a story. In other words the Pros were working *alongside* the Ams!

Indeed citizen journalism has pushed the boundaries of traditional journalism. Just like the BBC, many major news organizations have begun tacking on a citizen-powered news stream. Due to so many events taking place in parts of the world that are hard to access, it has created the perfect conditions for niche media outlets providing snippets of truth.

In Libya, a citizen journalist noted this: "Before the revolution, there was only one newspaper, that belongs to the government. But after the revolution, now, there are almost five newspapers."[5] He appeared jubilant that even he could play a small part in making that happen. His main profession while not being a citizen reporter? A dentist!

In June 2011, *The New York Times* opened up a story for citizen participation in making sense of a trove of email records (24,199 in all) from Sarah Palin, released by the governor's office in Juneau, Alaska. "We're asking readers to help us identify interesting and newsworthy e-mails, people and events that we may want to highlight. Interested users can fill out a simple form to describe the nature of the email, and provide a name and email address so we'll know who should get the credit." Likewise the *Washington Post* invited readers, saying "That's a lot of email for us to review so we're looking for some help from Fix readers to analyze, contextualize, and research those e-mails right alongside *Post* reporters over the days following the release."

Note the words: 'alongside *Post* reporters.' To qualify people didn't need to have a degree in journalism, just a computer and an Internet connection! ('Fix readers' refers to readers of The Fix, a *Post* blog on politics.)

Out of these 'snippets of truth' a larger story would be pieced together.

Others have been cooking up different recipes in the test kitchen of citizen participation. Media observers have been calling it 'non-profit journalism' and 'grass-roots journalism.' "Non-profit journalism organizations as well as citizen journalists are producing news that too often is overlooked by traditional media," observed Jason Stverak, President of the Franklin Center for Government and Public Integrity, a journalism non-profit organization. The distinction between online journalists and those who write for newspapers and magazines or work in radio or TV are disappearing, and their skill-sets are being cross-pollinated. Stverak rightly says that "not all those who write online stories are journalists—yet—but the ones who are should get the same access and treatment as those few still employed by newspapers, television and radio."

For the Ams, who are often videographers, bloggers and podcasters, access and 'treatment' are sticky issues, still. Consider these: Even when it comes to major events such as the World Economic Forum, (an event where bloggers and YouTubers provide up-to-the-minute and live coverage), press access is reserved for 'all accredited media.' Three bloggers, who called themselves "alternative" journalists, sued the New York Police Department for giving them the cold-shoulder treatment—denying them press credentials. In the UK, the Tameside council (a borough of Manchester) ruled that bloggers could not be permitted to tweet since they were technically not members of the press corps. The Council however permitted the *Manchester*

Evening News and the *Tameside Reporter* to use Twitter during Council meetings. In many instances like this, a person needs to prove he or she is an 'accredited representative' of the press. Which begs the question: would someone like Nabbous have been considered an accredited member? Probably not?

Jay Rosen, a promoter of the Pro-Am model for many years and a journalism professor at New York University, thinks that the profession has not been making much progress in this area for the simple

Could they listen? Mourner shelters from tear gas at funeral of a Bahrain man killed by a police car pursuing him—after he was mistaken for a protester.

reason that the Pros have not been making it easy enough for citizens. "The ergonomics of participation in Pro-Am journalism are poorly understood. We don't have enough experts in it," he says. In order to engage people in this model of reporting "they need to see and feel the connection between the small part they are asked to contribute and the big story that will result."[6] The participatory model could eventually earn more trust for both the Pros and the Ams. The symbiotic relationship has vastly evolved. Hong Qu, at the Nieman Journalism Lab says we ought to appreciate such a symbiotic dependence between dyed-in-wool journalists and citizens, since it "ultimately produces a more participatory, accurate and compelling news cycle."

INCONVIENT TRUTHS

Then there is the credibility factor. Citizen journalists do not have the built-in reputation of news organizations, especially if they are working solo. But this has been changing. As BBC's Michael Buerk noted, while talking to an Egyptian citizen journalist, "it's not important because of what old style journalism can't do, but for what they won't do." There is an upside to all of this, not just for the media, but for communities and for democracy. The "inconvenient truths" in a functioning democracy, says Sanjana Hattotuwa, editor of *Groundviews* (an organization featured in Chapter 5), is that with citizen participation "you risk the multiplicity of voices and you strengthen media literacy."

Groundviews featured stories of war, peace and the complicated democratic process in Sri Lanka. They were stories seen through the eyes of relief workers and even activists who were witnessing the protracted war between the government forces and the terrorists. Yes, it is messy, but you end up with an informed citizenry, which isn't a bad payoff. They, the *hoi polloi*, decide on which media they will believe, and as has been shown in Iran and Egypt until very recently, they often do not believe the official narrative coming from the mainstream media. This is especially so when 'mainstream' means state-sponsored in non- and faux-democracies. Through their small-scale snippets of a larger truth unfolding, Hattotuwa saw citizen journalists as "finding new ways for citizens to be heard, governments to be held accountable and the State to answer to failures of governance." He is quick to not over-promise what technology might deliver. New media and citizen journalism don't, in and of themselves, promise a stronger democracy, but set up key 'frameworks of transparency.' They build a wellspring of trust. Hattotuwa is right. By making sure we have these conversations about the 'inconvenient truths' we strengthen our republic.[7]

PROFESSIONAL AMATEURS

Some ex-journalists and entrepreneurs have spotted opportunities in this space and have begun to create business models, albeit non-profit businesses. One of them, *The Uptake* (www.theuptake.org), is a citizen 'fueled' news organization. "Online tools will not solve community development," says *The Uptake*. It stresses the need for a different type of citizen journalist—the Professional-Amateur. It explains how one person, wearing many hats, is not the norm in citizen-fueled news. Shooting the video, editing the story, and publishing it online is more than what a Pro-Am ought to be asked to do. *Uptake* recommends three core areas a citizen-fueled organization needs to focus on: train, organize and crowd-source. More importantly it looks at citizen journalism not as a reactive means to cover a story as it breaks.

Chuck Olsen, co-founder of *The Uptake* calls it 'committing an act of journalism.' Meaning, going out there and finding the story, not reacting to it. "Most acts of citizen journalism are simply documenting something—a London subway cell phone photo, for example. And that's very important," he notes. But as the model matures and takes on a Pro-Am status, he calls for more. "We want to elevate citizen journalism from being reactive to being proactive. Go out and find stories that interest you, and provide some training on how to capture and tell that story."

Interestingly, *The Uptake* trains its journalists to adapt the amateur camera (which can be an iPhone or a Nokia) into a device that records the video it streams live to a server. Why? Think about it. Most news is pre-recorded, pre-edited; it is passed through a few human filters before it gets to the audience. I still believe this is a good thing, to verify facts, and weed out bias. But in the context of dangerous investigative reporting, or reporting from conflict zones, the story could easily be censored; the reporter silenced; the equipment destroyed. Audio and video that does not reside on the device protects the raw story.

Nabbous mastered the value of the raw story. He did not work alongside the mainstream media because he was both Pro and Am. In fact, he had a degree in mathematics, not journalism. But as a citizen, he ran Libya Alhurra—what amounts to a TV station on the Web. It is still broadcasting. (Check it out at www.livestream.com/libya17feb.) In the last part of the video, you can sense he is terribly impatient, waiting as a large video file uploads to his computer from his camera. He knows the clock is ticking. There is gunfire and mayhem outside. "Where is the media?" he asks, rhetorically, distraught at being unable to get his story out even faster. It does not strike him that he was 'The Media'—the only media available to report that part of the story. "They should be there taking video of what's happening? The bombing hasn't stopped…"

It did not. Then the video abruptly ends.

Nabbous was killed just moments later, delivering to the world an inconvenient truth.

These pages sprang up overnight like a crop of magic mushrooms on a rich motherlode of corporate horseshit.*

—Chris Locke

---

* Chris Locke, *The Cluetrain Manifesto,* FT.com, May 2000.

9

TALK LIKE A WIKIPEDIAN

Wikipedia is one of the early examples of how a social Web works, with back-room conversations and animated disagreements in its 'talk pages' over content. If Wikipedia was a country, it's quite a chatty place!

It's been 11 years plus. And you're still not a Wikipedian? Even if you're not a communicator, does the thought of authoring a Wikipedia entry make you nervous?

I don't blame you if you've stayed off the turf, especially if you've heard that people do get rapped on the knuckles for accidentally violating Wikipedia policy. (I have!) But don't let it stop you. The world's first, free, crowd-sourced encyclopedia, like the Web, seriously needs editors. And writers. And curators. And persnickety fact-checkers, and content specialists, even punctuation freaks. In other words, Wikipedia desperately needs people like you who have the twin passions of yearning to inform and collaborate.

It's not difficult to become a Wikipedian. It's not some elite club that has been anointed by the Wikimedia Foundation. But learning to work within the parameters does take some practice. I asked a few

Wikipedians about some easy ways to get started. More on that in a moment.

There is another good reason to join this band of brothers and sisters—you may boost Wikpedia's credibility. Many people who regularly dip in and out of Wikipedia have reservations about the quality of its content. If you're one of them, that's precisely why I think you are the perfect candidate to join the ranks of about 10,000 editors, who improve the content of a resource that is evolving, maddening, and irresistible.

Wikipedia may be one of the earliest examples of how the social Web formula works. Its origins go back more than a decade, when Jimmy Wales set out to get contributors to Nupedia, an earlier version of an online encyclopedia that required content to be peer reviewed. Wikipedia did away with this requirement, and it quickly grew in popularity through word-of-mouth. Unlike most knowledge sources that use citations as footnotes, the wiki format that Wales adopted used hypertext to create a back-and-forth linkage.[1]

Wikipedia was one of the earliest sites that encouraged participation and a sense of community. It was very different from its predecessors such as WELL. Just like in Wikipedia topics discussed at WELL were specialized and also trivial, and there were rules of civility. But unlike Wikipedia, everything was not transparent. Some conversations were done in secrecy.[2] But a wiki is not the most sexy social space to dive into, considering that it is underpinned by a bunch of code. Considering what a global town square it is—Wikipedia speaks 285 languages—I often wish that some of Wikipedia's content was not so dry. On the Talk Pages, you'll see editors sparring over words, many who are sensitive to attempts to insert marketing language into content, or those with political axes to grind. But it is this tension that has kept an impossible project like this alive. That fact that no one really owns the content, and anyone can edit, delete or improve an article, is still a very disruptive idea. Think about that for a second. Would the editors of a magazine allow any passerby to 'improve' an article on its website? Would your Webmaster let some Joe Schmo add punctuation to a white paper or blog? Few want to go there.

And yet many of us do go there!

Like Jessica McCann, a Phoenix-AZ based freelance writer who says she visits Wikipedia often, and goes there for two reasons. "For my nonfiction work, it's a starting point for general information and research. Then, I dig deeper using the source links to find verifiable data, white papers, etc." That seems to be typical behavior when you ask students and even businesspeople—it's the start button when embarking on a search. Wikipedia takes seriously the 'verifiability' problem Jessica mentions. (It is one of the top three Wikipedia policies.) An article needs to be well referenced or it will be taken down. For this reason, since 2005, Wikipedia lets you author an article only if you register and log in. Editors often use page alerts to watch out for anyone who might insert fake sources or spam links.

There is another group—that includes those who accept Wikipedia, warts and all—who see the positive side of a knowledge source that is evolving, especially the concept of co-creation. People in this group include educators who use Wikipedia as a classroom resource. Jody Weissler teaches this stuff at California State University, Northridge. He shows teachers how to write articles and edit them using the wiki style. Teachers use it to demonstrate the difference between traditional citations and links to sources as an alternative method of verifiability. Others use it as a tool for teaching writing. Rallying against Wikipedia makes little sense, says Michael Netzley, a professor at Singapore Management University. What does make sense, he says, is "teaching students how to be wise (information) consumers in a knowledge age" Of course he agrees, we must be skeptical. He tries to inculcate in his students that Wikipedia is a great starting point but often a poor ending place. By looking at how Wikipedia works, they learn how content works in a more decentralized, networked setting, "They need to learn how to get better information, more diverse data and perspectives, more quickly, and process it all more effectively and efficiently than competitors, he adds. (By 'competitors' he also means graduates from other universities who compete for the same jobs.)[3]

Students are able to see very quickly how the editors of Wikipedia sometimes read and respond to an article posted. "Sometimes, students are taken aback to see that their edit is undone or commented on in a few minutes. "Sometimes those responses are polite, and sometimes not, but they are mostly accurate and engaging."[4]

There's a third group that is aghast at what's being served up. Three years ago, a middle school librarian in New Jersey put up signs over the computers saying "just say no to Wikipedia." Some educators have blocked the site in their schools because, as their complaint goes, 'anyone could edit' it. Considering the new interest in peer-production, and crowd-sourcing, I believe it's time for us to get involved in this 'information commons,' rather than snipe from the sidelines.

CURRENT EVENTS
Current event coverage is an unexpected development of Wikipedia. A current event gets updated rapidly by users. Over 50 percent of edits are made by less than one percent of Wikipedia users.

GET STARTED NOW!

But before you go there, it's worth picking up a few skills on how to work your way into this community. Yes there are policies and ethical practices that could make you feel like you're wandering into a foreign country. You need to get familiar with the jargon, as you would need to in any community. NOR, for instance, stands for No Original Research; NPV is a standard called Neutral Point of View; V refers to the big one, Verifiability. Just to take up one of these, NOR, it could be confusing, since Wikipedia wants editors to stay away from original research in the main body of the article. What? That's right, but this is what it means. It does not want an editor to add "facts, allegations or ideas (original research) for which no reliable published sources exist."[5]

Truth is, you don't need to know everything at once, since you are not supposed to be diving into the deep-end so soon. "The wiki culture has a deep acceptance of imperfections and incompleteness as both inevitable and perhaps even necessary for inspiring a working community," say the authors of *How Wikipedia Works*.[6] Yes, there's the wiki 'markup language' to help you format your contribution with the proper sized headline and subheads, and to create hyperlinks and bullets. But if you know just five of them you can get by; you will learn the others later. You can find some often-used markup language at the end of the chapter.

David Traver Adolphus, an occasional Wikipedian who's also an automotive writer, and blogger, says the biggest hurdle he faced was learning to conform to "the somewhat arbitrary internal protocols." This from someone who's authored seven articles! Editors are tolerant, and may put up an alert box above your article, or ask you about something in the talk pages. "It required quite a bit of trial and error to get things formatted correctly," says Adolphus—things such as image uploading, labeling and linking.[7] There is, indeed, a Manual of Style or MoS. You could search for it within Wikipedia using this short cut Wikipedia:Manual_of_Style.

TALK PAGES

Wikipedia editors do chat about the content, and the conversation threads run wide and deep. Most casual Wikipedia users seldom click on the discussion page named 'Talk' which is the next tab on any given article. You miss a lot of the richness of the encyclopedia by ignoring this area. Even the entry about what Wikipedia is (en.wikipedia.org/wiki/Wikipedia) invites animated back-chat. The conversations that go on about the 2012 Summer Olympics in London are a good example of this. Editors debate about dates, imbalance of entries, and the athletes bios. I find the Talk pages to be a fascinating insight into how content gets to stay on a page, and how such a large, diverse global community manages something as vast as Wikipedia. Think of it as a global chat-room, where people learn to disagree, collaborate, and hammer out ideas, and even detect vandalism, oblivious to each other's background, education or ethnicity.

Lane Rasberry, spends about eight hours a week editing material on Wikipedia. He even finds acts of vandalism, where someone tries to delete content or maliciously change something, exciting. His goal is not just to catch the culprit, but to send a message that this online space has flesh-and-blood people making it work. He says that "often you can convert them to becoming a constructive Wikipedia editor."[8]

The other reason to pay close attention to Wikipedia is because it is the epitome of how knowledge and ideas live in a 'link economy.' We often gush about the Web and what it has done for business, building community, freedom of access, and 'democratizing' knowledge. A wiki in general, but Wikipedia especially is a living, breathing example of how hyperlinks—what some early Internet geeks called 'Link Love'—play a transformative role in much of the online ecosystems we inhabit.

Want to try something quick? Go to the Sandbox, where the editors welcome anyone to try their hands on adding content on using the wiki markup language. Go to Wikipedia, and in the search box type in Wikipedia:Sandbox. Here, you won't be scolded for making a mistake, as content is cleaned up automatically. There is a better way, if you are committed to becoming an editor, and that would be to register with Wikipedia, after which you get your own sandbox. . Still nervous? You don't need to be. I'm no programmer, and when I got started it took me fewer than two hours to master the basics and start an article. I'm positive you could do it!

10 steps to create content in Wikipedia
1. Register. To author an article, you now have to sign up and log in. The policy was introduced in 2005, after a string of scandals. However, you don't need to register to edit an article.
2. Plan your article offline. It's intimidating to author a piece while in the Edit menu. Adolphus suggests you "assemble supporting documents, references and images ahead of time," and do it in Microsoft Word. I recommend you also include the wiki syntax. That way you can have a proofread, fact-checked document to simply cut and paste.
3. Find references and footnote every claim or fact. Wikipedia editors, even though they are mainly volunteers, enforce the Verifiability policy to a fault, meaning you can't make unsupported claims such as "It is largely believed that…," or "The world's largest manufacturer of..." You could also reference something using an internal link to another Wikipedia entry, too. (See Step 8 below.)
4. Stick to a logical format. If you write for other media you

would know this already. Chronology works well in most entries in Wikipedia. Often you are documenting the evolution of an idea, a historical figure, something about an organization—it's not like writing a press release. Categories for subheads could be 'Early years,' 'Later developments,' 'Controversies,' 'Final Years' etc. But you could be more creative than that, too.

5. Create a Stub. Take baby steps, and create what's known as a stub, which is exactly what it sounds like: a very brief, incomplete entry; a work in progress. Don't feel bad about doing so. Nearly three-quarters of all articles in Wikipedia are supposed to have started out life as a stub. Wikipedia describes a stub as an article "too short to provide encyclopedic coverage of a subject, but not so short as to provide no useful information, and it should be capable of expansion." Translated: let the community take it and run! There is plenty of help if you would like to become a 'stub maker.' Check here for more info: en.wikipedia.org/wiki/Wikipedia:Stub_Makers

6. Improve a stub. Like you, there are thousands of others who are doing the same, with incomplete articles that need your input. Some articles have been a work in progress for several years.

7. Start a list. How often have you searched Wikipedia and stumbled on a useful list? Editors and curators are needed to create those as well. These can be a list of films that received awards, lists of tallest buildings or waterways in a country, a list of stadium stands by capacity (a global list that clearly needs a lot of input, at the time of writing.) For more on this, here's how: en.wikipedia.org/wiki/Wikipedia:WikiProject_Lists

8. Add Wikilinks. A Wikilink is an internal link to another Wikipedia entry. Adding these improves the rich cross-referencing within articles. Try to add these to any article you create, so that it does not exist by itself. (See Sidebar for how to do this.)
9. Add a photo or illustration. These illustrate a dry entry, and shed light on a subject. Even if you are not a great writer, you could improve a page created by someone else by adding a photograph, a chart or illustration. Wikipedia uses a sister company, Wikimedia Commons, to supply thousands of these. Find them here: commons.wikimedia.org/wiki/Main_Page. They even accept contributions, including video and sound recordings.
10. Play in the Sandbox. As the name implies, it has been set up to get people like you started, to experiment with the formatting and not get dinged for violating any policies. Try it out here: en.wikipedia.org/wiki/Wikipedia:Sandbox

Indeed Wikipedia is not something frozen in time. It's a chatty place, if you dare to spend some time on the 'Talk Pages' that live up to their name. There are plenty of back-room conversations going on if you care to listen.

WIKI SYNTAX:

Wikipedia's syntax is the markup 'language' or the annotations you need to use in a Wikipedia entry. These annotations, such as the 'pointy brackets,' the forward slash, the colon, etc., and a convention of placing words or phrases within or next to these annotations let Wikipedia render a text entry in a consistent format. The following are a few of the common markup language elements you will need.

Adding A Subhead/Section Title The Original article name becomes the title and anything after than will be a subhead. To create one, use double equals signs before and after the subhead.

==Create subhead here==

Add an internal link or 'Wikilink' Use double square brackets around the word you link to another Wiki entry. [[wiki entry here]]

If the word or phrase has an entry it will link to it automatically. If not, clicking on one will take the visitor to a page that says there is no such entry for the word or phrase, and suggests he or she could start writing one.

Add an external link Use a hyperlink (a full URL with the http:// part) within a single square bracket like this. [htmladdresshere]. To give the hyperlink a name, use this format [htmladdresshere Name Of Link] As you may notice, there's a space between the html address and the name you give it.

Add a footnote/reference Reference Tags are the way to add links to verify a statement or idea. There are two ways to do this:

  A: Add the HTML within pointy brackets like this

  <ref>html address here</ref>

This displays just the HTML link as a footnote with a superscript (1, 2 etc.) after the word you cited

  B: More specifically use this convention:

  <ref>[http://www.arcamax.com name of article here]</ref>

This displays just the HTML link as a footnote, but in the footnote, the 'name of article' appears

Once you add a footnote, at the bottom of your Wiki entry, you need to add the category Footnotes. Use this:

==References==

Any footnote you added will automatically be listed here in numerical order.

Add bullets or numbering This is as simple as using an asterisk (before every line you want to bullet). Or two asterisks (before every line you want to number).

10

IF THESE PRESS RELEASES COULD TALK!

To a journalist, what the speaker, the majority leader, and the minority leader say is news, right? But most of what they say these days, all day, every day, is spin.[1]

—Andrea Seabrook

The Press Release happens to have the same initials as Public Relations. How unfortunate! It muddies the waters when people refer to PR as an activity that generates press releases, rather than an interactive, person-to-person behavior.

While public relations is now considered a relationship, a back-and-forth exchange, the press release is a tool. At its worst, it is a formatted device of communicating to a specific audience—the media. A one-way channel; a machine-generated template.

But like the PR profession itself, the Press Release has gone through several evolutions, having been under attack by critics, and under construction by more progressive thinkers in the field. Some of you who have worked on a press release, and struggled with the accepted language of a release, may have begun to wonder if the language and format is now inconsistent with how it serves the intended audience—the media. Many journalists search for stories in other places. They filter their inboxes, and apply what's crudely referred to as a 'BS detector' to releases filled with spin and gobbledygook. Even the marquee that announces "For Immediate Release' is circumspect, since the media, which operates on a 24/7 basis, knows that something for 'immediate' use begs to be let loose on a myriad of other real-time channels.

There has been plenty of discussion—books, blogs, panel discussions, white papers—on the press release as an ailing (or somewhat advanced in age) communication tactic. Linda VandeVrede puts it this way: "The press release as a concept should just be one arrow in an entire quiver of possible arrows, not the sole method on which the company relies."[2] Others have been ready to pronounce the press release dead; if not completely obsolete, lacking a pulse.

TOO MUCH 'TOP SPIN'

If the press release is on life support as some suggest, what might take its place? One candidate: the Social Media Release (SMR), something that was talked about five years ago. A quick recap if you are not familiar with the Social Media Press Release known by the acronyms SMPR or SMR. The idea of a Social Media Release was popularized by SHIFT Communications' Todd Defren back in 2007. Defren was responding to an attack—make that a death wish—by a Silicon Valley, California-based journalist called Tom Foremski, who in 2006 complained that "Press releases are nearly useless," with too much "top-spin," filled with "pat-on-the-back phrases and meaningless quotes." Often the press release is packaged with quotes from C-level executives, and ample servings of praise "from analysts, (who are almost always paid or have a customer relationship.)"[3] Foremski was spot-on, and some in the PR industry wanted to fix the problem.

When she first saw the social media release, VandeVrede felt slightly overwhelmed as it was very jumbled and disorienting. Today, she feels it more closely reflects the snippets of information that we are becoming accustomed to when scanning for a story hook. Having links to further information is a good thing. To borrow her 'arrow' metaphor, these outbound arrows (links) point to a variety of relevant, contextual information. More importantly, a SMPR "allows journalists to pursue their line of interests, rather than having to deal with too much information in one body of copy."[4]

The Social Media Release got its first iteration when SHIFT introduced a template that was optimized with online distribution in mind. It was a nod to the structural value of a link. Its architects were making a bold gesture to finally say that there was a story within the story, a story outside the parameters of the information released, and it was not handcuffed to the provided quotation. It was a recogni-

> "Press releases are created by committees, edited by lawyers, and then sent out at great expense through Businesswire or PRnewswire to reach the digital and physical trash bins of tens of thousands of journalists." *Tom Foremski, "Die! Press Release! Die! Die! Die!"*
>
> Silicon Valley Watcher (http://s.tt/14aCy)

tion that its embedded content—audio, pictures, video—would find its way, directly or indirectly, into blogs, social bookmarking sites, RSS feeds and other new media properties.[5] It was different from the traditional press release in spirit because it recognized that the digital assets linked through the Social Media Release had to add context, not hype.

There was one additional feature that, at that time, was being discussed but not widely implemented: the need for content to be optimized for search engines. Not many knew how to do it, and search engine optimization, or 'SEO', was highly desirable.

The press release was always a document with a singular intent—to earn earn 'press.' It was not supposed to be a stealth move, so when some try to turn it into an act of spin, everyone suffers. If you play tennis, you will know how crafty a top spin serve is. It tricks you into moving wrong in order to get to the ball. Before you know it, you're flailing at the air. There is a better sports analogy, from cricket—the 'googly.' The bowler, a leg spinner, delivers the ball as if it was a typical leg spin, and the batsman can see it is going to curve after the bounce, from the leg side (closer to him) to the off side (away from him). But the googly is a crafty delivery that tricks the batsman because even though he sees the bowler spinning his hand in that manner, the bowler (who wants the batsman to see this) spins it even further, thus reversing the direction of the spin. To 'bowl a googly' is to be truly deceitful in cricket.

> **IS A PRESS RELEASE PRINT-READY?**
>
> The practice comes up now and then, but is seldom addressed by the communications or media industry.
>
> In June 2011, reporter Steve Penn was fired by his employer, *The Kansas City Star*, "for using material that wasn't his and representing it as his own work." The material in question was from press releases. He was accused of also having used conclusions without attribution. The practice wasn't new. In 2008, a similar incident in the UK resulted in the firing of journalist Johann Hari of *The Independent*.
>
> Penn filed a lawsuit that in effect challenged the tacit agreement between PR and the media, particularly the media's policy of using chunks of content in a release. In a complaint filed with the court, Penn's lawyer observed that press releases are "widely-understood in the journalism industry to be released to the press" with minimal editing, and by those "who do not desire attribution as to authorship." Thus, said the lawyers, the accusation of improper practice is false.[6]

The social media release is the un-googly. It distances itself from any sleight-of-hand.

But something else has changed: the recipients of the press release. The 'arrows' were once aimed at the press. Today?

Shannon Whitley, who created the first social media release creation tool, PRX Builder, says that traditional PR which was once known as 'Press Relations,' has broadened in scope. Considering what social media has the potential to do, he has seen how the concept of the 'press' has been expanded to mean bloggers and group influencers. Whitley grants that it is still important to reach out to the press, but the release could also reach ordinary people. "Through Social Media, large groups of people are more available to PR professionals. With some work, PR practitioners can find places where the most important people for a campaign are already gathering. All one has to do is join the conversation."[7] Whitley is now an application developer who specializes in social applications for the Web, desktops, and mobile devices.

PITCH ENGINE

Jason Kintzler takes a different approach, saying we should not be obsessing with or targeting the press at all! A former journalist and anchorman turned PR guy, Kintzler has been on both the receiving end of a press release and on the publishing side. He co-founded Pitch Engine, a service that promises to 'free the press release.' Free it from what? As the company puts it, the service intends to free it from the trappings of a document, to "put an end to the 'Word doc PR era." The newsworthy announcement is instead placed in a social PR platform.

"Back when reporters would typeset paragraphs from press releases straight into articles, the press release served as a utility—like a Swiss Army Knife. It was the 'plug-and-play' of its day." When I asked Kintzler to elaborate on this, the word spam came up a lot. He was incensed by the fact that companies use a press release like an aerosol can to spray non-news across the wire services, with the intention of reaching thousands of journalists. Pitch Engine seems to be the grown-up version of the social media release. Kintzler shies away from calling it the social media release (the company has trademarked the word 'Pitch' instead). Why? He believes that the traditional wire services that created their proprietary versions of the SMR have 'watered-down' versions of what it could have been. "Truth is, all they did is put 'share buttons' on traditional press releases. You cannot make a press release social; it has to be crafted differently from the start—multimedia rich and conversational—something traditional press releases lack."[8]

There used to be a working group dedicated to improving the format and promoting adoption of it. But it is no longer active. Whitley was one of the members of that group (Shel Holtz, Todd Defren and Chris Heuer were also part of it.) Today, PR professionals are breaking out of the template-ridden exercise, with tools through which they can engage with the media and broader publics. "Components of the social media release continue to find their way into the release stream. For instance, it's exciting to see how HTML is now a major part of the downstream distribution from major newswires." This opens up many new possibilities for social tools says Whitley. This downstream flow he refers to is about content elements or assets in the release (video, podcasts, image files, etc.) that are 'search optimized' so not just a journalist, but a company's affiliates, vendors, potential investors or customers could get a more rounded view of a product or service they plan to be associated with. With social media's promise, of letting citizens creating or curating their own media, the question if often asked whether the media release should be crafted for those who want the content by bypassing the gatekeepers.

GET RID OF THE FILTER

Kintzler might second that, as he believes that the press release, um, the 'pitch' should be aimed at customers, not gatekeepers. "I believe that in the next few years, PR will become primarily consumer-facing. Brands are able to connect with consumers directly now, leaving little need for a middle-man or distributor in the process." What he means is that a pitch sent to a media organization is limited because it has to pass through multiple filters. It has to be considered 'newsworthy' to editors, then passed on to journalists, then incorporated into a story, sometimes losing the desired story angle of the pitch. Why bother with that? Just as audiences now get their music and news sans traditional distributors, the broader audience will be able to get to its information by bypassing PR distributors.

Press releases will continue to evolve. They may be not have the power of a direct message, a conversation between an 'agent' and a 'reporter' over coffee, but they probably will not go away. If press releases could 'talk'—ideally start different conversations with different audiences, that would be the magic bullet. Not everyone is cheering on the SMR as the solution, *per se*. Mark Blevis, a Canadian-based strategist on digital communications believes that press releases containing messages intended for 'consuming-audiences' are different from those intended for 'participating-audiences.'[9] As such, PR needs to focus on engaging content, not delivery tools; the voice of engagement also needs to change for different audiences. A 2010 survey of more than 770 journalists in 15 countries found that 75 percent prefer to receive press releases via email.

But despite that, some journalists like Dan Nelson give the SMR format a thumbs-up because "it significantly cuts down on the time it takes to get to the most important bits of information."[10] Nelson, a regular contributor to *The Seattle Times* and *Men's Journal* magazine, is your typical digital nomad working across multiple operating systems—a laptop, an iPhone, using online file storage and RSS feeds. He says he has tailored his work style to create, interact with and distribute content in the 'cloud'—a term that generally refers to using applications and services such as Gmail or Dropbox that reside on remote servers and not on a person's local computer hard drive. "What do PR people who work with press releases need to keep in mind in order to reach or interest someone like you?" I asked him. "Learn to work with PR in the cloud, and engage me in the cloud," he responded without missing a beat. A press release that is nothing more than a digital version of a paper press release won't cut it, he says.

> Before you fire off that next release to your database, here are three things Nelson wants you to keep in mind:
>
> 1. "Get Social"—Create your release with more social features—video, audio etc. If you have to connect with me, send me a very short email (with an emphasis on *very*) with a short URL to the pitch.
> 2. "Don't Send Me Paper. Ever." I don't want to read anything that comes through my front door. Besides, a digital release is easy to archive for later use.
> 3. "Don't Write The Story." It is futile to write up a full-blown story. We would never run it—or a canned quote—verbatim. What I am always looking for are ideas, condensed as bullet points.

11

THE REVOLUTION WILL BE UPLOADED

There was a cliché that journalists write the first draft of history. Now I think these people are writing the first draft of history.[1]
—Dan Gillmor

They're "Weeds." That's what Iranian president Mahmoud Ahmadinejad called those citizens who stood up and challenged the regime during the elections of June 2009.[2] Ahmadinejad couldn't have picked a worse metaphor with which to dismiss a pesky protest that was taking to the streets. Or, perhaps it was most appropriate.

Weeds aptly describe what we call grassroots movements that pop up in the most inhospitable spaces. They are hard to monitor, curb or eradicate. Citizen-driven grassroots organizations—as opposed to corporate-backed movements that contain a citizen element—emerge quickly, and are the bane of autocratic regimes. Within a week of elections, the protesters in Iran had come out in full force. Deprived of the oxygen of media, Internet and phone access, and sometimes electricity, ordinary citizens made sure information spread more rapidly than traditional media, according to the BBC that once used to be one of the only voices in a conflict zone.³ These voices became the *de facto* media. Videos were shot on camera phones, photos were uploaded to Flickr and other photo-sharing sites. When the government blocked access to certain websites and blogs, people got around it by using Blutooth connections, and when they could get on, Twitter. When Twitter users in Iran got to know that their tweets were being monitored, others passed them the addresses of proxy servers—safe access points hosted outside Iran—to keep the information flowing. Dissident voices couldn't be turned off.⁴

The more the Iranian government clamped down, the more information kept leaking out, with photos, videos, blogs and tweets. Twitter was still a young medium in 2009, and was full of social chatter. Few news organizations had found a way to leverage this one-dimensional, text-based platform. It didn't look anything like journalism. The Twitter account going by the handle @TehranBureau, however, appeared out of nowhere in Iran and acted as a clearing house of news, just like mainstream clearing houses such as Reuters or Associated Press. TehranBureau had begun life as a foreign affairs and politics magazine, begun by Iranian-born Kelly Golnoush Niknejad in 2008. By May 2009, it was launched as a virtual news bureau. She was interested in presenting Iran, a 'very complicated story,' through this virtual bureau.

Others use it to alert the network, with messages like this:

> rey_diaz WARNING FindTheRats is not a secure loc. Trackers working for Basiji track their links. BEWARE **#Neda #iranelection #iran #tehran #GR88** RT

Indeed Twitter was an important channel for protestors. One study found that 479,780 Twitter users contributed to the Iran election conversation, but just a small fraction were really active voices.[5] It was playing into U.S. foreign policy, since Twitter streams provided diplomats a glimpse of a potential revolution, and held clues as to what kind of support Ahmadinejad had. The State Department admitted that it did ask Twitter to postpone a scheduled maintenance on June 16, 2009. "We highlighted to them that this was an important form of communication," a U.S. State Department official was quoted as saying.[6]

But Twitter was not the only problem Ahmadinejad faced. Bloggers, website owners, and mainstream media were being threatened and punished. Saeed Malekpour, 36, an Iranian-Canadian Web developer was arrested and sentenced to death by the Iranian Supreme Court. His sentence was upheld on 30 January, 2012, and the International Campaign for Human Rights in Iran claimed Malekpour was under pressure to make a televised confession.[7] Another protestor, a 26-year-old blogger named Hossein Ronaghi Maleki, was arrested on December 13, 2009. He was subsequently sentenced to 15 years in prison.

The most telling image of the repressive force of the government (and the courage of a citizen journalist) came via a camera phone. It was a grainy, 40-second video of the killing of a young girl, Neda Agha-Soltan, who became an instant symbol of the movement. Subsequently a network of hackers set up NedaNet, in support of a democratic revolution in Iran. "Our mission is to help the Iranian people by setting up networks of proxy servers, anonymizers, and any other appropriate technologies that can enable them to communicate and organize—a network beyond the censorship or control of the Iranian regime," stated the welcome page of Nedanet.org. The anonymous reporter of that video forwarded it to *The Guardian* and the *Voice of America*, and was awarded a George Polk award, a prestigious journalism award. "This award celebrates the fact that, in today's world, a brave bystander with a cellphone camera can use video-sharing and social networking sites to deliver news," commented John Darnton of *The New York Times* who also the curated the Polk Awards.[8]

YOU CAN'T KEEP A GOOD TWEET DOWN

Repressive governments like Iran are on the march using hi-tech fixes to seal a leaky vessel. But for every fix, there appear to be a dozen work-arounds. Today it is micro-blogs and underground networks. In a few years from now different tools that enable people to connect and communicate will emerge. The masses, the 'weeds,' have not only found their voice. They have found their audience. Governments and organizations—even the not-so-repressive ones—that are resistant to having communication bubble up from below will have to prepare for this uncomfortable reality. As James Cowie, founder of Renesis observed, "If you put 65 million people in a locked room, they're going to find all the exits pretty quickly, and maybe make a few of their own."[9]

Women are blogging in Iraq. They are often doing the 'journalism' that no one else can do, writing about conflict, tragedy, and the human experience that doesn't come through when filtered through the editors and servers of, say, *CNN* or the *London Times*.

In a post by a woman at the Inside Iraq blog, who remains anonymous, we hear about a silly but potentially dangerous exchange she had with trigger-happy, somewhat racist soldiers. She is returning from a trip to buy medicine.

Fifteen minutes later I reached the security people; they were National Police. "Pull over!" Oh dear, the never ending issue of show-

ing the car documents. "Here are the papers, and here's my name on them and here's my ID." "Put them away!" He was almost shouting. What was wrong this time, I wondered. Louder still, and with eyes about to pop out of his head, "Why is that flag hanging from your rearview mirror? Are you a Bathist?"

I couldn't believe what I was hearing. At last I grasped that he was talking about a small perfume pad that my son had bought from an intersection in Karrada some months ago. It hung from the mirror by a short string. The pad was painted with the Iraqi flag—The Iraqi flag after 2003, I must add. It was an item sold in most intersections all over Baghdad by poverty stricken women and children.

Her attempts to complain don't help; they eventually let her leave.

He was still angry, "There is a law now against sporting that flag, you know. But people are ignorant and don't follow the news. Pull it out and throw it away!"

"Wallahi, I will not."

He reached out and pulled, broke the string and threw the perfume pad on the ground. I was furious by now. He threw my keys onto the cushion. In silent rage, I drove off.

I've heard similar terse exchanges in democracies and they are no different from those going on in autocracies. Heated conversations with immigration officials, school boards, soldiers and state representatives.

This tense conversation reads like a script from a TV documentary, doesn't it? Her recollection is so fresh, it could only come through in a journal entry like this. Her experience is raw and real, but she seems to keep her emotions in check, just enough to be what we expect of a real journalist. But it is not a bland report, either. She's frustrated and we can sense it: *Oh dear, the never ending issue of showing the car documents.* It is a blog, after all, and she's chatting with us, her readers.[10] You can't stop the tweets, and you can't keep a good blog post down.

Keeping journals, the act of logging an entry for others to read (which is where blogs—truncated from 'web logs' got their name) has now turned into a form of historical record keeping. Dan Gillmor, a former journalist, ascribes these citizen journalists the role of authoring the opinion pages, and often the scoops, in this digital era.[11]

THE RIGHT TO SPEAK

In Saudi Arabia, a different kind of citizen reporter sat down to record her comments. They were comments enough to rile the government and get her arrested. Thirty-two-year-old Manal al-Sharif was, however, recording her commentary in the driving seat of a car while driving around town in May 2011.[12] The video of her protest was posted on YouTube. (You can watch it here: http://www.youtube.com/watch?v=sowNSH_W2r0) Why was she speaking out? The problem was that in Saudi Arabia, women were banned from driving for religious reasons, even though driving was not technically illegal. Not only was al-Sharif defying the religious edict, she was talking about it to an audience that in a different era would have never known her plight or that there was such a law. An Internet connection provides people like her and the Baghdad blogger, people who have otherwise been silent, a powerful voice, and an instant community. A Twitter or YouTube account, a camera, a phone or a blog is incidental to all of this. They are simply tools, which by themselves have limited value. The real upheaval is that ordinary people are speaking out of turn, bypassing traditional filters, and talking back.

Or are the tools bigger than we thought we were?

Communication is a leaky bucket. Just like how prisoners communicate with each other by tapping on the walls of their cells in a maximum security prison (where communication is controlled), humans have learned to chat despite communication bans and network blocks.

FACEBOOK CHATTER

Consider what is often talked of as the Facebook revolution—the 2010 overthrow of Egyptian President Hosni Mubarak. Mubarak had been in power since 1981, after Anwar Sadat was assassinated, and Mubarak is supposed to have survived six assassination attempts. But ordinary people who organized themselves using social networks got

Wael Ghonim, Google's head of marketing for the Middle East and N. Africa, in Cairo. Ghonim organized protests that led up to the ousting of the Egyptian president, and was kidnapped hours before the revolution

this dictator out of power.

Wael Ghonim, a computer engineer turned marketing manager (he worked for Google in the Middle East), was frustrated with how young people in Egypt were so apathetic to their lack of freedom and a corrupt government. The dictatorship under President Mubarak had run on for four decades. Influenced by how young people in neighboring Tunisia had ousted their leader, Ghonim set up a Facebook page dedicated to the Egyptian protester, Khaled Mohamed Said, who had been killed. He then watched how the chatter via the social network took off—even without him to nurture the conversation.[13]

He was soon arrested that day and held in prison for 12 days, but the giant speech bubble he had given birth to took on a life of its own.

On the morning of January 27, he tweeted "Pray for #Egypt."

> **@Ghonim**
> Wael Ghonim
>
> Pray for #Egypt. Very worried as it seems that government is planning as war crime tomorrow against people. We are all ready to die #Jan25

The culmination of events from the violent repression by the government, to the resignation of Mubarak, had a subtext: young people with the ability to communicate with each other could now have their voices heard.

But it's not all about Facebook or Twitter. Think of it as the Twitter effect, the ability for people to intuitively know how to network, to work in uncoordinated, small clusters and pass information along a daisy-chain of human and digital networks that fly under the radar, and then find a loophole (those proxy servers) to make the story global. Or to help other mainstream channels such as *Reuters, CNN, Time, BBC* to knit together a richer story rather than one reported from the balcony of a hotel in a safe zone.

The reverse-Twitter effect is also in play. We have grown skeptical of monolithic channels so we patch together our own story from multiple feeds. As a story breaks, we can pull in a background piece from Christiane Amanpour via YouTube, receive a text message from Reuters, follow a hash tag on Twitter, check the latest iReport from a citizen journalist on CNN, and check Wikipedia as citizen editors debate the accuracy of facts and stats pouring in to the comments section.

> "This is about giving their voices a chance to be heard. One of the ways that their voices are heard is through new media."
>
> —Ian Kelly, *U.S. State Department spokesman*
> On asking Twitter to postpone a scheduled maintenance that would have cut off Twitter from Iranian citizens disputing the election.

Some have thought that social media did indeed cause the revolution in Egypt. These online media tools did create information flows where once they were stifled. Observed *Time* magazine's Kurt Anderson, "in police states, with high Internet penetration—Ben Ali's Tunisia, Mubarak's Egypt, Bashar Assad's Syria—a critical mass of cellphone video recorders plus YouTube plus Facebook plus Twitter really did become an indigenous free press."[14]

That's how information flows. That's how 'weeds' propagate. Deprived of nutrients, they sometimes take over the lawn.

12

VOICES ON

If we have too much of anything on the Internet, it's engagement: too many minds pushing the platform in new directions, too many voices arguing about the social and economic consequences of those changes.[1]

—STEVEN JOHNSON

The six-million dollar question: Should all employees be allowed to use social media at work? The word 'all' is a key part to the question, which invariably implies that only a few could be trusted. The bigger question really is, should employees engage horizontally and externally?

Social media always creates a tension, and that is often a good thing. It is not a simple switch you could throw on or off. There are no buttons and links that you could turn on or off to begin engaging with audiences. There are those who see social media as a sun-roof, or a transparency filter to let the sunlight in. There are also those who deride it as a lever that unlocks the floodgates to an unwanted stream of information and/or trouble.

Exhibit A: James Roppo was just doing his job. As vice president at Island Def Jam Records, he was promoting a Canadian kid, a pop singer who was appearing at a shopping mall in Long Island, New York. Roppo had sent out some tweets to promote the event, but when large crowds began to show up, the police asked him to cut it out and send out a message to fans, also on Twitter, so as to control the crowd. Roppo, probably relying on his promotional instincts for a bigger story, refused to do it, and was arrested and charged with 'endangering the welfare of children and obstructing governmental administration'. The 'kid' Roppo was promoting was probably going to attract a mob of fans with or without Twitter. His name: Justin Bieber.

Exhibit B: Brian Maupin, a 25-year-old employee at Best Buy in Kansas City, Missouri, sells mobile phones. But he also moonlights making videos. One of them, using cartoon characters, shows an employee engaged with an insistent customer who wants nothing less than an iPhone 4. The employee tries to tell the customer that he could have an alternative, the HTC Evo, which is a 4G phone. But the customer will not even consider. The exchange (it is sprinkled with profanity, so be warned—if you Google the words 'iPhone 4 vs HTC') is very funny. Even though the video was not made on company time, and never mentioned Best Buy, Maupin's bosses didn't think so, and placed him on suspension.

Are your employees allowed to talk to others about your organization on public media channels? Could they do it on their own time? Is your head spinning? Mine, too!

OWNING THE CONVERSATION

We seem to be liberated by social media at some times, but we could easily be unraveled by it. This swirling current of content, apps, and confusing best practices has many people, certainly many bosses, shaking their heads and wondering whether social media is worth dipping their toes into. I get asked the same questions: "Should Marketing be in charge of the blog?" and "isn't a blog just another form of PR, which means, should only those who understand PR be allowed to blog?" There are other issues, such as "could someone sue us for mentioning their name or company in a podcast?" and "what if an

SHOULD EMPLOYEES BE EMPOWERED TO USE SOCIAL MEDIA?

UNFORTUNATE: You may have not known comedian Gilbert Gottfried. However, if you live in the US, you may know him as the voice of the duck in the Aflac commercials. Gottfried was fired for Insensitive Tweeting a story that became instant news.[2] He had sent out these insensitive tweets about the Japanese earthquake: *"I just split up with my girlfriend, but like the Japanese say, 'They'll be another one floating by any minute now.'"*

LAME: "Britain's new MI6 chief caught in Facebook scandal." A true story of intrigue because it had the ingredients of a teaser—scandal, Facebook victims, and espionage.[3] Sir John Sawers was caught in the crosshairs of a security breach when his wife published family holiday photographs and other personal details on the Facebook. Trouble was that Sawers was Britain's ambassador to the United Nations. Lady Sawers' inadvertent posting gave the public more insight into his 'network' than was necessary.

SUICIDAL: Ketchum advertising's James Andrews, the company's Vice President, was flying into Memphis, Tennessee, for a meeting with the company's client, FedEx. He tweeted, *"True confession but I'm in one of those towns where I scratch my head and say 'I would die if I had to live here!'"* Unfortunately, a FedEx employee saw it and commented that "Many of my peers and I feel this is inappropriate. We do not know the total millions of dollars FedEx Corporation pays Ketchum annually for the valuable and important work your company does for us around the globe. We are confident, however, it is enough to expect a greater level of respect and awareness from someone in your position as a vice president at a major global player in your industry." Andrews is no longer with the agency.

employee who was featured in a series of customer service videos leaves the company? Should we take them down?" The questions get trickier. "Do we 'own' a conversation archived on a channel, long after someone has checked out of the company?"

These are fair questions when we get into the engagement business, wanting to not just promote, smooth talk, pitch or brand-talk our way in.

Corporate blogging has taken off in fits and starts. About half a dozen years ago, corporations such as Sun Microsystems and General Motors green-lighted the idea. Robert Scoble who worked at Microsoft then, was one of the best-known corporate bloggers, who practically set the template for how companies could engage customers via blogs. A good corporate blogger could stretch the rules to "see if the corporate membrane can handle it," he observed.[4]

With this in mind, keeping the doors to the outside world unbolted is a smart move. Why? Often the frontline employee is someone who will run into a customer issue before senior management does. If the problem shows up at 6:45 pm on a Friday evening, and the PR department has signed off for the day, good luck thinking it could wait until Monday morning.

Employee engagement is a big field of study today because it is more than a PR problem. It is a management—and 'bottom line'—factor. When employees are 'actively disengaged' they erode their organization's bottom line. The Gallup organization estimated that within the U.S. workforce, the cost of disengagement could amount to more than $300 billion in lost productivity.[5] Tracking these 'macro-level indicators' of an organization's employee activity and motivation could give an organization that cares about such things a better read of where it is so as to map its future.

Employee engagement is not something that could be imparted in a one-hour seminar by someone in the human resource department. It involves putting into place a system of incentives and feedback systems that let employees want to be the eyes and ears of the organization. I once worked at an organization where employees seriously believed that there were spy cameras sprinkled around the office, since the CEO was supposedly intensely paranoid. It's one thing to be asked to be the eyes and ears of an organization. It's another to feel that electronic eyes and ears are making sure you, the human eyes and ears are doing your part.

Josh Bernoff, co-author of *Empowered*, speaks of four types of employees: the disenfranchised employee, the rogue employee, the locked-down employee and the hero. The locked-downs are everywhere. In government, 36 percent of employees are locked down. In marketing and sales, 23 percent. They shrug their shoulders and walk away when they sniff a problem because they are not sure if they will get their knuckles rapped if they responded to an email, sent out a tweet or posted a video about an instant fix. "You can't expect people to paint beautiful pictures if their brushes and paints are locked way most of the time," observed Bernoff.[6]

EMPLOYEES GONE WILD

Indeed being able to communicate instantly, honestly, and without seeking permission is a mixed blessing. New legal issues keep cropping up every week involving Wikipedia ("should we ask employees to 'correct' a mistake in a wiki entry about the company CEO"), Facebook ("How do we block Facebook on non-approved laptops?"), and photo-sharing ("what if an employee takes a video of an HR meeting?").

The American Red Cross realized this one night soon after the earthquake in Japan. One of its employees mistakenly used the official Twitter channel @RedCross to communicate something personal with his friends. He was using Hootsuite, which is a dashboard-like application that lets you manage multiple Twitter profiles. It went like this:

@RedCross: Ryan found two more 4 bottle packs of Dogfish Head's Midas Touch beer.... when we drink we do it right #gettngslizzerd

> **CHIEF LISTENING OFFICER?**
>
> The job of 'communicator' is passé in a social business. Some believe that a high-demand job could be one known as 'Chief Listening Officer.' Jeff Lerner, a customer of Dunkin Donuts, received a direct message on his Twitter account asking for his phone number. Dunkin wanted to apologize. For what? Lerner had tweeted that the lid on his coffee cup had come loose while driving and it had ruined his white shirt. Dunkin had followed him within five minutes of his tweet.
>
> Lerner had never contemplated threatening the company with a lawsuit, as did someone in the past over a McDonald's coffee spill. "Sue the establishment? Not my style," he said in a long blog post about the incident. "This is social media. This is listening. This is engagement. This is everything that corporations should strive for." He had spoken out on "that great message board in the sky" just to vent. But someone had been listening in, and wanted to engage.
>
> Listening is not a technical App. It's emotionally driven. As Adam Keats, of Weber Shandwick said, brands that make persistent emotional deposits will have more success.
>
> > **@OneFastLerner**
> > Jeff Lerner
> >
> > The workers **@dunkindonuts** drive-thru need to be trained on putting lids on tightly so my new car does not get coffee everywhere #fail

It was picked up and re-tweeted like crazy, and looked like a dangerous faux pas. Notice the hash tag #getting slizzered. Creative, but in poor taste. After all, we associate the Red Cross with pints of blood, not beer. Images of Red Cross officials soliciting donations, drinking on the job and 'getting slizzered' isn't exactly flattering to its corporate image.

Well, with some careful calibration, and truly quick response, the Red Cross got itself out of hot water. How? First, it didn't ignore the issue. Second it brought it out into the open and posted it to its website, saying "Last night we accidentally tweeted from our @RedCross account something that was meant to come from a personal account." It even showed an image of the tweet in question. "We realized our honest mistake (the Tweeter was not drunk) and deleted the above tweet. We all know that it's impossible to really delete a tweet like this, so we acknowledged our mistake."

This, too is engagement. It takes guts to do this kind of damage control and talk directly with your audience soon after you inserted foot in mouth. Somebody in their community responded by saying:

"After I drop off a pint of blood to the @Redcross, I'm replacing it with a pint of @Dogfish beer. #gettngslizzerd"

In many instances like this, the initial response would be for an organization to clam up, to rethink its social media policy, add walls and make things so difficult that employees would give up. In case you are wondering, Best Buy did not fire that employee who made the video. In fact, it is one of those companies that have embraced social media across the organization. At Zappos, the online shoe retailer, some 400 workers are on Twitter. So too, are employees at Dell, JetBlue and other organizations who 'follow' and engage customers on Twitter. They chat with them, forging lasting relationships so as to solve day-to-day issues. In return, they get customers' honest opinions on services provided. It is a two-way exchange—just as how conversations always were. Many people today are in a hurry to credit social media for this complex human interaction. The channels we have available certainly open up new opportunities to listen, empathize, and deepen conversations, but humans once did have this capacity and didn't need fancy tools to engage.

There is another dimension to 'voice' that social media apologists seldom focus on: how voice validates a person's contribution to, and place in a social system. Think of the opportunity to 'voice off' as the psychographic necessity that affirms we are more than widgets in a soulless machine. Michael Lee Stallard puts it this way: being permitted to have a voice (whether it is being asked to be a spokesperson for a business unit's news segment, or being invited to blog) provides reassurance that "I'm not a dependant variable." Stallard, whose research into employee engagement lets him peer into several corporate cultures, believes that successful organizations are those that embrace any channel that gives employees a voice to express their ideas and opinions.[7]

We can't expect employees to have their 'voices off,' as is often expected of young students filing into class each morning. Employees will create those outbound links, and have those unscripted conversations. Whether you call it conversations or engagement, there are two aspects to it. The first part involves the ability dive in and join the chat. Most employees, even those who have not been in customer-facing positions, do not need training for this. The second part of engagement involves active listening. Unfortunately, it's easy to get drowned in the chatter, and forget how to do this.

13

BATHED IN BUZZ

It's not toxic... and we're launching a campaign to get people to stop calling it sludge. We call it 'biosolids.' It can be used beneficially to fertilize farm fields, and we see nothing wrong with that.[1]

—Nancy Blatt

Propaganda, PR, and image rehab are some of the choices world leaders resort to when traditional diplomatic communiqué's don't cut it. Modern republics and dictatorships have been skinny-dipping in the hot tub of buzz.

About ten years ago, a group of Libyan businessmen sought advice from a PR agency on how to improve the image of their country. Libya's reputation had been tarnished by Muammar Qadaffi's eccentric behavior, and terrorist links to his past. Qadaffi had been inextricably linked to the 1988 bombing of Pan Am 103 in Lockerbie, Scotland, after all.[2] The intention to engage in public relations may have been good—to improve Libya's tourism industry. But who would the PR be directed at?

What the world began to notice after that were such events such as the reopening of diplomatic ties between Britain and Libya, and the Qadaffi family's support of charitable foundations. Around this time the recluse leader agreed to give up Libya's weapons of mass destruction (WMD), and ballistic missile program and even compensate families of victims who died in the Pan Am incident.

To a certain extent, the image rehab campaign of Qadaffi and his country worked. Magically, in the first decade of the 21st century, his negative side was airbrushed—or overridden by a nicer profile. He was readmitted into the club of statesmen, and world leaders such as Tony Blair appeared in photo ops with him.[3]

You probably didn't hear about these in terms of a Public Relations exercise because in many successful PR campaigns, the 'wins' are not something for which a PR agency takes credit. If I may use a search engine analogy, positive links often bury the links to negative ones forever.

INFLUENCE PEDDLING

Contrast it to Libya's more recent PR. In February 2012, even as the citizens of the country began to take to the streets in opposition to the dictator, Qadaffi began using a powerful lobbying firm to polish his image abroad, primarily, in the U.S. The firm he worked with, The Livingston Group, proudly lists the foreign ministry of Libya as a client; other clients include universities, corporations and other countries—such as the Republic of Azerbaijan and the Republic of Turkey. A leaked email, purportedly from someone in the Libyan government, revealed how desperate Qadaffi's administration was to clean up its image and 'counter-balance' negative stories.

Interestingly Livingston is both a Public Relations and a lobbying firm. Not many people realize that PR is a very close cousin of Government Relations, or 'GR' and lobbying. Influence peddling and image management have come a long way since the other technique widely used by dictators: propaganda. Governments in the early part of the twentieth century did not hesitate to use it, employing Hollywood, for instance, to craft overtly propagandist films to stimulate patriotism, and the fear of the enemy—so as to support the war effort. Libya wanted something more subtle. In a letter supposedly sent to PR agencies by the country's ministry of information, it said that its need for PR was based on "good moral, political and legal logic.[4] It sought a firm to influence academics, 'existing and up-and-coming politicians,' journalists, etc.

Today PR and GR still involve a few of the tactics of propaganda such as posters, movies and articles planted in the popular press. But there are a lot more tools in the PR/GR firms' toolboxes. Their strategy might involve complex event coordination and seemingly spontaneous, but well planned, photo opportunities that target unsuspecting journalists. Recently, there have been cases involving paid spokespeople and fake grassroots movements (set up by agency people) to look like they are being spearheaded by ordinary citizens. The Public Relations Society of America cautions practitioners to not in¬dulge in such dubious practices; ever so often someone does, and gets caught.

> Subject: Mission for Peace
>
> Dear Sir/madam
>
> "We are seeking to employ your PR company to present our just and fair case to the world. Libya has been under an unjustified media and PR attack which led to NATO's military involvement since the 19th of March. We also face an armed rebellion that has been causing violence, terror and destruction in many parts of the country.
>
> We have good moral, political and legal logic supporting our position as the legitimate, sovereign and popular government of Libya. We also have proofs in written, audio and video forms to take our case forward."
>
> **Letter from Qadaffi administration official, Ali Darwish, Mission for Peace and Ministry of Information to PR firms worldwide.**[5]

I am not saying that PR for world figures is a bad thing. True PR is all about advocacy and how to manage information that is public. Many leaders, give or take a crackpot despot, need some advice. The senior minister needs help in how to conduct his personal and government affairs before stepping off a plane. Why? Because some of them who might be rather skilled politicians, do some really dumb things (no strategic planning) or are prone to say something embarrassing (poor media advice) in front of a camera or microphone. They dialogue with fellow parliamentarians all the time but they could sometimes be insulated from the rough and tumble chatter that goes on in the streets. The media is good at confronting public officials with provocative snippets of these plebian sentiments. If the official trips up, it enlarges the story and stimulates more conversations.

There appears to be no shortage of those who believe that buzz could disperse or muffle the real conversations going on in a country. Modern republics, even those that have impressive voting rights and people representation cannot help skinny dipping into the hot tub of image rehab.

BEING PROACTIVE

Creating buzz is not the prerogative of the West. A 74-year-old social activist in India, Anna Hazare, began a fast in 2011 to protest corruption in the government. But unlike other hunger strikers, Hazare used some savvy PR to make his campaign resonate with the public. Obvious tactics were his use of the Mahatma Gandhi imagery. But the real buzz was created by 'Team Anna' that turned the one-man protestor into a movement supported by candle-light marches, and street drama. Yes, the team was tweeting, and there were videos on YouTube, but the campaign got people talking because of street-level events.

In Sri Lanka, for decades, the government paid scant attention to public relations. The LTTE, a terrorist organization which began demanding a 'separate state' in the early 1980s, however, had a more aggressive way of managing its image, using bloody events plus foreign media to make its cause heard. The LTTE was defeated militarily in 2009, but the government's 'GR,' with regard to post-war events and media scrutiny reveals a lack of sophistication, if not strategic vision. In the middle of the war, it had not proactively come out and explained its anti-terrorism effort, even when it had a legitimate right to do it. It met propaganda with rebuttals from people who were not entirely credible. Its 'press statements' were old-school. Then, in 2007, it woke up and realized that it had to communicate better with many more constituencies than the press. In 2009, the embassy of Sri Lanka in Washington, DC, retained a law firm for advocacy, and to act as an intermediary between the embassy and the executive branch of the U.S. government and Congress.[6]

But what good is PR if the media will not give you a chance to speak and be heard? What good is a system of governance if you cannot engage with even your critics in a spirited dialogue? A young Sri Lankan diplomat, Bandula Jayasekera, a former journalist, broke with the old way of creating conversations, and took to making his own mission's point of view, on his own terms.[7] By then the government had begun engaging a variety of other tactics, including well-managed websites and some social media. Governments that have always managed crises through a 'ministry of information' or a media officer in a diplomatic mission, tend to believe their own spin, and often make the miscalculation that they know how best to manage public opinion. That mindset is now changing. If people have to talk, they calculate, there had better be someone who manages the conversation.

Consider how PR was engaged by another county, Kuwait. I'm not saying we ought to take a leaf from its book, but it is an interesting comparison. The government of Kuwait was known to have used about 20 PR, law and lobby firms during the first Gulf war. Twenty! One of them was a GR firm known as The Rendon Group which practically stage-managed the stories around the 'liberation' of the country. Rendon is an agency that specializes in crisis communications, political consulting, advocacy and public affairs. Observed John Rendon at that time, "if any of you either participated in the liberation of Kuwait City or if you watched it on television, you would have seen hundreds of Kuwaitis waving small American flags...Did you ever stop to wonder how the people of Kuwait City, after being held hostage for seven long and painful months, were able to get handheld American flags? And for that matter, the flags of other coalition countries? Well, you now know the answer. That was one of my jobs."

Like I said, it is not a great model to follow, especially when using deceitful practices, but it reveals the extent to which some countries think about their external relations. It could be as blatant as promoting a country as a brand.

In January 2011, China launched an image building TV ad in the U.S.—to coincide with President Hu Jintao's visit to Washington. The 30-second commercial, created by the same person who directed the closing ceremony of the 2008 Olympics, was managed by Shanghai Lintas Advertising. This image-building exercise by China is supposedly part of a long-term effort to promote "the soft power of national culture," using what China calls "external propaganda work and culture exchange." Government Relations, by another name!

But more often than not, GR falls somewhere in-between being blatant and highly invisible. Take Egypt. The Hosni Mubarak government was known to have retained several of these lobby-slash-GR firms over the past decades. They are firms such as Chlopak, Leonard, Schechter and Associates, Hill and Knowlton, and The Podesta Group. These firms employ some of the most powerful ex-politicians and influencers in Washington DC, including those who have served on senate committees, and presidential speechwriters. The Podesta Group is often cited as one of the most influential lobbies for Hosni Mubarak's regime. It describes itself as "a bipartisan government relations and public affairs firm with a reputation for employing creative strategies to achieve results." It is part of a 3-part lobby arm that services the Egyptian account. Likewise, the United Arab Emirates retains a few similar lobby firms as well.

There could be many countries, right now, working pro-actively on their image management. They may want to do this for different strategic intentions, and are probably retaining outfits like one of the above. I could bet that some are seriously exploring the role of social media, and how to bend it to serve some dubious ends. There has been anecdotal evidence of how governments are setting up fake social networking accounts to play in this space, attempting to influence the media and public opinion. The Rendon Group talks of converting "adversarial misinformation into an offensive client opportunity." That seems a somewhat questionable practice, but with so many countries in need of image-management today, I am not surprised there are firms who will fill their needs this way.

The level of advice they get falls across the spectrum of lobbying, PR, GR, legal advice and reputation management. Lobbying is described as "a form of advocacy with the intention of influencing decisions made by legislators and officials in the government." In some parts of the world such a blurry definition of influencing public officials is known as bribery, not advocacy. But some would say it's a matter of semantics; who you know, and what kind of legal defense you have, should you be found out, is what matters!

This is the new face of PR, crisis management and advocacy on a global scale. But absent real dialog, buzz drowns alternative voices, and only provides short-term gains. World leaders, however, never seem to learn from their predecessors. We citizens have discovered new ways to get ourselves heard. Our messages, our questions, our ideas could go viral in a heartbeat, without a PR machine. That's the kind of organic—as opposed to manufactured—buzz that our leaders should invite.

They could take a leaf from the page of the so-called link economy, and cultivate a little 'link love.'

14

LINK LOVE

It's not content until it's linked.[1]

—Jeff Jarvis

Most of us professional communicators, when asked what we do for a living tend to say we write, edit, design, update websites, or work in marketing, PR or media. But if we boil all of this down to one common role, we are all storytellers. To put it another way, we have audiences, and we connect with those audiences using different formats of stories: other people's stories, untold stories, fictional stories, timely stories, and our own stories.

> "Often, the function of the real-time Web is pointing people to the timeless Web."
> —Matt Thompson

No matter how we package content, whether in a media advisory or a 30-second commercial, storytelling has relentlessly focused on sending a message. We are fully aware that in an 'attention economy,' people are too distracted but we are consumed by the transmission of the content, rather than the content itself. The Web has turned audiences into 'content snackers' we are told. Our stories need to be designed to cut through the clutter, so we better shorten our preambles and sex-up our storylines. Sounds familiar?

I don't dispute the overcast skies of clutter. But there's another weather condition we storytellers might be flying into. It's the unrelenting force of the link economy. The link economy is one where the value of links is determined by the recipient of the links. Jeff Jarvis has a succinct way of describing it. "It's not content until it's linked," says the journalist, who is also a blogger, journalism professor and media critic.[2] Mainstream media has been skeptical and suspicious of it because it means linking outside to 'sources' and commentary that belong to someone else. Doing so has been not in their culture, and poses both technical and cultural hurdles for some. *The Associated Press*, a 186-year-old news gathering, distribution and syndication network vehemently fights content linking.[3] To be specific, it had a policy that disallowed bloggers and other news aggregators from quoting from, and linking to, parts of articles on its site. It was a genuine 'fair use' concern, but when so much of information gets forwarded, clipped and shared, it would be impossible to police. Others, like Reuters, have recognized the larger picture of linking, and have signed off on it.[4] They are in lockstep with Jarvis and others who observe that content has no intrinsic value if no one touches it, or sees it. "Content that isn't linked is the tree that fell in the forest no one heard," he says. Connecting a story makes it more nuanced, and adds a broader perspective. I like to put it this way: every story needs to have a beginning, middle and a hyperlink.

Many people ignore the power of the link economy because they believe they are only responsible for the production side of content. It's someone else's job to worry about how to distribute it. They ac-

> "Suppose all the information stored on computers everywhere were linked."
> —Tim Berners-Lee, *inventor of the World Wide Web, who wrote the specifications for URLs*

cept without question that 'it's all about the content.' This too sounds familiar? This content-is-king thinking is not completely off the mark but it's just too vague and has often come to imply that any content is terrific. It is why we hear such requests as "could you just throw some ideas together for our newsletter?" or "I need a few quick sentences from your PR folks to update our Facebook fan page." Such staccato signals of constant information don't really build an ongoing story. So it's time to stop thinking of ourselves as content machines and distribution hubs. It's time to think of our roles as conversationalists who swim in the link economy.

Tens of thousands of people with no financial incentive have invested more than a hundred million hours of their time, writing up bits and pieces, intensely hyperlinked, to create an enormous knowledge resource. We know this as Wikipedia. If nothing, Wikipedia is a statement of link love.

That's how the Web's architecture was intended to be—intensely hyperlinked. "Suppose all the information stored on computers everywhere were linked…" surmised Tim Berners-Lee when he designed the blueprint of the Web.

LINKS AS SCAFFOLDING

So how do you prep your storytelling skills for the link economy? Here's an assignment. First, go author and edit a Wikipedia entry if you have not done so already. (Go back to Chapter 9 for a primer.) It's hyperlink heaven in there. Sure the entries have to be 'neutral'—dry, really—to survive. But wikis teach us that in this information-obese, context-hungry world, hyperlinks are like super-nutrients. Dave Weinberger (in his book *Everything is Miscellaneous*) notes how a page in Wikipedia is not something that even exists; it is instead dynamically created to have the look and feel of a page, a collection of elements served up by multiple servers at the moment it is needed—a collection of *hyperlinked* content.[5]

Think about that for a second. The page you pull up using a search word didn't really exist until the second you called it up. It was built just for you because a bunch of hyperlinks, like virtual scaffolding, conspired on your behalf! Not all stories might live in such a context, but just the discipline of framing a story to ensure it could be dynamically pulled together by hyperlinks forces you to think about the broader universe in which your story will live in a borderless, timeless Web.

Hyperlinks serve another function. Before there were hyperlinks, one could have created any story out of a mashup of fact and fiction. To do any form of fact-checking was laborious. One had to take down notes, and remember to clip the article or record the segment. Hyperlinks bring an element of verifiability to the reader. Often this is something that could be done in real-time, via third-party organizations.[6] Today, as job seekers are aware, any little white lie and any scurrilous claim gets found out. A candidate's life story, her CV, has to line up with the larger hyperlinked storyboard that lives in the linked economy. Likewise, an organization's brand story is pulled up from a myriad of sources (servers), its links curated by millions of customers, suppliers, and product reviewers.

Another way to think of a hyperlink is to see it as the pores of the skin of a message or conversation. Some organizations used to have a policy of not adding outbound hyperlinks in information on their website. The thinking was that websites needed to be 'sticky' and therefore keep visitors glued to (or trapped in the glue of) the site's content. As we saw in the vignette of PepsiCo's internal newsletter, *PepLine* began adding links to certain stories, thereby solving one part of the problem of empowering employees to become brand ambassadors. But first, the company put all employees through social media training, known as SMARTU in May 2011, to educate them about the platforms and practices they could use.[7] The goal was to tell them it was OK to talk outside of the company on social media, as long as they followed guidelines. PepsiCo was keen—not worried—that employees share the knowledge, and not just inside the company but outside. But there was something it had to overcome. "We had done such a great job of explaining to employees in the past that they were not supposed to be talking to the press, or the media, that they immediately made the connection that they could not talk through the media," said Sharon Macintosh.[8] The revised newsletter now includes share buttons that gives all employees an opportunity to link outside, and to share the stories.

CURATORS AND AGGREGATORS

A story is today told and stored in dynamic spaces even broader than what Wikipedia represents. "Try to win the story," observes Matt Thompson, because news is "transitioning from an area of niche, into an area of networks." Thompson, editorial product manager at *National Public Radio* (NPR) in the U.S., has a very different idea of where storytelling is headed. We think of the Web as a collection of niches, but the timeless Web we have today grew out of (probably in reaction to) a closed, niche-media world. "We came from the early 20th century, with 677 different publications, seven daily newspapers in the Twin Cities, each of which spoke to a niche. But those publications didn't speak to each other." And so the audiences of those niche media didn't know each other, since the political party of trade publication was a person's only reading material and it kept him in that siloed world. "We then moved to a mass media where things began to conglomerate, largely influenced by graphic and economic trends, by advertisers who were seeking bigger audiences, and by the fact that people had begun moving away from city centers into the suburbs," notes Thompson.[9] The mass media favored monopoly with few concentrated mass media outlets.

But with the Internet the mass has begun to fragment in a different way. And this is where the link economy comes into play. Thompson is convinced that "We are now transitioning to less of an area of niche, and more into an area of networks. Where there is not much friction or distance separating one news outlet from another, where you could reach from one to another by a link." In other words the media were becoming just a few hyperlinks from each other, even though they did not welcome the development. Into this space leapt "a few systems with deeply focused, well-networked niche outlets served by a system of curators and aggregators. These are proving to be the new 'mass' in this universe." They will create a media product that ends up gaining a wide constituency. And what's a good example of this media product? Twitter! "Twitter is the definition of niche. Network effects are generated by Twitter, and you see a trending topic, even though a niche distributed audience, the curation system, is pointing everyone towards similar content." But Twitter is easy to misread as a headline-obsessed social network. "You look at Twitter and you see a big part of the Web on the latest thing. But there's another equally important part of the Web that Twitter reveals, and that is that news is time-less."

This is the new format of storytelling, Thompson points out. He is one of a handful of journalists who have been critiquing the practice of telling stories through the filters of 'recency' and 'immediacy.' Our story, he says, should be obsessive about context. In his recommendation to journalists, he asks them to aim to produce a work of journalism so excellent it'll get passed around for weeks even if it means creating the story as a nicely-packaged collection, a wiki, or something else you devise. "The key is that it should be long-lasting and distinctive."[10] What might save journalism is good medicine for us as well. Unless we tap into Network Effects, we will be lost in the noise, and lost in the niches.

Let me point you to two examples of understanding how this might work.

Living Stories: The project, now discontinued, involved two newspapers, *The New York Times*, and *The Washington Post*, that worked with a search engine, Google. It was known as Living Stories (Find it at www.livingstories.googlelabs.com) and looked at how the news business might harness the Web rather than become roadkill.

Augmented Reality: The second example is more audacious and involves a different kind of hyperlink. It's called Augmented Reality (AR). Magazines such as *Esquire* have featured a code on its cover and sprinkled across other pages. When held up to a webcam, it lets the reader experience 'content' in an unexpected way. (check out how here: www.esquire.com/AR)

> "The idea behind Living Stories is to experiment with a different format for presenting news coverage online.
>
> A typical newspaper article leads with the most important and interesting news, and follows with additional information of decreasing importance. Information from prior coverage is often repeated with each new online article, and the same article is presented to everyone regardless of whether they already read it.
>
> Living Stories try a different approach that plays to certain unique advantages of online publishing.
>
> - They unify coverage on a single, dynamic page with a consistent URL.
> - They organize information by developments in the story.
> - They call your attention to changes in the story since you last viewed it so you can easily find the new material."
>
> —Blog Post at googleblog.blogspot.com, Dec. 8, 2009

So what might we take away to learn to adapt to this different ecosystem? In Living Stories there's that eternal pull between real-time information and long-tail value of content. (Check out how the Swine Flu has been covered and curated here: bit.ly/c6Dj5j) Many of us, no matter how digital our work has become, still have old-media assignments such as creating PowerPoint decks, writing white papers and book chapters as part of our to-do list. These content pieces are seldom meant for real-time consumption. They are, to put it somewhat uncharitably, frozen in time. But as Thompson points out, we need to understand "how the real-time Web can point to the timeless Web."

We can be sure that new opportunities will show up as mobile devices and e-book readers become the new on-ramps to your real-time and timeless content. It's only if we experiment with the inputs, tweak our links, and stretch the 'skins' of our stories will we become better storytellers for the digital age.

LINK ECONOMY

Esquire's cover story in December 2009 did not live exclusively on the printed page. It was written in a way that could address the reader directly — in the voice of actor Robert Downey Jr., sitting awkwardly on a QR code. It highlights the fact that this is "a living, breathing, moving, talking magazine."

Once the edition of a magazine using such a device became a back issue, it could be turned into a living story with new voices and new conversations added for the timeless Web. This gimmicky, nascent, print-to-Web experience is enhanced only by the reader taking action — in this case pointing the magazine at something. He could also tilt it to 'navigate' through the content. When was the last time you used paper as a pointing device?[11]

15

AMATEURS WITH MICROPHONES

Imagining then a Semi-Circle, of which my distance should be the radius, and that it were fill'd with auditors, to each of whom I allow'd two square feet, I computed that he might well be heard by more than thirty-thousand.[1]

—Benjamin Franklin

For a microphone, it is an odd wireless device. The People's Microphone is waterproof, bulletproof, and best of all, it does not need to be connected to an amplifier to work. In fact, you can't purchase it anywhere.

You see, the People's Mic is not even a piece of hardware, making it impossible to confiscate or (as in the case of cameras and recording equipment used by investigative journalists) smashed.

And yet, it is a powerful communication tool.

In a time when most major communication innovations are invariably part of a social media ecosystem (think QR codes, Google Voice, Facebook) it is striking to see this patently social 'technology' being adopted without an online component. Because it does not fall into the 'shiny new object' category, it makes it even more valuable, with a promise of wider adoption.

The People's Mic gained popularity in late 2011 during the protest movement known as Occupy Wall Street, but its 'invention' could be traced back to the 1980s when ordinary people took to the streets to vent against nuclear facilities in the U.S. It later showed up in the anti-globalization rallies in the 1990s in Seattle and other U.S. and European cities.[2] You probably never heard about it then because that was in a pre-YouTube era. Indeed, there were cameras, but few people had a video camera handy, if at all, when something disruptive took place down their street.

> On October 19, 2011 the Urban Dictionary's Word of the Day[3] was Human Microphone. The entry read:
>
> "A tactic protesters can use to circumvent police bans on electronic amplification of speech. One person starts to speak to a large crowd. After a short sentence, everyone within hearing distance repeats whatever was said at the top of their lungs, allowing people outside of hearing distance to hear the speech."

And one more thing. The People's Mic isn't connected to a recording device, and doesn't require wires or batteries. But it is tethered to a grid, and just amplifies a person's words.

As a 'device,' the People's Mic is more technique than tool—a means of transmitting information using human ingenuity. This ingenuity actually pre-dates this century, going back several hundred years when oral cultures spread information via semi-professional storytellers, known as jongleurs and troubadours. Using a repertoire of stories featuring literary works, entertainment acts and music, the thirteenth-century jongleur was a sort of a cultural transmitter in Europe. But the 'information' moved slowly as he traveled in a caravan that meandered through taverns, brothels, livestock exchanges, and churches. When word got around about a larcenous king or a bumper crop in the next village, his stories probably got more colorful and the fellow received more invitations to narrate his tales. "Come give us the inside scoop about Sir James," they would say. "We will give you free board and hot soup if you do!"

You're still wondering what's a People's Mic, aren't you? Now that you have some background it gets more interesting.

PEOPLE'S MICROPHONE: TRIBAL LOUDSPEAKER

The People's Mic is essentially this: Someone stands on a milk crate under a tree, and speaks to a small gathering of people. As he speaks, the audience draws closer to hear what he's got to say, but as the crowd swells, the people at the back have no chance of hearing him. So those folks closer to him begin to repeat each short sentence, in unison, and the people at the back also begin to repeat what they have begun to hear. The effect is like turning up the volume on an amplifier. In effect, the speaker's words radiate outward.

But, as you may have guessed, there are several problems with this kind of broadcasting arrangement. What if someone at the back doesn't catch a sentence? What if the speaker's sentences are very complex, with no neat pauses? Interestingly enough, humans have found ways around this. Because the 'microphone' only powers up if there are many people repeating the words of the speaker, a person at the back who may have missed a sentence can hit the pause button, so to speak. She could pause the speaker by simply shouting out the magic words, "Mic Check!" (This is also the way someone initiates a speech and invokes the People's Mic by just shouting out 'Mic Check!') The audience repeats the words "Mic Check" and this gets the speaker's attention, even if he cannot see who needed the pause. It is a slow process, but it gets people to focus on the deeper conversations.[4]

The crowd that powers the microphone could also involve itself in another way. People could voice their agreement or disagreement with a speaker without causing cacophony. The goal is consensus. All they have to do is use a convention of hand signals. Hendrik Hertzberg, writing for the *New Yorker* described this process well: "The listeners register their reactions silently, with their hands. Four fingers up, palm outward: Yay! Four fingers down, palms inward: Boo! Both

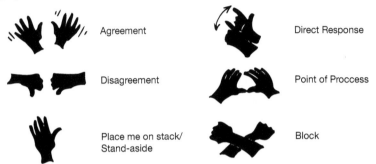

The language of Occupy Wall Street—hand gestures used by the movement's 'General Assembly'

hands rolling: Wrap it up! Clenched fists crossed at the wrists: No way, José! There's something oddly moving about a crowd of smartphone-addicted, computer-savvy people cooperating to create such an utterly low-tech, strikingly human, curiously tribal means of amplification—a literal loudspeaker."[5] The idea of the People's Mic came out of a way to circumvent the ban on amplification technologies at sites where many Occupy activists gathered.

It is therefore a bit of both—a tribal device to amplify chat and the human loudspeaker. But lest you scorn this kind of behavior, know that even in modern broadcast studios, radio and TV hosts and producers resort to hand signals, while the mic is live. A finger swiftly draw from left to right under the neck indicates to the speaker to cut it out or 'wrap it up' etc.

Indeed, there's something intriguing about a group of grown-ups repeating every sentence of a speaker. It has the feeling of a classroom where the teacher says "now repeat after me" and the students do exactly that. Students have no choice but to echo their teacher. Using the People's Mic does not assume there will be such obedience or

> **THE *INHUMAN* MEGAPHONE**
>
> A good example of how a digital replacement doesn't work comes from an app designed to mimic the human microphone. It's called the Inhuman Microphone. Here's how it works: Someone getting up to address the crowd at an 'occupation' speaks first into his smart phone loaded with the Inhuman Microphone app. His words are uploaded in real-time to a server and becomes accessible to anyone in the crowd who uses the app. The individuals hold up their phones and play back the words through the speakerphone; the server synchronizes the playback, creating an echo effect.
>
> There appears to have been very little thought given to whether the technology was a way to boost or replace the human activity. (It was developed in one weekend in December 2011, in London, during an event known as Music Hack Day.[6] After all, the influence of a movement that brings people together is only as powerful as the number of voices, ideas and community, not its amplification.
>
> Amateurs do use software and hardware fixes, but a movement that came about because of the need to have its voices heard, and to add to the national conversation, eventually earns its legitimacy from people not just the cool tools they bring.

hierarchy, but the fact that the crowd follows the 'rules' voluntarily, makes it a powerful process. Some who have participated in the Human Mic say that it feels like democracy in action, where people from all walks of life gather, impromptu, and pay attention to a person, with opportunity to 'vote' on the message. Give or take a few funny hand signals![7]

NOT FOR POLITICIANS

More than that, some say that this decidedly non-digital practice forces people to become participants, not spectators. Social media advocates like to talk up the benefit of 'engagement.' This is audience engagement, with a double-shot of espresso after a swig of Red Bull! No wi-fi required. The slow pace of the ideas being repeated ensures people listen carefully. "It encourages deeper listening because audience members must actively repeat the language of the speaker," notes Sara Van Gelder. The technique—crowd-powered—allows democratic decisions to be taken, and it encourages consensus despite the diversity because the act of hearing oneself repeat something one doesn't even agree to makes it powerful.[8] There is no such thing as a sound bite here, and the speaker has to choose his or her words carefully. Language must be simple, so the chance of jargon creeping in is small. It would be irritating if a speaker was Mic Checked several times a minute because he is full of you know what!

It is therefore highly unlikely that politicians would grab a Human Mic, even though they do engage in street talk. But often when they talk on the street, their trainers caution them about sticking to a script, and to guard against off-the-cuff remarks. To permit an audience member to Mic check a politician would be unnerving.[9] For the same reason, a CEO's speech would not work in this format. The Occupy movement is an attempt to contradict the logic of leader-follower, speaker-listener communication. The radical, "body-flip of the old model by a seemingly rowdy crowd, demands a participatory format."[10] But when you think about it, the best speeches of our era would work with a Human Mic.

We may not always acknowledge it, but as in the use of hand gestures and tweets, the digital realm and the analog do exist side by side. One of the early digital tools used by the movement was an iPhone app called Vibe. It let those in Zuccotti Park, New York, post messages to each other, with videos and photos. But they were able to limit who could see these messages, using what was called a 'geo-fenced radius' So, in effect, someone could create a 'whisper' campaign that would be only seen by other OWS people in the park within a few hundred feet. Vibe also let the message have wider reach through options ranging from Whisper (50 meters), to Speak (500 meters), to Shout (50 kilometers), to Yell (500 kilometers), to Bellow (worldwide). What also seemed clever was how the sender could set an expiration date or time for the message.[11]

Apps are all the rage now, but what feels disingenuous, and even hollow, is when an attempt is made to replace the analog system of the Human Mic with something wholly digital. Those in the movement bristle at a reference to an iPhone app known as the Inhuman Microphone!

So here's the challenge if you are involved in crafting words that need to have wide audience reach and engagement. Is 'amplification' your thing? Do you need widespread distribution? Or do you prefer audience (and employee) engagement? Do you really want feedback from the audience, and are you ready to pass the mic? These are important questions communicators need to ask themselves and their organizations' senior management.

When you choose your next medium, or launch your new tool, would you be able to build in some elements of the People's Mic? The tool or the concept will change over time. It always does. Twitter was a gift to those who saw it as a unique form of 'asynchronous communication,' but it turns out that synchronicity is not its only advantage. It was also supposed to be symmetrical, but there are a lot of messages that have gotten to be asymmetrical. In other words, the unintended effects of any device will be hard to see at the outset.

Could your blog, podcast or live-streamed town hall meeting leverage the Mic Check option? Would you allow someone in the audience to interrupt the flow of your script, storyboard or agenda just to enhance participation? It is hard work, it is messy, and it upsets all the models we once used—top-down, I-speak-you-listen, written-in-stone, etc. But just as the 'microphone' has been adapted to become a listening device, not just an amplification device, a lot of other communication tools we take for granted can change. Amateurs, not pros will probably make this happen.

Maybe you could ask your audience for some ideas, as you will discover in the next chapter.

16

CROWD-SOURCING IDEAS (MANAGERS NOT REQUIRED)

> *We want questions as well as answers, and we need to get them from a broader community because the same old people asking the same old questions in the same old way is not moving things fast enough.*[1]
> —Harvard Catalyst project

Tired of the same-old ideas from same-old people? The crumpled 'suggestion box' in the lunch room may be a tad obsolete. There are gazillions of ideas available, if you care to ask. George Bernard Shaw once said, "If you have an apple and I have an apple and we exchange apples, then you and I will still each have one apple. But if you have an idea and I have an idea and we exchange these ideas, then each of us will have two ideas."

The best ideas in any organization are usually kept down. Not by some control freak in Human Resources or a Creative Director with an oversized ego and an undersized portfolio. Great ideas are often trapped, like pockets of air in the earth's crust, in a layer of the organization known as the 'cubicleosphere.' In this inner-space, below the mantle of crusty been-there-done-that managers, everyone sits in his or her cubicle (mantra: "just doing my job"), and once in a while someone bores a hole into this rich layer and releases some ideas. We famously call these breakthrough moments brainstorming sessions. So the question is, why don't organizations do it more often—bust into the inner layers? Why is there such a low level of employee engagement? Seventy-one percent of American workers are "not engaged" or were "actively disengaged" in their work, according to a 2011 Gallup study.[2] They are emotionally disconnected from their workplaces and are therefore less likely to be productive. Is it too expensive to engage people in the workplace? Or would doing so potentially be too anarchic?

Whenever I have been involved in face-to-face brainstorming sessions, I never fail to notice how organizations are trapped in the "let's have a meeting to discuss this" mode. Structure is not a bad thing. But when structure becomes a box with no air vents, it makes it hard to blend planned idea-generating sessions with loose idea-busting conversation threads. Organizations like the focus group for similar reasons. It keeps ideas tidy.

Ideo, a design firm for innovation-seeking companies, uses an 'unfocus group' to get ideas flowing. It is a qualitative research method that involves putting people who are radically different in one group. Why does all hell break loose when a person tries to implement an idea that did not come up in the Monday morning meeting? I can tell you why. Managers require cubicle dwellers to put their heads down and do the busy-work first, and talk about their hare-brained ideas later. There are people who still try to schedule creative output like they schedule the cleaning crew or set the timer on the coffeemaker. Crowd-sourcing ideas is messy and unpredictable. It breaks hierarchy, and lets non-experts compete with professionals. That could be a good thing.

NOVICES WANTED

Victor Garcia was a Mexican immigrant who arrived in the United States at the age of five. He ended up in a community college, doing odd jobs to support himself, not sure of what he wanted to do. He soon registered in a technical college in California and pursued a career in design—to design automobiles. Around Jan. 2011, he was a relatively junior staff member of a company designing automobile products. Thirty days later, he was one of the most coveted designers in the company. DARPA (which stands for Defense Advanced Research Projects Agency), the Department of Defense research group had set a challenge, espousing bottom-up change, basically throwing open a challenge for anyone—not just designers—to come up with a design for the next generation combat support vehicle. The reward was $10,000. DARPA specifically said that it sought "to engage the crowd." It didn't care about the resume of the designer, or how the idea was submitted. It welcomed "experts, novices and the curious" to participate.[3]

Out of 20,000 submissions, Victor Garcia's design won the contest. Aneesh Chopra, the then White House Chief Technology Officer, told this story as an example of how it doesn't matter where ideas come from, or what a person's pecking order in the organization is.[4] If the organization is flexible enough, and the system of encouraging bottom-up ideas is in place, any low rank employee could be empowered to bring an idea to fruition.

So is it time to release the best ideas in your organization? The first thing to do is to create an environment of cross-pollination, where conversations between diverse groups can occur.

Before we get there, let's look at why people still cling to the clunky approach of idea generation and employee feedback. There are good (though wrong) reasons why people only chat among their division, their tribe. There are three things that typically keep the ideas from flowing.

1. **Habit.** Managers love silos. Blending job functions and integrating offline and online conversations is messy and politically risky; it upsets lots of apple carts. Managers also want the wheels on the apple cart to be properly aligned. By force of habit, managers keep things in air-tight receptacles because unscheduled ideas may cause cracks. "We're in the business of making apple sauce, folks. No apple cider experiments here, please!"
2. **Fear.** We fear good ideas. Hard to admit this, but though some of us (even non-managers) like to say we welcome any good ideas, we are terrified that they may go against the status quo. Easier to tape people's mouths shut (translated: not inviting them to certain meetings) than letting free ideas reign. Heard of the 'not invented here' syndrome? Some folks instinctively oppose ideas that don't originate in *their* department, at *their* meeting, on their watch. Novices instill fear.
3. **Overload.** We've never been trained to handle the idea torrent. If 33 people in a room come up with 12 good ideas about improving workflow, who is going to prioritize them, assign team leaders, track progress? "Let's table that idea for next month's meeting, shall we? We have quotas to deliver, so let's not get distracted for now."

Even if you can be trained to slay the first two dragons of habit and fear, managing a torrent of ideas takes a lot. I have good news and bad news for you, however.

Bad news first. The tools and platforms are now in place to force idea generation and feedback on your organization. Employees are now speaking up! You don't even have to ask for ideas. They will give it to you. The good news? Managing the flow of ideas in the workplace is getting to be a lot easier—with one caveat: You will have to give up the role of censor that you've secretly enjoyed. While most organizations are terrified at the prospect of employees collaborating and chatting over internal social networks, there is plenty of evidence to calm managers' nerves.

INNOVATION TOURNAMENTS

Wal-Mart set up mywalmart.com, which has more than 1.2 million users. It is a platform for discussing change management, voting on issues, announcements and 'story sharing.' It had 12.3 million page views in February 2011.[5] A more recent example comes from a University of Pennsylvania group called Penn Medicine, at bigidea.med.upenn.edu/how-it-works. Penn set up what it called 'Innovation Tournaments' to solicit ideas from employees to help Penn Medicine improve its patient experience. The ideas submitted are ranked and get placed in 'rounds' that move forward. Here's how they describe it:

> "Innovation Tournaments help identify great ideas. Think of it like 'American Idol' which begins with many performers and ends with selecting the very best. 'Your Big Idea: Penn Medicine's Innovation Tournament' will start with a large pool of submissions from Penn Medicine employees and, through a series of rounds, will be narrowed down to a final few that will receive funding and the resources to be put into action."[6]

Sure everyone has a voice, at least in theory. But the group has a way to knock sense into anyone with an ax to grind, the belligerent chap, the one who doesn't have the interest of the group. The 'wisdom of the crowds' is often hard to wrap our minds around. It is a term coined by journalist James Surewiecki to explain why large groups of people can be smarter than an elite few.[7] According to this view, the 'crowd' is right most of the time. For instance, the TV studio audience in 'Who Wants to Be a Millionaire' guesses correctly 91 percent of the time, whereas the so-called 'experts' are right just only 65 percent of the time.

The system works a bit like how Wikipedia does (For more on how Wikipedians contribute, see Chapter 9). When you think about it, an online encyclopedia that anyone could edit is counter-intuitive. Wikipedians—self-appointed editors—make sure that only verifiable, unbiased content gets updated. The existence of such a large body of 'wisdom' by people not sanctioned or selected by the Wikipedia organization, but by the crowd, proves that knowledge does not always reside in an elite few, but it emerges from the crowd that gathers around a subject. On a Wikipedia entry, click on the 'Discussion' tab of any article and you could read a debate over words, punctuation, bias, etc. which seldom ends.

Organizations often talk the talk about being committed to unleashing the ideas that lie trapped within, but it takes more than a link on a website soliciting suggestions, or a series of meetings to get things rolling. The Media Lab at the Massachusetts Institute of Technology is one hotbed of ideas. But it didn't get to be that way by accident, but by sheer design. Students and researchers at MIT are encouraged to rub shoulders with corporations, with very few guidelines. If there are guidelines, the only two are that an invention should significantly improve the lives of people, and that the idea must be radically different from anyone else's idea.[8]

For organizations that need to tap into their own 'crowds' of employees, there are some good tools out there, and more are on their way.[9] Here are five to give you a flavor:

- IDEASCALE—A tool for community-level conversation tracking **www.ideascale.com**
- IDEASTORM—Dell's initiative that gives customers a voice and opportunity to share ideas and collaborate, but also to hear what products or services customers would like to see Dell develop. **www.ideastorm.com**
- CONCEPTSHARE—Where teams of designers and creative people could collaborate and generate ideas. **www.conceptshare.com**
- GETSATISFACTION—A tool for customers and employees to interact to gather 'social knowledge.' **www.getsatisfaction.com**
- ONE BILLION MINDS—A platform to solve problems in Science, Technology, Design, Business or Social Innovation. **www.onebillionminds.com**

FAREWELL TO THE CHAIN OF COMMAND

Organizations are recognizing—grudgingly perhaps—that the best ideas don't only come from people up the chain of command, or from paid consultants. Some of the greatest money-saving ideas come free, if you only ask. We have a fancy term for it in the online world—User-Generated Content or UGC. This act of 'crowd-sourcing' makes people who love hierarchies somewhat uncomfortable. After all, the crowd doesn't know or pay heed to a chain of command—a term that is itself redolent of a bygone industrial age. Ideas could range from the practical to the lunatic, as they are encouraged to be at MIT Media lab.[10]

Sometimes unasked, the ideas are game-changing. Starbucks saved up to 6 million gallons of water every day, when a customer in one of its UK coffee shops questioned the company about the practice of leaving the taps on throughout the day. It was 'company policy' for its 10,000 coffee shops worldwide in order to maintain health standards, they said.[11] But they took the idea anyway, and the policy was reversed. Like UGC, user-generated ideas are being put into practice.

I'll leave you with two great examples of how the wisdom of the crowds works.

- The first is how the Department of Labor in the U.S. recently asked citizens to vote on the best tools and career sites (www.dolchallenge.ideascale.com). The crowd-sourcing program was powered by IdeaScale, a tool for community-level conversation tracking (www.ideascale.com). For two-weeks in January, some 16,000 people took up the challenge. A simple task of evaluating and prioritizing what's valuable to the public used to be what a typical government agency does—based on the assumption that it knows better than us. Online tools driven by social media prove that ideas can be outsourced for free.

- The second example has deeper implications. A Harvard medical research group ran a challenge—a social networking challenge—asking people for insight to fight Type 1 Diabetes. It used a crowd-sourcing site, Innocentive, to find ideas from people who were not necessarily PhDs. Why would guys with PhDs want us to tell them how to go about their business? Why would Harvard seek broad input from the community? Here is how they put it: "We want questions as well as answers, and we need to get them from a broader community because the same old people asking the same old questions in the same old way with slightly newer technology is not moving things fast enough or broadly enough for us to cope with these incredibly complicated diseases."

Questions as well as answers! We seldom encourage people to engage with others on the level of questions, and people tend to fear being the one to ask the 'dumb question.' But often the best answers and the best conversations come out of dumb questions. (If you read the FAQs of any service organization, you can't help but notice how a lot of them, evidently written up by someone who has an idea of what the typical questions are being asked via email or phone calls, are what one might call the dumb questions.) I coach a robotics class, and my team competes in annual tournaments set up by the FIRST Lego League, a foundation backed by inventor and serial entrepreneur, Dean Kamen. The FLL stresses the importance of 'questions, over answers'.

MIT's Media Lab has four principles for its idea generators: **1.** The power of passion, and a 'no rules' environment for pursuing one's curiosity. **2.** A principle that recognizes 'disappearing disciplines' where someone could come at an idea from outside of an established discipline, not governed by what a solution should look like. **3.** Playful invention and 'hard fun,' encouraging students to work on fanciful ideas. **4.** Serendipity by design. The lab is an environment that truly believes that the most unlikely, random sparks will bring about an invention.[12]

I wish we could always adopt the idea of 'hard fun,' as contradictory as it may seem. So if you're a manager or a senior executive, welcome to the discomfort zone! The Web 2.0 world is not the Internet you once thought it was. It is a place where the *same old* can be improved upon; where great ideas are just waiting to be released, if you let people link up and speak out.

Social media didn't change marketing from a monologue to a dialogue—it changed it to a multilogue.[*]

—Jason Falls and Eric Decker

---

[*] *Jason Falls and Eric Decker, No Bullshit Social Media: The All-Business, No-Hype Guide to Social Media Marketing,* Que Publishing, September 2011.

17

TEXTING UNDER THE INFLUENCE

I don't get why people voluntarily present themselves for online inspection.[1]

—Bill Gates

What was the most embarrassing text message you sent someone in a fit of fury—or passion? Do you wish you could take it back? There is a seldom-used feature in Microsoft Outlook that lets a person 'withdraw' an email not intended for someone. But we all know that the act of recalling an email only prompts other recipients to revisit it and see what was so inappropriate or wrong in the first place.

Sure a Facebook Wall post can be scrubbed—at your end, at least—and reposted. This is a useful feature especially if you post something with a really bad typo. But the operative phrase in that sentence is 'at your end.' Wiping clean a post off your Facebook wall does not erase it off the hundreds of other Walls of your friends, or your friends' friends who may have seen it. Someone actually came up with an app that could clean your profile, wiping off any incriminating evidence. How? It lets you seek and destroy a "dirty word" list. It's true! It's called (what else?) 'Facewash.' If you're particularly unlucky, someone may have copied it and pasted it (emailed it, tweeted it) to other groups. Basically you're now in deep cow manure!

So now there seems to be recourse for folks like us. (Yes, I've made some bad typos in my time!) There is a market for auto-erasing text messages, to prevent content from being archived forever. Remember those messages in old spy movies that, once opened or played, would magically combust or disappear? In an age of textual indiscretions being practiced by teenagers and angry (meaning 'dumb') managers across the social media universe, I would think there could be a huge market for communication that self-destructs.

They are designed for those who are texting under the influence of poor judgment. See if you can identify which one of these services is real and which is a figment of my imagination.

BushTalk. The former U.S. President George Bush had a predilection for saying the most embarrassing things. Called *Bushisms*, they were both slips of the tongue and also genuine, bad mistakes. (Such as this gem: "I know how hard it is for you to put food on your family.") Now there's a piece of code that you can launch and the nifty little bot goes out into the search engines and websites and quickly corrects the mistake. It takes a few days, because it has to seed an exact, competing post, so the search engine spiders see both, and realize one is worth deleting. It's a bit like the 'Replace All' feature in word processing applications that lets you substitute words, dates and typos in one click. But it can save your bacon, and improve your legacy.

TigerText. A neat little application you download to your cell phone to avoid the consequences that Tiger Woods faced. In case you missed it, Tiger chatted a lot! Tiger sent a series of raunchy texts thinking he was having a nice little private chat with a mistress. He probably erased his digital fingerprints from his phone, just in case his wife or children saw them. But what Tiger didn't know was that some chats live forever out there in the ether, or on some cloud. So one company thought this would be a problem worth solving and invented what it calls TigerText. It puts an expiration date on messages so that they won't be retrievable and won't come back to haunt you. No more digital paper trails. Apparently it is also great for discussing sensitive topics such as financial matters and patents. It's also great for text chatting with journalists 'off the record.'

GobbleDeMail. This is for people who want to clean up their email indiscretions, especially when they chat online on free email services on Google and Yahoo. Designed by Google Meta Labs, this still-to-be released app is sort of Gmail for dummies so to speak. Real dorks. You could say whatever you want in an email, but you pre-authorize it to spot the words you never intend to say (for instance swear words, phrases that might have racist or sexist overtones) so the worst phrase comes out cleansed. Some words may even come though somewhat meaningless, but it's better to be cleansed than sorry, right? Phrases such as 'son of a barbeque' and 'total freezing nightmare' are not likely to upset anyone. GobleDeMail has a mobile app as well, so a compulsive Twitter user could sleep better knowing that no matter what she tweets about, it would not hold up in court.

So what do you think? They all seem like nutty applications, don't they? On the other hand, they all seem plausible because they address the problem about which we worry ourselves—and our bosses!—sick. As managers, we all try to protect our corporate brand from being tarnished by employees' irresponsible communication, and by someone saying something out of context. Words or phrases that could be repeated by a blogger, turned into an attack story in the media. Our chat republic is fraught with the problem of too much smack talk.

Ok, here's the answer. The real application is the one inspired by Tiger Woods' problem.

TigerText (find it at www.tigertext.com) is an application, not just for people who dabble in salacious stuff. The text message that goes out through the service provider doesn't actually live in your phone, and certainly not on the servers of a mobile phone company. Here's how the company puts it: "Face it, we're human and we're prone to communication mistakes." Call it "text regret." It says that TigerText is different because, even though it has the look and feel of a normal text message, the sender can deleted it not just from his server, but from the recipient's phone.

"Let's say you send a text. You realize it's not what you meant to say. A rush of terror builds up inside you as you stand there terrified about what your recipient is going to think after reading it. So you tap "Recall" and, voila, you are recalling the text. You have deleted it from their phone, your phone and everywhere in between. It's a face-saving, do-over that might one day save your relationship, your job and your hide."[2]

Messages are displayed on a sender's and receiver's phone until the 'lifespan' (set by the sender) expires. So someone could mark up a message to expire say, 60 seconds after it is has been opened and read. Those expired texts are wiped off the servers every minute of the day, the company assures. TigerText, which has mobile apps for the iPhones and Android phones, was based on the idea that social sharing should be possible without sacrificing privacy, and that individual control should be key to the text messaging experience.[3]

There is one business sector where text deletion is useful—in healthcare. Information sharing between healthcare providers and patients are protected by HIPAA laws—the Health Insurance Portability Accountability Act, a U.S. federal law which specifies physical and technical safeguards to assure the confidentiality and availability of a patient's health information records.

Privacy of health records aside, you don't need me to tell you that in a world that has gone neck deep in digital communication, there appears to be no software to pull you out of a reputation quagmire you create for yourself.

Well, there is. It's just that you may not realize it's available to Android and Apple users alike. It's an app that's already installed—in your head. In a folder labeled 'common sense.'

18

OMG! THE STATE DEPARTMENT'S ON FACEBOOK!

The Internet has become the public space of the 21st century – the world's town square, classroom, marketplace, coffeehouse, and nightclub.[1]

—Hillary Clinton

What's the difference between Public Relations and Propaganda? It's easy to understand what propaganda is after the fact, when the motive of the one sending the message is revealed. But it is harder to sniff it out in the middle of an event. Is a blog just propaganda or another way to tell a particular story? If you pay a spokesperson to say something on your organization's behalf, is it just an endorsement or blatant act of propaganda?

Oddly enough, communicators who use various channels and engage audiences with 'outreach programs' don't think too hard about propaganda. But some institutions, especially those in government, need to consider how their communication strategy could unwittingly embroil them in propaganda. A good example of how to navigate these choppy waters is to watch what the U.S. State Department has been doing. But first let's recap what is considered propaganda. Two classic definitions are worth evaluating.

Propaganda is the control of opinion by significant symbols, or, so to speak, more concretely and less accurately by stories, rumours, reports, pictures, and other forms of social communication...the making of deliberately one-sided statements to a mass audience.[2]

Harold B. Lasswell

Modern propaganda is a consistent, enduring effort to create or shape events to influence the relations of the public to an enterprise, idea or group.[3]

Edward L. Bernays

Many of you who were born after Bill Clinton was in the White House would probably assume that PR and digital media are joined at the hip. No one seems to complain about spin just because the White House has a YouTube channel, or that the U.S. Department of Health, NASA, and the Department of Energy have blogs. We appear to have skirted the PR vs. propaganda debate by accepting that more information, even tempered with opinions, is better than a government institution that's tight-lipped, and very uptight about saying anything outside of sterile press releases.

Ever wondered why? It was not too long ago, in July 2008, when a major shift appeared to be taking place in how the U.S. government was approaching social media. The big news was that a cabinet secretary, Michael Leavitt had started to blog. The timing was critical. This was in the pre-Obama era, when the Bush administration was largely managing communications in a top-down mode. Leavitt, who said that he was no professional blogger, made many pundits wonder if it was not a disaster waiting to happen, since government officials are so often misquoted.

"MESSAGE FORCE MULTIPLIERS"

To understand why this shift was significant, we need to step back to 2002.

The Assistant Secretary of Defense for Public Affairs at that time was Victoria Clark who was convinced that the government needed to make a cohesive case for going to war with Iraq, using the media. She was behind the idea of recruiting and placing a cadre of 'influentials' to promote the war effort. These 'influentials'—advisors and analysts—would sell the idea of war to the media first and thence to the public. More than 75 retired military officers were hired to do this. They were referred to as the government's Message Force Multipliers.[4] The media used their advice and chatted with them, seldom questioning their bias. Some of the analysts even authored Op-Ed columns. They were paid by the government to do this, but this was not disclosed by the media outlets that used them. The extensive, sneaky, message-dissemination was clearly not PR. It was, in Edward Bernays' sense, a classic case of propaganda.

Fast forward to Michael Leavitt. He was secretary to the Health and Human Services (the equivalent of Health Minister). Where does a blog, authored by a senior cabinet secretary sit on the spectrum between opinion and propaganda? Leavitt clarified it this way: "I use my blog as a short cut to communication," he said at a meeting explaining why a man of his stature (who had so many underlings paid to do it) needed to communicate with the public. Responding to several media people in the audience, he went on to explain that he blogs about what mattered to him, not a topic chosen by a reporter. He considered communication such an important function of his job that he made time for it, writing out draft posts on airplanes, and while exercising on a Stair-master. He fired off these posts as Blackberry messages to himself, and these were later turned into blog posts. "Information goes where people are, and public policy-makers should do the same," he urged.

Leavitt may be a forgotten name now, but he may have been a turning point in how Washington communicates. He was the new wine being poured into the old wine skins of government. He proved that those values of transparency and openness could be embraced by the folks at the top as well. Even those who were in an age bracket that is suspicious about social media, and work in institutions that are known for being tight-lipped.

DIPNOTE: DIPLOMACY UNPLUGGED

Soon after I discovered Leavitt, I began to notice another interesting initiative by the U.S. State Department. It was a blog called Dipnote. This blog was certainly well managed, but not well known. Even its name, Dipnote, a truncated word, was a bit of insider jargon.[5] But it had stories that suggested they were not contrived. They were human-interest stories bubbling up from the bottom, and from across many divisions of an organization. Heath Kern, editor-in-chief at Dipnote, observed that, given the green light to start a dialogue with the public, she was "a little surprised, by the genuine disbelief that a cabinet level agency could have started a legitimate blog complete with criticism and contrary opining. Readers seemed to appreciate this. One wrote that 'Diplomacy, after all, is not a conspiracy,' and that 'the success of our diplomacy will continue to depend on its inherent honesty and openness. Deprive us of that, and we are deprived of our strongest and most effective weapon.'"

It seemed odd, coming from an institution that is very concerned about staying 'on message'. The State Department has had a history of being a tight-lipped outfit. After all, it is involved in negotiating relations with other nations.[6] You have to admit that managing foreign policy is a tricky beast; communicating it is no walk in the park. One word, a misplaced phrase, or a photo taken at a wrong angle can break out into an international furor. Just as traditional PR departments in large corporations never allow anybody to act as a company spokesperson, those who manage a country's image are extremely sensitive as to who gets the microphone, who hits the publish button, and who is on camera. The move to start blogging and to dive into all forms of social networking at the State Department reveals a huge shift in that mindset of that office.

What made it change? What turns an organization that is inherently given to secrecy to up-shift into information designed for public consumption? Is it the people or the realization that communication could be an integral part of policy, not the end product?

Let's start with the watertight compartments that keep information in and people out. In government, as in the top secret R&D labs of manufacturers, people go to great length to stop leaks. Information surrounding back-door negotiations with other governments or briefings on national security threats aren't supposed to be in the public

> **'SOCIAL MEDIA' IN THE 6TH CENTURY!**
>
> Herodotus writes of an incident involving Histaeus who was a ruler in late 6th century BC in the court of the Persian king, Darius. When Histaeus needed to send a message to his brother-in-law to urge him to revolt against the Ionians in Persia, he realized his communication might be intercepted. All networks (the roads, that is!) were being closely watched.
>
> Histaeus came up with a good plan and set up what was the equivalent of a tweet or an SMS. He took his trusted slave, had his head shaved, and tattooed the message on the slave's scalp. Then he waited until the slave's hair grew back and sent him on to his brother-in-law.

domain, for obvious reasons. Until recently, to maintain this level of command and control, it was easy to limit access to servers, screen outgoing email, and have strict policy on classified information. But mobile phones—especially phones with cameras, voice recorders and email—change all of that.

It is common knowledge that the former Secretary of State, Hillary Clinton, is a big believer in the use of social media, not as an end in itself, but as a sort of connective tissue that ties the hard decisions of diplomacy with the 'soft power' of public affairs. She has coaxed her ambassadors to get into the habit of using Twitter and Facebook, requiring every diplomat being groomed in the foreign service institute to get social media training.[7] While she places a premium on social media in helping the U.S. connect with the world, she also places a big value in how other nations use the Internet. In a speech in February 2011 on Internet Freedom, she noted that "The Internet has become the public space of the 21st century—the world's town square, classroom, marketplace, coffeehouse, and nightclub. We all shape and are shaped by what happens there, all two billion of us and counting." She noted that "the goal is not to tell people how to use the Internet" but that the U.S. will provide the support in "expanding the number of people who have access to the Internet."[8] That's code for saying the U.S. will step in to help when it sees the need for Internet freedom.

And it did.

In 2011, it helped the dissidents in Libya, months before Muammar Gadhafi was ousted. Clinton has talked of the tools of engagement as enablers of 'participatory democracy' that make leaders more responsive. Not just leaders, but every employee becomes as a potential node in the response network. The State Department has field officers filing their reports minus the diplomatic euphemisms.

Not all agencies take the same approach. The Department

of Homeland Security (DHS) maintains a blog but it is the very antithesis of Dipnote, where all you see are long, boring statements from high-ups. Over at the Transportation Security Agency, or TSA, the folks who manage airport security may come across as humorless government agents while you wait for your shoes and belt to come through the scanner. But on their blog (at blog.tsa.gov) they take a human approach to communications, as does the Federal Emergency Management Association or FEMA. Their blog (at blog.fema.gov) is a marked departure from the double-speak, gobbledygook and tight-lipped statements that emanated from those three big agencies just a few years ago. (A good example of Bush-era double-speak is made by Tim Lynch at the Cato Institute.[9])

So what does this mean to you? Chances are that your job does not involve coordinating humanitarian efforts in Darfur or pushing for a tricky arms control treaty. Your Web copy might ignite a trade war, not a nuclear one, but there are some lessons to be gleaned from how Dipnote works.

1. Tell your side of the story—but don't assume (or obliquely suggest to your audience) that you know everything.
2. Mention if there's a conflict of interest issue. Kill cynicism early.
3. Feed the conversation thread. Recognize that you may not have the final say in the story, but respond thoughtfully to irrational or impolite comments.
4. Separate opinion from fact. Some stories may be highly subjective, as many blogs tend to be. That's fine. But differentiate these posts from factual stories, or posts that correct factual errors.

In your bid to do PR, be wary about striking deals with people in order to control your organization's voice. There's a PR scandal that is now a classic case study of how not to cross the line. It involves Wal-Mart, and the world's largest PR agency, Edelman Public Relations. In early October 2008, a blog showed up written by a folksy couple named Laura and Jim. They appeared to be traveling across the U.S. from Las Vegas to Georgia in a recreation vehicle (RV). As most people who do this find out, parking a large RV in a city is difficult and they often do so in a vacant spot near a mall or a corner of a parking lot at a Wal-Mart store. Laura and Jim were documenting their experiences using the store as their focal point. They called it 'Walmarting across America'. It was all very cute until word got out that the couple was doing it on behalf of Wal-Mart, which had paid for their expenses.[10] The whole 'story' was rife with deceit—including the couple, one of whom turned out to be a freelance writer. There was more. The organization known as "Working Families for Walmart" which appeared to be sponsoring the blog, turned out to be a fake grassroots organization. The idea of an organization that pretends to be backed by people (not corporations) is not new. There is a term for it: 'astroturfing'—a term coined in the 1980s to describe fake grass-

> "But engagement does not end with digital interactions—as is the case with our traditional shoe-leather diplomacy—relationships that begin online must be nurtured away from computers, through real-world interactions."
>
> —*Victoria Esser, Deputy Assistant Secretary of State for Digital Strategy in the Bureau of Public Affairs.*

roots organizations.[11] Tobacco companies and political parties have used the tactic. 'Working Families for Walmart' however, became the Internet-era's update of 'astroturfing'.

But the lessons we could glean from unethical *quid pro quo* practices go back further than this, to a little-known incident in 1951 involving the State Department and...Iran.[12] It involved using press, radio, and posters in a campaign to develop better agrarian practices in Iran.

There was a hidden agenda: to dissuade the Iranian people against communism, and cultivate an anti-Soviet attitude. The U.S. had said it would supply personnel, material and equipment so the Iranians could develop in on its behalf. "If skillfully handled anti-Communist material, in fairly large doses can be administered to this audience, however it must be strongly emphasized that...no direct reference can be made to the Soviet Union, its satellites, or Soviet personalities."

It is hard to imagine diplomacy without secrets, or at the least withheld information. But in a time in which it is dead easy for a cover-up to be outed, the U.S. State Department, which knows how to be engaged with different regional audiences and global ones, also appears to understand how to stay away from such old world tactics.[13] It has Twitter feeds via nine foreign languages: Arabic, Farsi, Chinese, Russian, Spanish, French, Portuguese, Hindi, and Urdu. And, OMG! If these one-time risk-averse bunch of guys are on Facebook, what's making your organization so uptight about social media?

19

LOW-HANGING FRUITCAKE

Your marketplace's mother tongue is human—it speaks press release robot as a second language.[1]
—David Meerman Scott and Brian Halligan

When was the last time you got home from work and said, "Hi honey, I'm home! Let's put the offspring to bed and make a strategic investment in a cutting-edge piece of cinematography?"

It sounds funny, because we never use 'CEO-speak' at home. But here's the brutal truth. Many of us show up at work and immediately switch to an argot of English that we never impose on our family and friends. I've been railing against this practice for the past two decades, but have to admit that when I sit down to write a proposal, a little jargon app fires up in a part of my brain, too. I realized that un-

> Steve Crescenzo talks of CEO-speak as a malady—what he calls 'homicide detective syndrome.' Basically it is a person's ability to switch between a code language spoken in the workplace, and normal language a person would use when ordering a sandwich. On TV, he says, the homicide cop always says things like "we apprehended the alleged perpetrator." When the detective gets home he would say "We caught the dirtbag!"

less I am highly conscious of this, this sneaky little gremlin squirts a few puffs of noxious vapor, which spreads like mold. In business, this stale vocabulary creeps between the floor boards and dry walls of our communication channels. It seems to thrive well in a few square inches of a PowerPoint slide. It lodges in-between words we use in email, and whenever there's a white board and a set of markers, there's an invisible drop-down menu with dozens of buzzwords urging us to use them liberally.

Synergistic. Best of breed. Paradigm shift. Boil the ocean.

Long before blogs showed up and taught us that you don't need highfalutin PR words (yes, even words like 'highfalutin') to convey something with immediacy and passion, there was a book called *Why business people speak like idiots*.[2] In it, Brian Fugere, Chelsea Hardaway, and Jon Warshawsky described why it was OK to be human in any form of communication. They used an example of *CBS* news anchor Walter Cronkite to illustrate. An editor apparently handed Cronkite a wire service report that had just come in, and he quietly paraphrased what must have been the most important broadcast of his career: an announcement that President John F. Kennedy had been assassinated. He didn't stick to any script. He *ad-libbed it!* Had he simply read the report, it would have gone over like a lot of colorless 'breaking news' communiqués.

"Templates are your enemy," they note, making a point that information we pass on to others is often too big or too important to fit in a news template. They say that the 'polish' we apply to communication reduces its impact. "Whatever efficiencies come from cue cards, notes or scripts, they make it obvious that what we're saying is coming from the page rather than from our brains." Words that come from technical handbooks and phrases we pick up at conferences have a way of often wandering off the page (and off the stage) into our mouths. They make our stories confusing, colorless.

Here's a fine example, from the opening sentence of a press release I received. The company name has been replaced by an X.

> X company Inc., headquartered in Hollywood, MD, was recently ranked third in the nation for 8(a) Prime Contractors by Washington Technology. X company is a minority-owned 8(a) certified research, development, test and evaluation firm currently producing innovative unmanned air and ground solutions providing battlespace awareness, force protection, and force application capabilities for the warfighter.[3]

How riveting!

It's the same old template. Company (add brand here), located in (insert city here) has been named/ranked/recognized as the best/fastest/world-renowned (choose one) organization for (insert adjectives such a 'bleeding edge' here).

The problem is partly with the baggage we have inherited from the language of press releases, which, it turns out, is generated by many in the industry who use weasel words such as *cutting edge, innovative,* and *best-in-class*. When we write just as we chat, when we use more spit than polish, it makes our communication more authentic. Being rehearsed, articulate, and clear, or adding color and context is not the problem. The trouble begins when we use the prep work and cue cards slavishly. "Your marketplace's mother tongue is human—it speaks press release robot as a second language," advised David Meerman Scott and Brian Halligan. What they were struck by was how the band, Grateful Dead (in spite of having managers who looked after its PR) were decidedly un-slick, getting on stage looking their scruffy selves—a lot like their fans. It doesn't make sense to hide behind a scripted persona, they say.

FROM THE GUT

Like Cronkite, the best anchors know just when to depart from the teleprompter and cue cards, and when to inject a personal comment—the language of ordinary speech. Brian Williams, a veteran television news anchor for NBC Nightly News, is someone who frames stories every night in the language of common speech. Williams is very conscious of the language he delivers on the set, despite it flowing through the invisible teleprompter. You will never hear a buzzword slip out of his mouth. He recognizes the latent power of words. "I'm writing a blog everyday…It's gonna be right, because you know every word you write or utter in the Internet age has the weight of page one *New York Times*." Sometimes, as he explains to a non-journalism-savvy audience, you are relying on words that have to flow, and these words have not been vetted by anyone. "You're standing with a camera that's attached to a satellite truck. The teleprompter we use to put our writing on a glass sheet, so you're reading your writing while you're broadcasting…you don't have any one of those in the field. Your broadcast comes from your gut."[4]

Circle back. Monetize. Low-hanging fruit. Mission Critical. Bleeding edge.

If we aren't careful, given the volume of jargon and gobbledygook thrown at us, our brains become warehouses of a lot of meaningless templates. These are words such as 'leverage,' and phrases about 'thinking outside the box' and 'low-hanging fruit.' Speaking of which, some people say that low-hanging fruit is usually the last type of fruit anyone should pick—literally or metaphorically. The reasons for this involve avoiding bug-infested fruit and working with smaller pickings first, good pointers to remember, even though they come from fruit pickers, not language experts![5]

Boilerplate paragraphs are also prone to jargon. That's often because a small army of communicators labor on a paragraph, each adding a minor tweak. Whoever observed that if a committee designed a horse it would look like a camel must have grown up on a diet of boilerplate information. A sure way to lose the respect you may have got in the opening paragraph is to inject a moldy word at the end.

Here's a story that grew out of a press release flagged with one of the most loved phrases in corporate gobbledygook, Mission Critical. It was a story of a rugged tablet computer, known as the Toughbook. The name invites the reader to envision an accident-resistant device, but alas, the press release was studded with jargon, especially this 47-word opening salvo.

> **Syracuse, NJ, October 19, 2010** —Panasonic Solutions Company, provider of collaboration, information-sharing and decision-support solutions for government and commercial enterprises, is working with partner Activu Corporation, an information technology and services company delivering true end-to-end *network solutions for mission-critical command and control environments,* to deliver state-of-the-art command centers for public safety agencies. These command centers merge the most reliable hardware and intuitive software to enable public safety officials to focus on protecting their communities...[6]

The emphasis, however is mine. But where's the reference to the device? The first sentence sprinkles terms such as decision-support, end-to-end, and state-of-the-art, as if one of them was inadequate to make a 'tough' device sound manly. Was there some sort of contest among the Syracuse, New Jersey, PR department to see how many buzzwords it could fit into a sentence without getting arrested? The partner mentioned in this release, Activu Corp, is wrapped in similar language about "turnkey, net-centric, software-based visualization." If you ask 10 people the meaning of turnkey, I am certain eight people will give you a blank stare; one might throw up in your lap. The other will probably say, "what-ever!"

FINDING OUR VOICE

I listen to a lot of podcasts and marvel at how the spoken word can get away with so much that the written word cannot. I am talking about podcasts by wing-tipped corporate types. While written material generated by them always sounds buttoned down, self-conscious, and über grammatical, its spoken-word counterpart walks around in a mismatched t-shirt and dirty sneakers. In these podcasts, unfinished sentences, messy grammar, pauses and even flubs don't seem to matter. But you know what? These unscripted chats bring out a level of authenticity and clarity that rises above the fastidiousness of being correct. Yes, some of them are probably scripted,[7] but many podcasts, especially those that are conversations, not lectures, seldom run out of juice. Or listeners.

Communicators often struggle at finding their voice. The reason? A rookie writer who sits through seminars, and hangs out with public relations therapists (the kind that caution us to only use words and phrases from a talking points memo) learns the art of the corporate voice, but buries hers. Podcasting is a sure-fire way to loosen up, toss the talking points, and find your voice. In Chapter 22, we will take a deeper look at humanizing our communication, irrespective of who we are or whom we represent. But unless we are ever vigilant, we begin to echo the people we hang out with, sounding like marketing clones. There is reason people make fun of the 'fake DJ voice.'

BEING OBSCURE, CLEARLY

There are plenty of books on the topic of gobbledygook, but one of the earliest ones nailed it. *The Cluetrain Manifesto*, which I referred to in Chapter 5, preceded—nay, anticipated—the social media-infused era of marketing and corporate communications by about a decade. Its authors talked about the dead wood lying around us in the form of the corporate newsletter, and the memo. "The memo is dead. Long live email. The corporate newsletter is dead…." The four authors, who happened to be corporate types and publishers, rightly observed that "we are so desperate to have our voices back." They seemed to be pumping their fists celebrating how the Web took off the voice handcuffs forever. "We say anything, curse like sailors, rhyme like bad poets…just for the pure delight of having a voice." (Bear in mind this revelation that the Web lets people speak out predated Twitter and blogs by seven years!) David Weinberger lamented that our business voice is virtually the same as everyone else's, but "managed businesses have taken our voices."[8]

It was impossible to imagine then that just six years later, CEOs would be extolling the power of blogs in regaining their voice. Jonathan Schwarz, CEO of Sun Microsystems at that, time observed that in this new participation age, the ability to speak like a human, without depending on the media filter, was like pouring "kerosene on the fire."[9] Spiro Agnew, the 39th Vice President of the United States, was given to use some of the most poignant language that has come out of the White House. He had a terrible aversion to journalists, calling them "nattering nabobs of negativism" and "hopeless, hysterical hypochondriacs of history." Though some of his speeches were authored by a speechwriter—the well-known *New York Times* columnist and Pulitzer prize winner, William Safire—Agnew was given to call things the way he saw them, often too negative even for President Nixon's liking. He once called Nixon's talks with the Chinese 'ping-pong diplomacy.'[10]

It's not just managed business that has forgotten how to talk with authenticity. Many people talk "Stengelese." I bet you haven't heard of it. It sounds like a legitimate language, but it is a quaint term given to the language of obfuscation. You see, Stengalese is a 'language' that was spoken by Casey Stengel, manager of the New York Yankees. According to Larry King, who held nightly chats in his *CNN* studio with thousands of eminent, ordinary, and controversial people, Casey Stengel was someone who raised to an art form the technique of answering a question without really saying anything. He recalls one 'performance' before a U.S. Senate sub-committee on July 9, 1958. Questioned by Senator Estes Kafauver of Tennessee (during an anti-trust and monopoly hearing) whether Stengel supported legislation that was now before the sub-committee, Stengel went on about ballplayers' pensions. The senator persisted, "I am not sure I made myself clear." To which Stengel responded, "Yes, sir. Well, that's alright. I'm not going to answer yours perfectly, either."[11] Do you know someone who speaks Stengalese, or its dialect, in your republic?

This kind of language, be it 'Stengelese', marketing-speak, or geek-speak, has crept into another established instrument: the employee newsletter. Many have been quick to proclaim the death of the employee newsletter. But the corporate-written employee newsletter is hardly dead. PepsiCo has upped the ante of what it could look like, in its *PepLine* newsletter, written by professionals, but widely read and shared, not deleted. [I referenced *PepLine* and how it engages employees in Chapter 14.] The corporate newsletter, described by Dom Crincoli, a communication consultant, is "about as sexy as the petrol-leathery smell of ink drying on an offset press." He thinks it does still have its place, though. He calls it the communicator's best option in trying to reach 'non-tethered employees.'[12] In other words, don't kill the newsletter. Just kill the bland voice that makes it unsexy.

I know what you are thinking. You can't distance yourself from people (like your boss) who write this stuff and unleash 'low-hanging' vocabulary at every turn. Are you yearning to be released from the handcuffs of business-speak? You could still edit it out, or dull its impact. But first, you've got to train yourself to spot it. Here is a partial list of some of the most egregious words and phrases to avoid.

- *"Low-hanging fruit." It is supposed to suggest an easy-to-reach goal, but someone borrowed the farming image, and made it seem like a business-class statement. Did I just say business-class? Oops!*
- *Paradigm shift. The word paradigm is complicated enough. The term has been used so much it's now a cliché.*
- *Synergy. Derived from the Greek, synergos, which means working together, it means being mutually beneficial.*
- *Best of breed. Another way of saying top-drawer, or best. Best-in-class is a similar, abhorrent phrase.*
- *Circle back. People used to say "let me get back to you" but that didn't sound forceful. Even that lifeless word 'revert' is nicer.*
- *Re-language. Supposedly used by those who can't stand the shorter word 'Edit'.*
- *Scalable. A word used by technology managers who want to convey mathematical certainty to something expandable.*
- *Bio-break. Since bathroom sounds a bit dirty to some, they have borrowed from hospitals and schools that perform 'bio clean-ups'.*

- Bleeding edge. *A way of making something advanced look like people shed blood to achieve it. Overuse of the term simply begs for a bio clean-up.*
- Gamification. *The game business says it means "applying game design thinking to non-game applications to make them more fun and engaging." If you're not in this business, stay out of the game.*
- Strategic alliance. *The word 'relationship' has five letters less, but 'strategic alliance' makes business hand-shakes look posh.*
- Baked-in. *What's so inadequate with the word 'included'?*
- Boiling the ocean. *Just like spinning your wheels, to boil the ocean is to indulge in meaningless overwork.*
- Open the kimono. *An exotic Asian reference to allude to transparency, with a hint of flashing! Perhaps 'sarong' and 'kilt' sound a bit vulgar.*
- Mission critical. *Investopedia defines it as an activity, device, service, or system whose or disruption will cause a failure in business operations. Often the word 'essential' will suffice, but it sure sounds more important when tagged onto Strategic Alliance, doesn't it?*
- Blamestorming. *I've never heard anyone use this, but Merriam Webster appears to have! It gives an example of its use: "They spent the whole meeting blamestorming about the quarterly losses." Pointing fingers, eh?*

Symbiotic realignment. Platform agnostic. Contractual elasticity. Mission Critical.

A few years back, a fellow IABC member, Wilma Mathews, gave me a calendar that dealt with buzzwords. The body copy described how it was once possible to attend a business meeting and comprehend what people were saying, until "everyone started thinking outside the box and taking critical path to seamless world-class value propositions." It featured words such as 'symbiotic realignment,' 'scalable exit strategy,' and something called 'robustivity.'[13] The funny (and scary) thing is that I actually know people who could write such words and maintain a straight face. Wilma is certainly not one of them, and taught many communicators a lesson or two about calling a spade a spade. Consider the following sentence by a company that was a sort of corporate rock star in its heyday.

"We have robust networks of strategic assets that we own or have contractual access to which give us greater flexibility and speed to reliably deliver widespread logistical solutions."

Who comes up with this stuff? How many cups of coffee did they have before they got to the third word? (I wonder why they didn't add *mission critical* and *scalable* into the mix?) Let's prod the 'corporate horseshit' (a term used by Rick Levine) out of the above sentence to decipher what's being said. 'Robust networks' seem like a collection of durable things that are linked together. Make that bolted together. But dropping an empty phrase like 'strategic assets' after it is designed to suggest that these are not mere pieces of hardware, like servers or staplers, or even small offices, but fuzzy things like billing procedures or accounting practices. Tacked on to 'robust networks,' the word 'strategic' seems to give the company some (magical) muscular prowess in 'logistical solutions.' To my mind, 'logistical solutions' appear to be what you get when you cross a fighter jet and a FedEx truck. Of course this leaves us completely befuddled as to what exactly the company does. Could it be like Wal-Mart? Or a company manufacturing smart ATMs? Guess again.

Turns out (and you won't be disappointed!) this classic boilerplate describes a company that elevated corporate horseshit to a fine art. That company of course, was (drum roll, please) Enron. That's right, Enron, a company that successfully misled government regulators, stock markets and even its own employees with plenty of gobbledygook, and sometimes borrowed from exotic names for its off-the-books divisions from *Star Wars*.[14] As people became 'lawyered up,' it became very difficult to represent the company, and it filed for bankruptcy in December 2001. Shareholders misled by Enron lost nearly $11 billion, and many of Enron's executives were indicted and sent to prison. If there's a lesson in all this, it's this: *Your strategic language won't come to your contractual assistance in a robust, bleeding edge, jailhouse.*" Or, 'speak clearly, dude!'

Prior to *Cluetrain*, prior to the hype of PR, George Orwell ruthlessly struck out against such pretentious use of language. He took this sentence:

"I returned and saw under the sun, that the race is not to the swift, nor the battle to the strong, neither yet bread to the wise, nor yet riches to men of understanding, nor yet favour to men of skill; but time and chance happeneth to them all."

and translated it into this, using meaningless words to make a point of the dangers of opaque language:

"Objective considerations of contemporary phenomena compel the conclusion that success or failure in competitive activities exhibits no tendency to be commensurate with innate capacity, but that a considerable element of the unpredictable must invariably be taken into account."

If Enron had been around in 1948, Orwell would have been a much sough-after copywriter! "Modern writing," Orwell observed, "consists in gumming together long strips of words which have already been set in order by someone else, and making the results presentable by sheer humbug." He noted how in the first sentence, which comprised just forty-nine words, there were only sixty syllables. The second was shorter, with thirty-eight words, but had a whopping ninety syllables.[15]

Things don't appear to have changed a lot since Orwell's era. You would think that ever since *Cluetrain* exposed corporate rhetoric for what it was—the 'self-centered drone emanating from Marketing departments'—companies should have learned to bring their PR and marketing down to earth. David Meerman Scott, who reminded us that the marketplace's mother-tongue is human, has expounded on weasel words, too, in his *Gobbledegook Manifesto*.[16]

Yes, you will still run into people who speak 'Stengelese' and gobbledygook. Just don't accept their low-hanging fruitcake.

20

SHUT-UP AND COMMUNICATE

Modern art is a disaster area. Never in the field of human history has so much been used by so many to say so little.

—BANSKY

Chances are that cutting through the clutter is just one part of your job. It's an age old problem we confront no matter how much smarter our tools get. So I wondered if we might gain some insights from how we handled it before we had Flip video cameras, iPhones, Facebook and widgets. Maybe it could to help us be more grounded, as we anticipate how to handle what lies ahead.

In April 2009, one example popped right in front of me in Trafalgar Square, London, amid the usual din of advertising, protest messaging, music, vendors, and pigeons. A street protestor was 'communicating' with an audience in a way that put a lot of things into perspective. This public square is no different from a lot of online venues for sure. Chances are that, as a communicator, you're very familiar with such cluttered hangouts. You've joined a few online networks and are struggling to keep up with the volume of communication coming at you. You find it impossible to respond to everyone who wants to follow, friend, or 'Like' you. You've been sent dozens of surveys you haven't taken, on top of emails that you have not even looked at. Now think of what your customer or an audience you are trying to reach is going through. How do you break through to them?

Let's get back to the pigeons and protesters. A noisy plaza is not the kind of place to easily cut through the clutter. The protestor was drawing quite a crowd. How? He was not ranting, he had no easel or soapbox. He was painstakingly creating a 'sculpture' on the pavement using contributions from passersby. The contributions: coins. More specifically, pennies, dimes and the occasional 20p—tiny insignificant bits thrown at his feet that quietly grew into a short message that was

User-generated content? An activist in Trafalgar Square, London 'sends a message' to Western leaders using coins from passersby

hard to ignore. The message he was creating: "G-20 ecological crime in progress." His purpose: to raise awareness that the financial crisis was caused by the greed. At least that's what he told me when I asked him what message he was trying to send. He was a man of few words, shy almost, to make a verbal statement to someone paying attention to his message.

CONSUMER-GENERATED CONTENT

I have been writing about technology and communication for more than a decade, so why did something as low tech as this stand out as something significant? When we think about competing for attention in an over-communicated world, the first things we tend to reach for are the new technology tools. In our search for the next big thing, in our lust for a way to make a message resonate, we spend a lot of time worrying about audience size, the potential for word-of-mouth, how to build loyalty or make the message 'sticky'. But there are some basic elements that our man-on-the-street seemed to understand, drawing on a long tradition of connecting, creating and communicating. Street artists know a lot more about engagement than all of us savvy Facebook users put together.

Let's draw some parallels to see what really matters. Whether your tools are tweets (or coins) and your 'platform' is a blog (or a sidewalk) it's sometimes good to ask yourself these questions.

Do I need to shout to get attention? People don't only pay attention to the loudest voice in the room, plaza or website. The street artist wasn't trying to compete for that kind of attention. He stood out by doing precisely what everyone else was not.

Is my pitch too wordy? Is my copy too long? Since he was making a form of 'protest,' he could have written a 'manifesto' and handed out photocopies. But he condensed his message to just five words. Five! As with billboards or bumper stickers, the message needs to be quickly grasped.

Is it user supported? The coin sculpture was an aggregate of user contributions. It redefined what we think of as user-generated content. Users in this case are those who tacitly approve what the protestor represented. Everyone who threw in their two-cents' worth (literally) was adding to its impact.

Does it pay? The protestor was basically asking for what we now call 'micro-payments,' but instead of begging for them (I saw no hat in sight) he was making his content pay for itself.

Will it drive traffic to the site? The five words were laid out in a well-trafficked area. It was right at the foot of the steps of the London Portrait Gallery in Trafalgar Square. Its location and context didn't seem accidental. The message was in close proximity to other 'content creators'—artists, musicians, etc.

Is it in the Creative Commons? We know that locking down content is a sure way to limit its spread. The protestor had no problem with me photographing his creation. In fact he did not seek ownership of his work. I asked him to whom the pile of money belonged; he answered smugly, "her majesty's head is on the coins. I guess it belongs to her." He then sauntered off, perhaps to his next site. To him, this message belonged to his audience.

Is the timing relevant? We all worry about how best to time our messages. (We never issue a press release on a Friday, for instance.) This message must have been carefully planned. The day was 1 April, 2009, the day the world leaders—and the media—poured into London for the G-20 summit. The city was buzzing with spring tourists as well.

Does it start a conversation? Street art and guerilla marketing have a way of making people talk. (For a different view, check out Bansky, the-best-known street artist in Britain.) But so do expensive or obnoxious messages. The problem with risqué campaign ads that are hungry for buzz is that they have very short shelf life. (Anyone remember the 'shockvertising' print ads for Abercrombie Fitch? Thought so!)

Is it adaptable? A pavement may seem like a boring 'platform' compared to TypePad, Google+ or YouTube. But the street artist was not confined to the rules of the place. He could take his message to the base of Nelson's column or Westminster, and change his 'headline' if he so desired!

Is it creative enough? If you give ten people a bag of coins and ask them to create a statement, the chance of someone coming up with a simple device like this would be slim. It's hard work, it's clever, and it is creative in a way that doesn't appear in art books.

BANSKY

He is thought to have been born in 1974 in Bristol, England. He slipped into the graffiti scene during the 'great Bristol aerosol boom' of the late 1980s. His 'art' expresses a characteristic contempt for government.

In 2008, Bansky added four words on a wall in Westminster, with an illustration of a child-like figure that appears to be painting them. "One Nation Under CCTV" was an open criticism of Britain's move to install cameras in public spaces to monitor citizens. It got a lot of people talking.

We have more things to deal with than pigeons droppings on our clever copy. Competing for attention is one of the biggest challenges we all face, whether our job involves managing a website, sky-writing, churning out press releases, or working on stories for publication. Do we speak too much? Do we over-saturate our channels and social spaces in the hope that a *media blitz* (the old media term whose evil twin is the *email blast*) will get us more customers? Our tools will always change, but what remains constant is how we connect with our audience and how we help it identify with our message.

21

TALKING LIKE HUMANS

One way the opinion guys kick our ass and appeal to an audience is that they talk like normal people, not like news robots speaking their stentorian news-speak. So I wish more broadcast journalism had such human narrators at its center.[1]

—IRA GLASS

Lindsey Hoshaw wanted to tell us a dirty story.
She pitched her story idea to a very small online community because she wanted to report on an issue that few people wanted to talk about. The story? It was about America's trash. Not just any trash heap, but an enormous pile of trash, a large island of garbage, literally, that was floating around in the Pacific Ocean. Some people were calling it the Great Pacific Garbage Patch. To call it a 'patch' was a misnomer. It was a 'soup' of material roughly twice the size of Texas.

The community she pitched her story to, known by its website, Spot.Us, is a model of open-source journalism. Spot.Us was founded by David Cohn, someone who had worked on citizen journalism projects, hell-bent on trying to understand how the social Web interacts with journalism. In late 2008, with a $340,000 grant from the Knight

News Challenge, Cohn set out to test the idea of how open-source journalism could be made sustainable—what he called "community-funded reporting."[2]

Hoshaw had noticed that reporters covering the Garbage Patch had not been bringing up the garbage-human connection. Indeed, newspapers had been doing similar environmental stories, especially those around 'sustainability' issues; they had been reporting that plastic was causing havoc to marine life and fragile ecosystems. When the Garbage Patch story had been covered, (in a niche publication) it had been mentioned on the same page as a story about Britney Spears. Hoshaw says she also noticed one other thing: no one had told this story from a first person point of view. No independent journalist that she knew of had ever gone out there to the ocean to report on it. She was convinced that she could do it in a first person narrative. She wanted to focus on the human-garbage connection, and tell this powerful story as a human being first, and a reporter second. It would be a story told in her own voice. Spot.Us gave her the green light.[3]

This was the first real breakthrough, since Hoshaw is no 'citizen journalist.' She was professionally trained at and graduated from Stanford University's graduate journalism program. Prior to that, she had worked as a reporter at several newspapers. Before she got involved with Spot.Us, she had pitched her idea to the *New York Times*, which showed interest in it. *The Times*, however, did not guarantee it could carry her story, but she decided to go ahead and make the trip and report on it, backed up by the Spot.Us community. Reporting from the Pacific Ocean wasn't going to be easy. She found out that the cost of doing the story would be $10,000, mainly to secure a seat on the boat, pay for safety equipment, medical supplies, insur-

> In April 2013, UNESCO declared 'Garbage Patch' with a population of 36,939 (for the 36,939 tons of garbage) as a state. Seriously! This new nation's flag is blue.[4]

ance, and of course food for three weeks. She also needed a satellite phone for updating her blog from the boat.

Yes, she had a blog going. Although Hoshaw was a mainstream media journalist she considered herself a blogger, too. Which brings up an interesting issue. You have probably heard of the friction between bloggers versus journalists in the early days of citizen journalism. It was once considered an either/or choice. The bloggers versus journalists issue got to such a point that newspaper editors wrote scathing editorials about the bloggers working with 'aggregators' who stole their content, and that bloggers were somewhat socially challenged, "slightly seedy, bald, cauliflower-nosed young men sitting in their mother's basements and ranting,"[5] etc., etc.

Would a community be willing to pay for a story that would be done for them, details of which would also feed into her blog? Would it sully her reputation as a journalist? She had to give it a try.

CROWD-FUNDED STORIES

The pitch was very basic. Hoshaw recorded what she describes as a low-quality video explaining the story idea. The pitch on Spot.Us was posted in July 2009, but there was no rush of community support. For a few weeks, her mom was the only major contributor! It was discouraging. She worried that the 'crowd-funded' model may not work, as it was unlikely that people would be willing to part with a portion of their paycheck for some new journalism idea. This was, after all, soon after the financial crash of 2008!

Then a stroke of luck, from an unexpected quarter. An editor of *The New York Times*' Sunday edition, Clark Hoyt, wrote an article praising the endeavor, and mentioned that he was donating money via Spot.Us toward the cost of the story.[6] Think of that for a moment.

A mainstream media outlet supporting a freelancer. No strings attached. After that, the donations poured in.[7]

To get back to the boat trip, telling the story in the first person may sound powerful, but if it is even considered serious journalism, it is often associated with amateurs in general, blogs to be more specific. It is very different from the 'who-what-when-where-why-how' format we have grown up with.

Writing in the first person is not the only problem. The '5WH' model is the creation of journalism schools, where stories are packaged after they address these pertinent questions, and they only get printed or broadcast once the assignment is complete. Hoshaw's story was updated every day on her blog as the story unfolded. She was talking to her audience every now and then, and they could talk back, as communities often do. If this was a news assignment, she had it approved not by a media filter, but by the media audience.

ACTS OF JOURNALISM

Spot.Us is an experimental model of journalism that brings the human side of storytelling front and center. It begins by asking its community members to recommend what issues matter to them. Then it finds citizens—essentially freelance writers like Hoshaw—and pays them through community-generated funds, so the citizen journalist can meet his or her basic expenses. But that is not all. Spot.Us then asks media companies, the ones who own the printing presses and antennas, to bid on these stories so that the story could be theirs. In other words, the story could work in two realms: the blog community and on the pages and servers of Big Media!

On one level, Spot.Us brings us the type of journalism we always craved, where we get to chat with reporters. They write the story for us. A few of us, not a few hundred million of us. They often consult us and listen to us. They use language and nuances we would use if we get chatting with someone down by the barber shop. The challenge today for journalists, said Ira Glass, a prominent radio journalist, is "to sound like human beings, not know-it-all stiffs."[8] There are other challenges besides language at Spot.Us, and that is making sure readers vote, suggest ideas, and contribute financially in micro-payments. A 'crowd-funded' model—as opposed to an advertising-funded model. The former seeks small change from a large number of people; the latter looks for big money from a few.

I liked the Garbage Patch story for two reasons. It was a story that did not fall into the typical buckets of stories that mainstream media usually gives us: "Gotcha's," political hot-button issues, celebrity stories, crime, etc. This was not one of those stories that assignment editors—the air-traffic controllers in the news business—would typically pick. Or to put it another way, it would not sell. Stories that come via Big Media have editors who decide ahead of time, usually every day, what issues or topics might be relevant to its readers that day or week, and assign the time and space for them accordingly. If they are interested in reader conversations, it is usually an afterthought.

The other reason was that a story like this puts the onus of being informed, on the community—the consumers, not the producers. "Essentially (the experiment is about) seeing if the nation will put money where its mouth is," said Cohn. "People complain about the amount of mainstream journalism coverage there is. But the fact remains that covering those issues is cheaper and guarantees a bigger audience than reporting on garbage, city hall budgets, etc., etc."[9]

One reader at Spot.Us sniped about the fact that someone was actually being paid for a story like this, and Cohn had to come back and defend the crowd-funding of Hoshaw's story. "That is a real and high expense for this story (it is in the middle of the ocean)—so that is where ALL the money is going," he said. "The reporter here isn't going to pocket it."

Hoshaw is a freelance journalist, but just like her, there is an expanding cadre of citizen journalists going after stories for niche me-

> **DIFFERENT TYPES OF CITIZEN JOURNALISM**
> David Cohn explains the differences between the emerging classifications of citizen journalism
> - Citizen Journalism – This falls under the class of "Participatory Journalism" – but it is not "professional."
> - Stand-alone Journalism – This happens when the individual isn't reporting out of happenstance. The reporter, who is not acting as a 'professional,' makes a conscious choice to go out and report on a topic.
> - Pro-Am Journalism – when professional and amateur journalists work together, through basic comments on an article. Those comments add extra information or new views that the original writer left out.
> - Networked Journalism – Like stand-alone journalism, there is a conscious decision for large groups, rather than a lone reporter, to do the work. Networked journalism rests its fate on two principles: the 'wisdom of crowds' and 'distributed reporting.'
> - Open Source Journalism – Like networked journalism, it is collaborative. It has multiple points or 'sources' of information. It either involves a) the re-release of stories or b) sharing information among competitors. These make a project "open."

dia, and are sometimes being courted by mainstream media outlets. The definition of Citizen Journalism is murky. To some it's oxymoronic, since one half connotes someone untrained and amateurish, while the other refers to an activity of professionals. It has also been described as Pro-Am journalism, which refers to someone who's a hybrid of professional and amateur.

This definition gets massaged a lot, especially during crises such as natural disasters and terrorist attacks, when distinctions between a Pro journalist and the amateur blurs.[10] "Can we take good ideas like...distributed knowledge, social networks, collaborative editing, the wisdom of crowds, citizen journalism, pro-am reporting...and put them to work to break news?" asked Jay Rosen, one of the earliest proponents of open-source journalism. This was back in 2006, when the cracks were beginning to appear in traditional journalism.

The *Huffington Post* had arrived on the scene a year earlier with a model of "short-form, rapid fire posts" and began covering the usual entrées such as politics, business, entertainment, going green, etc.[11] When the *Huffington Post* got onto people's radar, it was because it functioned like a regular online newspaper, but was using a community of bloggers to contribute content. The professionals were not amused! Many believed that this online newspaper was essentially a spiffed up blog, and it would fail. Today it is one of the most resilient journalism models, vindicated by the fact that AOL acquired it in 2010 for 135 million dollars.

There have been many isolated acts of citizen journalism, where an individual, who was obviously not a paid journalist, bore witness to a newsworthy event and broadcast it. "Acts of citizen journalism in this sense happen by mere coincidence," observed David Cohn. "People are everywhere and when disaster strikes, someone usually has a camera." He explains the new nomenclature of citizen journalism that ranges from accidental, happenstance amateurs (who happen to have a camera when a story breaks), to a more formalized band of networked journalists fanning out to cover a big story.

CITIZEN VOICES, CITIZEN APPETITE

What would a world without traditional media and editors look like? What would information we use to operate with be like if we got it from niche media and citizen journalists? Would we be better informed? Would the 'crowd' be a good source? There is no easy answer. A world without the rigor and passion of full-time journalists could be nothing more than one where headlines and unchecked facts get passed around. On the other hand, when citizens add the dimension of the 'fifth estate' through social media, a new kind of news bubbles up. The truth is, citizens want to be a part of the production cycle of the news they consume.

> Parts of the media ecosystem are embracing failure and what I'd call the 'agile and iterative' process—which includes failure.
>
> —David Cohn[12]

For the past five years, there have been two large trends: The first is a palpable shift in appetite for citizens' voices and citizens' stories. People have been gravitating toward a different kind of journalism. A 2007 study by the Pew Research Project for Excellence in Journalism found that 70% of the stories which users selected came from blogs or websites such as YouTube and WebMd. Many of the stories that users selected were not the top stories in the mainstream media coverage. Most interestingly, it found that domestic events were popular.[13] In other words, news consumers cared about events closer to them. People seek stories from sites that do not focus on 'news' *per se*. Most stories they chose appeared only once.

The second is the hybridization of the media as we know it, which makes available the voices of the 'outsiders'—citizens, freelancers, Pro-Ams, and other accidental reporters. Technology companies are becoming media companies. So it makes sense that media companies should become technology companies, observes Cohn. In this 'melded future,' the best way media companies could protect their values, traditions and beliefs would be to create the platforms themselves not wait for technology companies to show up and build it for them.[14]

Citizens sometimes speak up and raise the importance of a story, and 'contribute' to it in unexpected ways. In March 2012, a teenager was killed in a gated community in Florida by an armed man, who happened to be a neighborhood-watch volunteer. He apparently shot the teenager in self-defense. The story went relatively unreported. One reporter, Ta Nehasi Coates, had stayed away from the story, feeling somewhat reluctant to cover what appeared to be a hopeless stereotype: black man killed by white person. Coates, senior editor for *The Atlantic*, was also a prolific blogger. He noticed that during his silence, his blog readers had been discussing the story. He began covering it. Within a few weeks, the local story went on to become a national issue, and part of the larger conversation about not just race issues, but gun laws and racial stereotyping. "When you see your readers talking about it before you, you realize that you are not alone," said Coates.[15]

The bloggers vs. journalists debate ought to have ended, but there is still a some friction around the edges of mainstream journalism as to who 'these people' are. But like Coates, and Hoshaw, who don't see a big red line dividing where they write, or on which channel they should tell their stories, the distinction is all but inconsequential. They don't write for a 'platform'—they write for an audience. Their words are not filtered through some cool media algorithm. They use a very basic alternative—the human algorithm.

BLOGGING FOR THE ASIAN TSUNAMI

In 2004, exactly eight months after I started blogging, a tsunami devastated many coastal towns of my homeland, Sri Lanka. Text messaging served us well, but wasn't enough. On impulse I turned my blog, *Hoi Polloi Report*, into a tsunami relief conversation space. With many local and international agencies willing to help, I could see the need to connect the dots, between donors and those affected. The blog made it so much easier, as people in other cities and countries began asking for advice on how they could engage. I was not sure what I should do. Should my blog act like a clearinghouse? A bulletin board for supplies? A space for citizen journalists? There was no time to think, so it was 'all of the above.' The blog at that time was an experiment, anyway, so I didn't care about its 'brand' identity.

In the initial hours after the tsunami, when roads were impassable and cell phone towers twisted like giant pretzels, the true picture was not easy to come by. Non-media people kept speaking up, talking like humans; citizens began gathering data, painting a truer picture than the mainstream media: people missing, how orphanages had been swept away, a train lifted off its tracks, and villages devastated.[16]

Some who travelled around the country began 'filing' reports to me via email. I promptly posted some of these stories, and asked people like Joey Caspersz, director of tea firm, Finlays, if he didn't mind being a citizen reporter. Another friend, Andrew Samuel, who had been volunteering for an NGO, sent updates. I was not sure what my blog was really serving. It was all a blur! Here's one of these reports, in January 2005:

> *Joey Caspersz reports from Galle - 4 January, 2004*
>
> *i was in galle yesterday and the devastation along the coast is heartbreaking and unbelievable. thousands of houses and buildings have beensmashed to their foundations by the force of the waves.*
>
> *yet, i saw signs of hope. people were returning to their non houses, sitting among the ruins, chatting, cleaning up and so on. in some places a single light bulb hung from a pole in the ground shedding light on the ruins.*
>
> *just past abalangoda lie the remains of the death train and the army has moved in heavy equipment and tanks to lift it up. children were playing cricket on the beaches and on land laid bear by the waters. i had grit in my eyes.*
>
> *actually people are pretty amazing in more ways than one.*

This whole experience wiped out my initial skepticism about what a blog could do. It was a forceful reminder that this untested thing called citizen journalism, of people speaking with 'grit in one's eyes', was where all communication would follow. It could be a personal journal, but it could also become a place-holder for collective action.

Hoi Polloi Report was one of the two websites that I managed to support the cause. Around the same time, word got out that my family was collecting supplies to send out to Sri Lanka. Complete strangers came by with truckloads of clothing, water purifiers, canned food, medical supplies, toys, and blankets.

Our minds have been conditioned by past models, so we tend to judge and predict a new medium by its nearest cousin. Journal keeping and acts of journalism, asynchronous communication, and making connections between strangers could obviously live under the same skin of a social medium. I learned that the hard way.

22

YOUR PODCASTING VOICE

When you speak with resonance, your whole body is vibrating in the same frequency, as well as your surrounding area ... Voice without resonance is thin and dull. It has less or no power to engage, influence, and inspire.[1]

—Cynthia Zhai

I happen to think that podcasting is the most powerful engagement medium in all of social media. Other tools and techniques to hold conversations come and go, but podcasting, which is not by far the hottest medium, has had a tremendous staying power. It's an important factor to consider when mapping out a communications strategy that pulls in all the threads of traditional and social media. Why? Because it is the best format and space in which to speak about an organization or an event in a human voice. It is also the best medium to 'listen in' to the people and culture that reside behind the turrets and moats of an organization. The walls, being the marketing department, human resources, legal affairs, and public relations. They never set out to build these fortifications and trenches, but looking from the outside in, they do seem zombie-like and insufferable.

Podcasting is one way to open a few 'loopholes' in the fortification.[2]

Have you ever tried your hand at podcasting? It may feel quite different from anything you have done, but once you get past the fear of the microphone, it begins to feel a lot like how you tend to communicate best—in normal conversations, sans scripts, teleprompters, and style guides.

"Podcasting is like blogging out loud! It gives you a voice," says one of the earliest handbooks of the industry, *Podcasting for Dummies*.[3] As simple as this sounds, it points to the often-missed connection between two powerful outlets of expression today, the podcast and the blog. There are many podcast formats available today, from highly-produced 'shows,' to ad-hoc rambles and coffee-chats, to journalistic-styled reports, and lectures converted to MP3 formats. Plus, there are more, especially with the growth of citizen journalism. The reporter with a recorder can quickly turn a short report into a podcast with little or no coding or editing experience. Podcasting as a form of citizen journalism has become common with the convenience and connectivity of cell phones. The first 'reports' that came out of Haiti after the 2010 earthquake came via a 'phonecast' using a service out of the United Kingdom known as ipadio. Mark Smith, who founded ipadio, says that his goal was "to give voice to people wherever they are." There's hardly a place in the world, he says, from where ordinary people have not been podcasting—from the middle of the ocean, tops of mountains, inside corporations, and from disaster zones.[4]

So what style and format does a communicator pick to 'blog out loud' in a world awfully cluttered by 'corporatized' communication?

To find out, I decided to ask some well-known podcasters themselves, including Evo Terra, one of the co-authors, of the *Dummies* book, C.C. Chapman, Krishna De, an Ireland-based podcaster, and Toni Sant, a Malta-born podcaster who now lives in the United

Kingdom.[5] I also wanted to get a sense of what has changed, because I have seen so many new tricks and fixes that have transformed what seems like an act of audio engineering, into something as easy as pressing two buttons on a smart phone or video camera and just talking. In our splintered but connected Republic of Chatter, there are even services that allow you to pick up a phone, call a number, record your voice, save it, and add music and other elements to turn it into a podcast. It's that easy!

But let's back up a bit. Let's say your organization has a rich-media site, lots of videos, presentations, and a well written blog. Now someone has been talking about a podcast. You have never been on radio, or recorded a voice presentation. What should you know about creating a podcast that will complement rather than hurt your PR and communications? When I started out with a podcast at my job at Decision Theater, a scientific visualization lab at Arizona State University, I ran into many hurdles that I bet you will, too. The first question I was asked is why should we podcast? We were just one business unit of a four-campus university which, after all, had a fully-equipped media relations division that handled videos, website content management, press releases and articles.[6] Why should we tell a separate story, and where would these audio files be hosted?

The short answer to 'why have a podcast?' was because the spoken word was the right media for people (we had more PHDs than you could shake a stick at) whose work tends to be hidden in journals. When you work for a large organization with some 11,000 employees and about 65,000 customers (students, in this case) who interact with you on a daily basis, you are usually asked to work in sync with others, not go rogue. But I will let some of the experts who do this, address some of those issues. First things first:

DURATION: What's a good length for a podcast?

I realize that this is as useful a question as 'how long is a piece of string?' But it's still a relevant question to ask. "Do not ask how long your episodes should be," says Terra, "ask yourself how short you can make them." Podcasts like *For Immediate Release*, by Shel Holtz and Neville Hobson, wrestled with the issue of length early on, when they were podcasting twice, weekly, but today—some 700 podcasts later— their shows run for one hour a week. "Will you make them choose to drop something in favor or yours?" asks Evo Terra, or can you make it small enough that it's an easy decision to fit it in?" In other words, will your podcast have content that is compelling enough?

BEST BET: At the outset keep it short—under 15 minutes. It will prevent you or your guests from rambling (and sometimes give you the club that talk-show hosts use: "I am coming up on a hard break. Could you explain that in two sentences?") Once you get the hang of it, and understand your audience, you can adjust the length.

FORMAT & STYLE: What's a popular format for a podcast?

The interview is, hands-down, the best format to start with. Two voices on a show are much more interesting than one. The interview also solves other concerns, such as not sounding like a repeating groove. It opens up the possibility of creat¬ing content around several angles, and still keeping to an overarch¬ing theme. "The best podcasts are conversational, not didactic," says Donna Papacosta, a Canadian podcaster. She notes how some podcasters envision the person they're speaking to: always an individual, never a large group. Mitch Joel, in his excellent marketing podcast, *Six Pixels of Separation*, rolls in a panel discussion on media now and then.[7] The podcasting platform Blog Talk Radio, at its basic rate, lets you host a 2-hour, live podcast every day, with up to 50 concurrent callers. This means you could design your 'show' to include a call-in line for customers, listeners, or employees, and make it less about you!

BEST BET: Draw up a list of guests in advance. Authors will be always willing to discuss their latest book. People in your community are always looking for outlets to get a message across. Music is a great common denominator. Adopt a conversational style—shun the lecture; talk to people, not *at* them. Toni Sant, who features music on his show, has audiences in many parts of the world.

FREQUENCY: How often should we podcast?

Television and radio have trained us to think in terms of weekly schedules, says Evo Terra. But consider too, that podcasting is not like 'appointment TV' where the listener sets a timer so she doesn't miss the show. Time-shifting is a big thing in podcasting.

BEST BET: Set up reasonable expectations. Listeners to your weekly podcast should not have to waste time coming to your website or iTunes only to find you have not updated for months. Don't call it a weekly show if you only do it 'whenever.'

SIMPLE PODCASTING PLATFORM:

Your cell phone could be your microphone, with ipadio, an international podcasting platform. Technically, the podcast-by-phone service is called a 'Phonecast'. Just follow these steps:

- Register your Phone. Go to the ipadio website at www.ipadio.com.
- Call ipadio: Use a local ipadio number if you are based in the U.S., U.K., Canada, Australia, Germany, Ireland, Iceland, Italy, or Belgium, or dial the nearest international number (found on the site).
- Verify your Identity: You will be asked to enter your personal PIN.
- Start Talking: No software to configure. Each recording can be up to 60 minutes.
- Be Heard: Your 'phonecast' is automatically available, unless you set it up for editing first.

EQUIPMENT: What kind of hardware should we invest in?

You have a lot more options than were available a few years ago. In 2009, Bryan Person began a podcast about online communications, media, and technology called *The Daily Boo*. Why the odd name, Boo? He recorded on his iPhone, using an application called AudioBoo! Evo Terra gives big props to the Zoom H4n, and a microphone such as the Shure SM-58. The iPhone makes it even easier. It has a very good recorder, as do most other smart phones. They may be difficult to set up for an interview, but the upside to this is that a phone being passed back and forth may not be as intimidating as a microphone, which causes people to freeze up. Ipadio and Blog Talk Radio are two services that require zero hardware—just a phone. A podcast could be streamed live or recorded for later publishing. Both services offer free podcast hosting options for 30-minute and 60-minute podcasts. Both could be embedded in a website.[8]

BEST BET: C.C. Chapman, the master of high energy, short podcasts on marketing, *Managing The Gray*, and a music podcast, *Accident Hash*, recommends recording directly to any computer if you are not going to be doing interviews. "I would recommend getting a good microphone though. If you are just starting out, a high level headphone/microphone combination or one of the new USB microphones will do the trick."

AUDIENCE: Who would listen to my podcast?

You have to try out many things before finding your audience, no different from using any other digital channel, where audiences are finely segmented. An internal audience may be a good start. This audience may first seem like 'all staff,' but not everyone in the company may have access to a computer (for example, linesmen at a utility company), or an MP3 player. So be careful when you decide whom you are targeting. Some (mechanics or teachers, for instance) who may have an MP3 player may be in a noisy work environment. The audience determines the style, how content is packaged, how often they may seek new content, etc. If you are talking to people who are tuning in from a noisy workplace, you may not want to add more background effects, such as a music track running under the voices. Krishna De the Irish podcaster, host of *Talking Coaching Podcast,* a commentator and digital marketer, says she is in constant conversation with her audience, and often gets feedback from face-to-face meetings at live events.

BEST BET: Ask often, using all the social media channels available. Audiences are always willing to tell you what they like, or what they find irrelevant or annoying. Krishna De: "I also invite feedback in my newsletters and on my blog and through Twitter/Facebook/LinkedIn. I had someone tweet how good a podcast was that I had recorded over 2 years ago!"

PREPARATION: If Podcasts are unscripted conversations, how much prep work is needed?

Some preparation is important; no matter how off-the-cuff you may want to appear to be. However, I particularly like those podcasts that leave in the flaws and natural pauses. A bit of self-deprecation, even, will make you come across as authentic, and not too 'corporate.' C.C. Chapman and Toni Sant say they write down names of bands, songs, and a running order on the back of an envelope, to ensure accuracy. The rest is up to the spirit of the moment. Chapman regularly comments on his flubs

NEAT HOSTING IDEA:

Even if you record your podcast on your computer and host it on your site, you can still make it available on BlogTalkRadio. Here's a neat trick for doing that. Krishna De sometimes uses the service to 'play back' shows. How? She adds an intro and 'outro,' then uploads an entire podcast, and lets BlogTalkRadio play it at the scheduled time. This does mean that she has to be online throughout the duration of the show, because it is still considered live.

with comments such as "O my gosh, did I just say that?" It does not take away from the feeling that this guy does have a plan for his show. He's just human!

BEST BET: Make notes, but only to keep content flowing. Scripts are good, as long as you are not a slave to them, and allow yourself and your co-host enough freedom to deliver the content naturally.

Finally, you probably wonder what your podcasting persona ought to be. A good rule of thumb is to represent yourself, rather than try to be some stilted spokesperson for your organization. A podcast is not a press release, even though it tells a story. It's worth repeating: A podcast is not a speech! Nor is it a soap-box for someone you bring in as a guest. Like a blog, a podcast is a great way to bring out a level of humanity that is absent in so many other forms of communication. It is a chat zone. A hype-free, buzzword-free chat room. Krishna De advises, "it's important to be congruent with who you are."

Podcasting could be as complicated or simple as you want to make it. If you're aiming for 'radio quality' and want to have slick editing, go for it! But people are willing to accept a certain 'handmade' quality as long as the content is compelling. The equipment you need is inexpensive and most likely free. I have used a no-frills twenty-nine dollar Sony recorder to capture a conversation with an interviewee on speakerphone (with his permission of course!). I have used Web-based platforms with nothing more than a regular phone. I have used cell phones and a professional Zoom H4N. But in the end, podcasting is more than the hardware and software—and there are so many options.[9]

It's all about the ability to hold stimulating, engaging conversations.

23

RETHINKING DIGITAL STORYTELLING

You won't find press releases here—we have that in our Intel newsroom. You won't find a lot of Intel marketing materials, if I can help it.

—Bill Calder

What comes to mind when you hear the term digital storytelling? There's much more to it than just tweaking the format or adding hyperlinks. With so many opportunities to tell stories on so many different platforms, a number of definitions are emerging. Organizations such as the Center for Digital Storytelling, an international training and research nonprofit, offer workshops in the craft of producing digital stories using images, video, and music. Begun in San Francisco in the 1980s, the CDS soon became aware that people with little or no prior multimedia experience could use new technology to craft their own digital stories.

Such training is good news for many of us today who are working cross-functionally, taking on the roles of data journalist, content curator, and editor. Digital storytelling has its challenges. Author Nicholas

Carr believes that moving a story online might actually dull the experience, in effect diminishing our contact with the "intellectual vibrations" of words put together by authors. Carr, who happens to be a prolific blogger, is no Luddite. His latest book, *The Shallows: What the Internet Is Doing to Our Brains*, is controversial, but needs to be taken seriously if only because it speculates on the erosion of people's habit for "deep reading" when online. "My mind now expects to take in information the way the Net distributes it: in a swiftly moving stream of particles," he writes. "Once I was a scuba diver in the sea of words. Now I zip along the surface like a guy on a Jet Ski."[1]

So what do we do if our audience is swimming (or skimming) in a fast-moving current of information, unable to take much of it in? Matt Thompson, editorial product manager at *National Public Radio*, suggested that digital storytellers could sidestep this problem by obsessing less about immediacy and more about giving the story longer shelf life.[2] I asked two people, Vadim Lavrusik and Bill Calder, how they would approach storytelling, from their respective areas: social networking and brand journalism. Their ideas dovetail nicely, but depending on what channels you use, there are some differences worth exploiting.

SEPARATING TRUTH FROM NOISE

Vadim Lavrusik has given a lot of thought to digital storytelling via social networks. He is, after all, the journalist program manager at Facebook. He often talks about the building blocks of our stories and how we need to move them beyond lazy, webified formats. Indeed, he says we have unthinkingly crammed our stories into the boxes determined by Web software and site architecture.[3] Lavrusik is also an adjunct professor at Columbia University's Graduate School of Journalism, where he teaches social media.

"Today's Web 'article' format is in many ways a descendant from the golden age of print," he explains. "The article is mostly a re-creation of print page design applied to the Web. Stories, for the most part, are coded with a styled font for the headline, byline and body, with some divs [that is, a <div> tag, used in HTML code] separating complementary elements such as photographs, share buttons, multimedia items, advertising and a comments thread, which is often so displaced from the story that it's hard to find."

Lavrusik has been conducting a study on how people are engaging journalists on Facebook, with hopes that the findings will provide journalists with some best practices and insights into how to better engage with and distribute news using the ubiquitous social media site.

Consider how you last clicked on a story someone sent you via LinkedIn or Facebook. Maybe you read only a snippet of the story before getting lost in the comment thread, rather than focusing on the deeper points of the story. The writer might have included many more issues than you had time for. Lavrusik talks of "separating the truth from the noise," whereby the journalist as communicator has evolved to something that is far more complex: "I think the role of the journalist has shifted from [being] not only a storyteller and reporter, but also an amplifier of information."[4]

LOOKING FOR OVERLOOKED STORIES

Business communicators are more than agents of the organization that speak or blog on behalf of their employers in some cautious corporate voice. They

People need a business narrative which advances the conversation.

—Springfield Lewis

have begun to see their roles as storytellers, performing what has been loosely termed brand journalism. These 'stories' are often created outside the realm of public relations and marketing communications.

Bill Calder, managing editor of Free Press at Intel Corporation, takes a strong position on how this nascent idea might work. Free Press, a beta news site, covers stories that tend to be ignored by mainstream media, or reported with inadequate context. A one-time journalist, Calder oversees how the organization's stories can be told to an online audience. He expects his writers—geeks with journalistic integrity as he puts it—to look for the overlooked stories and "weave in tidbits and facts that are interesting, without falling into the trap of marketing or PR-speak." Free Press is very clear about its approach. "You won't find press releases here—we have that in our Intel newsroom. You won't find a lot of Intel marketing materials, if I can help it," Calder said.[5]

If it makes you wonder why Intel is trying to be a media organization, rather than 'stick to its knitting,' that's because many progressive companies have recognized that the line between traditional media and digital has blurred. Intel knows the risks, and also the benefits of being authentic. "We're trying to take an editorial approach with a journalism style and integrity at heart, while doing it objectively and transparently," says Calder. In other words, Calder sees storytelling from a corporate entity as a third role, beyond sales and public relations. "We are not trying to be the next Engadget or CNET....But if we look hard enough, there are always untold stories waiting to be told, but also waiting to be told outside of the tired templates communicators have gotten used to," he explains. Intel's Free Press stories are "a series of stories and video and pictures about things you may not see in the regular press and in the Intel newsroom, so we're really in between," he adds. He even invited outsiders to submit story ideas, corrections, and complaints.

I really like how this brand journalism inspires the story angle. They are certainly not dull. Some examples of articles are "The Battle for Female Talent in China" and "Revolutionizing Computing with Lasers." Even short videos with no mention of a product, are fair game. In one story about "What is an Ultrabook?" the montage of edits reveal that young, would-be customers have no clue about what an Ultrabook is. It's almost like a video survey. There is no editorial slant, even though it would be easy to give it one, considering Intel's investment in this series of thin laptops. Is this where digital brand journalism is headed, where you leave it to the listener or viewer to find an angle? "You have to think more like a journalist and not do the obvious," he says. You need to ask, "what kind of unique angles are there? Who are the people behind the technology or the products?"[6] This is how most organizations need to think in order to become 'media organizations.'

Creating content is becoming a priority for organizations. Why? Because the "hard-to-categorize mix of traditional, personal, shared, commentary-rich, experiential, remixed media" is part of how businesses educate their markets, says Chris Perry, writing for *Forbes* Magazine.[7] There are good reasons for wanting to tell your own story, and create your own media company. Newsrooms today have shrunk, and are 30 percent what they were in 2000.[8] Whereas Public Information Officers (the PIOs) were once there to push content at the media, the digital storyteller in an organization, the Chief Content Officer, is the one who educates without the high-handed push tactics; she is a storyteller, not a hack.

What are the best examples of digital storytelling? When I asked Lavrusik, he pointed to ProPublica (an independent, nonprofit newsroom for investigative journalism[9]) and its coverage of "The Opportunity Gap"—how states in the U.S. are (or are not) providing equal access to education. This was not a 'sexy' story, or even a story in the traditional sense, but "it told a story through data," Lavrusik says.

Facebook collaborated on the "Opportunity Gap" story so that a reader could republish it via a Facebook app. Speaking of apps, when you are building digital stories, it is worth looking closely at what is possible at Storyful, a 'storybuilding' site that encourages content curation. Its app, Storyful Direct, for Apple and Android devices, lets you drag and drop different social media elements into a story and then publish it through a variety of channels. With digital storytelling taking off in so many directions, where might we be headed? "I don't have a Magic 8-Ball," says Lavrusik. "A good story is a good story. It doesn't matter the platform. Digital storytelling leverages the technology of the Web to enhance the way the story is told and consumed by a person."

> **DIGITAL STORYTELLING Will.i.am STYLE**
>
> One way to tell stories was for corporate communications or PR to take the reins of the story, craft it, and distribute it. That's the old way. The new way is to let someone *not* inside the organization do it. In other words, you 'lose' control of who says what, when, where, and how. Intel wanted to promote its ultra-thin laptop series, the Ultrabook, without using the usual suspects. It gave Willl.i.am, rapper and member of the Black Eyed Peas, one of these Ultrabooks and let him travel to Tokyo, Las Vegas, and Mexico City as part of the Ultrabook Project.

Here's another take on storytelling. It is easy to become too distracted by the tools of spreading a message, and not the quality of what is being written, videoed or shared. Digital storytelling is obsessed with delivery mechanisms, notes Springfield Lewis, a former journalist who is now vice president of strategic communications at Newsroom Ink. As the name suggests, Newsroom Ink is an outfit that builds online newsrooms for organizations. Lewis, a heavy social media user, believes that a newsroom needs to be hard-wired and aligned to a business agenda. "There's no lack of content but people need a business narrative that they could follow along, one which advances the conversation." In other words, static information, and information that provides no context is of little value. The newsroom he has built is built around foundational pieces, and its storylines, with 'brother and sister storylines,' all track to the central story. Newsroom Ink builds media microsites, or a dynamic news platform as a sort of content factory. The content invites interactions between the organization and readers.

But what about the uncomfortable reality that information in any organization could not really be managed? That stories or rants can be easily published by employees, without the imprimatur of the organization? Faced with this, is a centralized newsroom relevant? It is, in the same way that a marketing department is relevant, even though employees who are not in marketing are often the best brand voices. Employees are eager to 'wallpaper the marketplace' with posts on social media sites, but many who do it would be hard pressed to figure out how to tie it back to a business objective.

> **TOOLS OF STORYTELLING**
>
> **Storify** (www.storify.com) is a tool for telling stories using social media. You can search multiple social networks from one place and then drag individual elements into your story. You can also reorder the elements and add text to provide context for your readers.
>
> **Storyful** (www.storyful.com) was founded by journalists who wanted to separate the news from the noise of the real-time Web. It was set up to discover "the smartest conversations about world events and raise up the authentic voices on the big stories."

Lewis is a big believer in storytelling that follows an editorial calendar approach. This sounds counter-intuitive, since we all realize that each week brings new issues, new story angles, new crises. Organizations that are big on storytelling need to be prepared to respond quickly, or even preemptively, to issues in the marketplace. But Lewis warns of distractions, what he calls the 'squirrel in the attic problem.' A lot of companies use the squirrel (some temporary snag) to drive their activity as opposed to having a good roof and having your eaves all in place. His prescription: Follow a calendar, but do leave room for 20 percent of stories that come out of nowhere, when something goes amiss or something horrific happens.

24

CAN YOU HEAR ME...NOW?

In this new world, something is amiss. And that something is attention.[1]

—MAGGIE JACKSON

Not listening to the Blogosphere can hurt you!
 Harry, an eight-year old, was fascinated with planes, and his dad said Harry would draw a few hundred pictures of planes in a six-month period. So Harry wrote to the plane company, Boeing, and he got a plain rude response. The corporate office at Boeing replied with a letter saying it did not accept unsolicited designs, and that Boeing had destroyed Harry's picture.

It turns out that Boeing was not trying to be a child-unfriendly company, but it sure did appear that it did not want to hear from little kids with airplanes on their mind. The letter they sent back to Harry starts off by saying nice things about the company "being encouraged by this enthusiasm because it tells us that people around the world want to be better connected and protected." But—and this is a big ugly 'but,' as you may guess—the letter Harry received was a Form Letter, something children don't have experience with. These are the letters that companies send out when they have no time to answer people. Most form letters start with a nice layer of sugar coating to disguise the insincerity, or soften the bad news that might follow. The letter quickly steps into corporate voice. "Experience showed that most ideas had already been considered by our engineers and that there can be unintended consequences to simply accepting these ideas. The time, cost and risk involved in processing them, therefore, were not justified by the benefits gained."[2]

Basically, "thanks but no thanks."

We have smart guys who don't need a little person's sketches; we have gone down this path before, and it's not been worth it. But hey, we do understand how people like to fly and want to try to connect with us!"

This is not an uncommon experience. Some organizations don't want to engage, especially if there is no monetization attached to the engagement. I like to think that the person at Boeing who received the letter and replied probably didn't have a clue about other branches of the organization that were simultaneously doing lots of PR and outreach to invite participation from passengers and businesses.

The odd thing is, Boeing may seem tone deaf, but I happen to know that it is, in fact, just the opposite, an organization with a history of participation and collaboration, one that listens, and one to which unsolicited ideas are welcome. When I interviewed Dr. Cyndi Laurin, author of *The Rudolph Factor*, a book specifically about Boeing, she spoke glowingly about its culture which encouraged sharing. Boeing had given Dr. Laurin access to all levels of the company.[3]

Harry's dad, who was the chief executive of an advertising agency, happened to have a blog. So he decided to write about it, and ask his blog readers what they thought.[4] The comments were what you might expect: Some recalled similar rebuffs from organizations, a few remembered how in a previous—pre-email—era, they did get a thank you packet in the mail. But one parent, a communications professional, recommended this to Harry's dad: "draft a new letter to replace the one you received in the envelope. Use the first two paragraphs from the original, and then replace the next three paragraphs with this." In other words, tell the boy a big white lie about Boeing. If you're a parent you would have probably wrestled with this kind of dilemma.

Meanwhile, back at the ranch at Boeing headquarters, the company did have a social media initiative, and they had just begun using Twitter. The company's Communications Director, Todd Blecher, who would later say he was a 'Twitter convert' having been skeptical at first, had noticed the online chatter about Boeing soon after the incident. He responded in a comment on Windsor's post, and ended up calling Harry, inviting him to visit the company.[5] "We don't have a more children-appropriate response for things like that," Mr. Blecher admitted. "We're expert at airplanes, but novices in social media. We're learning as we go."[6]

Blecher says that the company started out on the wrong foot, by asking the wrong question, "How do we get onto Twitter?" The ninety-six year old company had a broad communication strategy, but was "very technical, engineering oriented, and boring...stories weren't interesting, focused on the product not the people behind it." Yes, those were a Boeing execs words. It had unwittingly become so focused on technical products it had forgotten how excited people—especially children—get about things with wings. Today Boeing's communications department is moving into social media, albeit cautiously, to listen to conversations.

We have a term for the act of listening, and keeping our antennas tuned to the environment. We call it due diligence. But what exactly comes to mind you hear the term 'due diligence'? Focus groups?

Competitive analysis, consumer research? Would it surprise you that a blog, which never arrived in the same respectable attire as say, a Nielsen tracking study, can be all of the above?

BLOG AS RADIO TELESCOPE

Erase for a moment what you may think about the pajama-wearing bloggers with an excess of bile, and a fascination with celebrity trivia. Today blogs have a bit more street cred. People from advertising, Search Engine Optimization (SEO), and even government are rediscovering the other side of blogs, and so can you.

"Your website is your radio telescope. It is how you're listening to the marketplace," said an SEO expert Avinash Kaushik, best known as the analytics guru for Google. He writes one of the top ten ranked analytics blogs.[7] It is a great way of thinking of a blog as a tracking and collecting device a listening tool—a listening tool, rather than an instrument to amplify your voice. A blog, like a radio-telescope is a 'directional' antenna that can pull data from a specific area.

If you haven't set up a blog for your organization or yourself, the 'listening post' function may be the single most reason it could get buy-in from your boss. Sure a blog has other neat benefits, from 'personal branding,' to the ability to bypass mainstream media and become an independent publisher, and a zillion other things we have discussed in the previous chapters.

In truth, listening posts involve a lot more work. And why would you need such a listening post? Consider the alternative. Malcolm Brandt (not his real name for reasons you will find out in a minute) is assigned to answer customer service calls and emails for a major U.S. airline. He goes to work every day looking forward to solving the problems customers have when flying, and who doesn't? These range from the typical bereavement-related cancellations, to missing a connection, to poor on-board service. In his previous jobs, Malcolm was used to listening with a sympathetic ear, because he had been trained to walk in the passenger's shoes, so to speak, and design a solution that would be a win-win. "Today it's a 'win-lose' solution," he says. "I get a script, and set of criteria. I listen, but I know at the back of my mind that I am not supposed to consider all that I am hearing." I stopped him to check if I heard that right. "Did you just tell me you are not supposed to pay attention to a passenger's problems?" Yes, he said. "The script is staring in front of me, so in effect I am listening more to my boss than the customer."

Is he disappointed? Indeed. Malcolm has worked in other major airlines and knows it used to not be as bad as this.[8] Moreover, he is not privy to social media channels in his organization, even though his job is specifically to 'listen to the customer'—a line that is used over and over again in companies like this. More recently, another U.S. airline, Delta Airlines, began to use a Twitter account specifically to respond to customer service issues. The account, @DeltaAssist, frequently has tweets using words like "I'm sorry about this," and "my apologies…" It is managed by 14 employees. Fourteen pairs of eyes and ears.

CONVERSATION TRACKER

Think of how this listening post feature could work for you. Let's say your company markets a packaged good with ingredients sourced from Australia and China. Your blog features stories submitted by your media team, but also by customers who also use it as an information exchange and chat room. Suddenly there's a contamination scare in China, and one of the ingredients may have been tainted.

Your Australian supplier has not been affected.

Before you know it, you'll find people searching for information on product recalls and safety guidelines. They may arrive at your blog in droves via search engines. Some customers may pose questions, others may respond to them to debunk the rumor, while others may be very alarmed or angry and ask your company tough questions. By looking at the sources of concern (country or origin, domains, which search engines direct traffic, time of day, etc.) and checking the source of 'trackbacks,' you can tailor your crisis response to decide what channels to use to respond. (A trackback is how another blogger acknowledges your blog post. For more information on trackbacks, go to http://tinyurl.com/mnjspd)

Unlike a phone call or a focus group, a blog can dial down the temperature of an issue. The shouting match can become a conversation. You can pick up on certain keywords to address the concern; you can even adjust your messaging at the point of sale, and you can brief your sales team based on what you are 'hearing,' on a daily basis. The best part is that you could do this not within days, but within a few hours of the crisis breaking.

You won't be the first to adopt this approach. Comcast, the largest cable company and digital service provider in the U.S. uses a blog for the specific purpose of addressing prickly customer service issues. They listen and respond to technical problems that used to be previously handled on the phone. At Comcastvoices.com a team of 24 bloggers do just that—listen! "This blog is also about your voices: we look forward to conversations about your favorite (or not so favorite) topics," it says. "We want this blog to be a conversation. You can comment on all the entries here, and we hope you do."

This strategy of listening didn't just happen. Many years ago Comcast was accused of turning a deaf ear to customer complaints.

It was savaged on YouTube, in chat rooms, and on blogs set up by angry customers intent on exposing the bad practice.[9] By comparison, Comcast's blog strategy today is considered a great example of how to have an ear to the ground. It can intercept problems before they break out into flame wars.

DEEP LISTENING

The listening post function is not only valuable in times of a crisis. Paying attention to who your visitors are and what they are saying might tip you off to new opportunities in the market, possible competition, and shifting lifestyles. Outside of the blog—or even before there's a blog—an organization needs to incorporate a mindset that turns it from a reactive organization to a listening organization.

Jason Baer and Amber Naslund outline three levels of listening that organizations could consider.[10] Level 1 Listening, for almost every business, is a passive listening operation that could be manned by one person spending just a couple of hours a week, utilizing free online listening tools. Level 2 Listening steps up the game to two employees engaging in active listening, up to 20 hours a week. What's interesting here is that in Level 2, the listening intent shifts from a passive to an active role, with a good portion of time assigned to analyzing and reporting the findings to other branches of the organization that could build on the knowledge gleaned.

LISTENING TOOLS

Radian6 has a dashboard that combines social media monitoring, engagement, and workflow management into one area. Built to help organizations participate in the social web, it lets you filter chatter by language, region or media type, or organize keywords into groups to monitor competitors and industry terms. This information could be seen raw, via bar graphs or pie charts, or you could dig deeper to get a big picture of the post.

Then there is Level 3 Listening for those who are dead serious about being a listening organization. It involves up to three staffers spending 40 hours a week, using paid tools to man the listening post. The team comprises people from different business units, overseen by a social media person. Here what's important: all knowledge gleaned is routed to 'dedicated response teams' who could initiate or join a conversation.

Managing and parsing out the torrent of information is what makes a listening strategy effective. When I worked at Arizona State University, in the early days of social media, a few of us communicators spent a lot of time bringing other departments up to speed on why Twitter was a useful listening tool. Everyone was keen on 'following' others, or amassing followers as some kind of validation for spending time in a space that many felt was a waste of time, or creepy! Tweetdeck and Seesmic were barely a year old then, and soon the lightbulbs went off. Administrators began to look at these Web-based dashboards as a way to keep track of conversations going on in four campuses, and to be able to turn the knowledge into actionable reports.

> **ANALYTICS MADE EASY: 3 TOOLS**
> - **Google Analytics** is an easy-to-master analytics tool to monitor visitors to a blog in real time. Clean dashboards, and custom reports. It is free, but a premium version is also available at www.google.com/analytics
> - **Piwik**, the alternative to Google Analytics, is open source Web analytics software that you could download and install on your server. Get it at www. http://piwik.org/
> - **Clicky** provides real-time data about who's visiting your blog, and from where. Filters let you sift through bounce rate and time spent. It also has Twitter analytics built in, which is useful if you're integrating Twitter with the blog. www.getclicky.com

Today there are paid services that let you listen in on the chatter. But as Baer and Naslund emphasize, listening is only one part of the equation. You need set up a more robust 'radio telescope' to tune in to the conversations (and the monologues) that are going on, whether you participate in them or not. Picking up the chatter means answering "the new telephone," they say. You just cannot ignore these 'calls' coming in via the slew of social channels. Sometimes it means responding in ways you previously were not supposed to or were trained to. Radian6, a Canadian-based Web analytics company, is one service that does this.

HELLO? IS ANYONE LISTENING?

David Carroll was a customer with a gripe, so he started out having several conversations with a company. But it was all one-way. No one seemed to be listening. Carroll, a musician, had taken a flight on United Airlines from Halifax, in Nova Scotia to Omaha, Nebraska. Along the way, at a stop in Chicago, O'Hare, he had spotted his guitars being flung around by the baggage-handling crew. He filed a complaint. When he got to his destination he noticed that his guitar had snapped at the neck. This time he filed a claim with United, but was told that he had failed to make the claim within the company's stipulated "stan-

LESSONS FROM 'UNITED BREAKS GUITARS'

In Dave Carroll's happily ever after ending, where the corporation was forced to listen to the little guy, there were some points worth noting:

- Some things you can't repair. In his video statement, Carroll said that United offered "generously but late," to compensate him. When forced out of the company, it's not the best damage control outcome. The customer's voice is what's remembered most.

- Better late than never. United did finally connect with Carroll, and he was unexpectedly complementary of the customer service person—the infamous Miss Irlweg—whom he had first ridiculed for obstinately sticking up for the company.

- Put the handbook aside. Information in a handbook is designed to help employees understand the ground rules. Yet, to Carroll the handbook seemed like a "system is designed to frustrate customers." Company policy thwarts conversations. Human policy lets some fresh air in.

dard 24-hour timeframe." In frustration, since subsequent talks broke down, the musician wrote and produced a song, titled "United Breaks Guitars."[11] Suddenly they were willing to talk.

But how did he get United Airlines to listen? By uploading it to YouTube! It became an instant hit, viewed by millions of people worldwide, creating a black eye for an airline that values its global reputation.

Carroll had originally offered United a chance to be part of the story. He kept his promise. He made a statement, on July 10, 2009, also on YouTube, about the resolution that came "generously, but late." Interestingly, he made it a point to mention the customer service rep, Ms. Irlweg, whom he had chided in the first video. He said she was a great employee, unflappable, and someone who merely acted on the policies of a company that she represented. Watching this denouement, you get the feeling that it is a veiled warning to all those who act on 'policy,' especially if that policy doesn't include listening. In his subsequent videos on the subject, Carroll rubs it in: "If you just come to your senses, accept the consequences...we could be best buddies, but our friendship has been muddied," he croons.[12] "United Breaks Guitars" will go down as one of the great customer wins using social media.

There used to be a television commercial for Verizon Communications in which a technical person roams the country across different terrains, holding up a phone to his ear. The so-called 'Test Man' was constantly checking to see if the person he's connecting with can hear him clearly, repeating that phrase, "Can you hear me now? *Now?...Now?*" It was both a memorable and annoying phrase. It addressed the problem—and tried to convey a solution—that many early cell phone users faced about abruptly dropped calls, when people moved around, especially in and out of buildings, or while driving. It also gave the impression that the company was constantly 'listening' to these complaints, and that it was always tuned in, trying to make sure people's conversations were not interrupted.[13] [The Verizon ads, which began in 2002 were discontinued in 2011. Quite ironically, the 'Can you hear me now' guy was not allowed to speak about his contract.[14]]

United and Boeing are not the first, and certainly will not be the last to be targeted for not listening. We have had our share of tone deaf companies.

TELLING TEN MILLION

In the past we 'filed' a complaint—maybe a letter, or asked to speak to a manager, and that was it, right? We assumed it would not go any further up the org chart, but we asked to be heard, anyway. Social media has upturned that model. We don't have to ask to be heard, we make sure someone does listen, not in some private format or in the customer service office, but in a public space.

"Conventional marketing wisdom long held that a dissatisfied customer tells ten people," noted Paul Gillin. But "in this new age of social media, he or she has the tools to tell ten million."[15]

I have taken a few extreme measures myself to get a company's attention, one of which included a call to my local television news station, Channel 12, which runs a "Call to Action" segment. They often get the ear of people who would listen to a news reporter rather than a customer.

A better example, however, was with a technology company. I was miffed after taking in my son's laptop to Data Doctors, a local computer repair franchise. The technicians had performed a diagnostic service for which I paid, and recommended I replace the hard drive.

I decided to buy one before I went back, but when I asked that they install it they said they could not. (I should've bought it from them,

> **@TheDataDoc**
> Ken Colburn
> @heyangelo I totally agree with you, especially since it's not our policy. Please DM me your contact info.

they said.) It reminded me of Dave Carroll's experience. Sorry mate, but it's our way or the highway. No ifs, no buts. Company policy. Being unable to get them to listen, I contacted the company on Facebook, and asked for some consideration. I also sent out a tweet about this.[16] Within a day I had two responses. The company CEO, Ken Colburn, sent me a reply, via Twitter saying "@heyangelo I totally agree with you, especially since it is not our company policy. Please DM me your contact info."

It's impossible to miss Colburn's choice of words that suggested he had his ear to the ground. He *totally* agreed with me; he thought I had a right to good service. He asked that I send him a 'DM' (for the uninitiated DM refers to the direct messaging feature in Twitter where simply using the letters DM in front of the person's Twitter address keeps the exchange just between ourselves), so we could take this conversation to a private chat, which we did.

At that time, I happened to be co-hosting a radio show out of Phoenix. The show, called "Your Triple Bottom Line," was all about how organizations were incorporating sustainable business practices and we focused heavily on the intersection of social media and employee engagement. I felt this was an extremely relevant topic to the show and would open a good point of discussion. My co-host, Derrick Mains, a CEO at that time who had been behind many companies, was someone who was a big user of social media. [Mains now enjoys his own 'concierge service' with a communication service provider after using Twitter to not just bitterly complain, but to start a conversation. The customer service rep is now a good friend.]

When Colburn contacted me, I asked him if I could feature our conversation on the next show, and he agreed. His comments were extremely poignant as it demonstrated that, in spite of me being a ticked-off customer, he truly wanted his organization to reconnect with me and work it out through a direct conversation. Not through some PR slave, not by offloading the problem to some low-ranking customer service person, but the CEO himself.[17]

I know of plenty of examples where someone using a tweet has had immediate or a better response than a call to the organization's toll-free number. Maybe Twitter is the new 1800 customer-complaint number, because it doesn't go through a phone tree, and is staffed by real people, often around the clock.

Before YouTube, before Twitter, before all these fancy channels and listening tools, it was a given that employees listen. That shouldn't have changed. As customers or as citizens, we miss the time when people did listen to us. We live in the midst of chatter, bathed in speaking channels and listening systems. As managers and marketers, public officials and communicators, we gloat over the fact that we are truly plugged in. But it's good to do a regular reality check and face up to the fact that to engage in chatter is to engage our ears, not just our vocal chords.

25

YOUR CHAPTER

If this is your speech bubble, how would you fill it?

This book may be 'complete' as a project, but the chapters are open to revision and updating. I deliberately left this chapter for unfinished business. Conversations don't have neat beginnings and endings. Why not a book? We interject, update, revise our words, and admit others into our circle. Even if you picked up this book by accident, I would like to hear from you. Interject!

Help me update the ideas in this book through your contributions to this chapter. Share your experiences, your discoveries, and your analysis of things going on in your neck of the woods in our Chat Republic. Jot some thoughts on the blank pages here. Scan them and email them to info@chatrepublic.net. Or visit ChatRepublic.net for more information on how to do so. It really doesn't matter how we share ideas, in digital or analog formats.

CHAT REPUBLIC

Afterword

WHAT FOR THE TALKING?

When texts replaced calls...the game changed from conversations to composition.[1]

—Katy Steinmetz

"*What for the talking?*" This phrase, in classic Sri Lankan English, captures our exasperation with idle talk. Roughly translated, it means, "What's the point of all this chatter?" Or, "Tell me about it!"

"The censorship bill is making its way in parliament for the third bloody time!"

"What for the talking, my friend?"

"My board of directors has a few more questions about your website proposal."

"What for the talking, for heaven's sake?"

We spend a lot of time chatting, don't we? Teenage chatter. Political chatter. Forums online. Heated conversations on blogs. Text chats and Twitter blurts. Most people agree that Homo sapiens are programmed to chat. Or at least, maintain 'ambient' intimate noises through short-form content. That's why someone who does not is quickly scorned as being 'too quiet,' weird, a poor conversationalist, etc.

So where might we take our chatter-box proclivity? In a world where boundaries and identities have blurred, is our spot in the borderless Chat Republic a better place than ten years ago? If a lone activist with a Webcam in a country in the throes of a revolution could pave the way for more voices of governance, if a cancer patient or an airline passenger could bring about change by engaging with others, then many of us facing much less complex day-to-day issues could make this world a very different place.

The implications of our connectivity and our conversations run deeper than the cute social networking stories you often hear on the evening news. As we saw from examples of how activists use voices and hand signs, a 'communication network' sometimes doesn't ride on a wireless signal. Governments that focus on visible chatter will be caught off-guard by human ingenuity that creates ways for people to talk on their homegrown proxy networks. Or the poor-man's Internet: flash drives passed on from hand to hand. I have shown how the Chat Republic we live in includes the realm of corporate communications—internal and external. Organizations that empower word-of mouth must learn to tap into both organic buzz and amplified buzz. It's hard to ignore the evidence from business and government, which proves that inviting new voices through the highly-suspect phenomenon called 'crowd-sourcing' can solve intractable problems.

Bearing down on all of this is the inexorable force of mobile. Large numbers of their citizens, armed with virtually nothing but cell phones, continue to challenge the status quo. People on the edges are proving to be more media active that they were expected to be, and this means they could fight corruption, fact-check—and unseat—those who have evaded scrutiny for a long time: politicians, advertisers, global organizations, governments, journalists. People will talk! Online, offline, and without corporate or political approval.

AFTERWORD

CHATTING OVER-THE TOP

The mobile chatting experience has been around for some time —it's been 20 years since the first text message was sent out. It's early 2013. We, the one billion plus people who own cell phones are poised to make giant strides in how we will engage. Chat Apps, which are third-party applications for cell phones, have swooped in on our phones, letting us send text messages without incurring SMS fees. Chat Apps such as the popular 'WhatsApp' are those that create over-the-top (or OTT) messaging. Two indicators of what a big shift this is:

- By the end of 2012, Chat Apps overtook text messaging—19.1 million vs 17.6 million in the previous year.
- In the first quarter of 2013, smart phones 'out-shipped' feature phones for the first time ever, paving the way for such apps.

As more Chat App services such as Kik, Viber, ChatOn, WhatsApp and iMessage take center stage in the mobile experience, expect a new wave of peer-to-peer conversations in your republic.

The human urge to engage in chatter is a very disruptive app. It is that 'killer app' that is—pardon the geek-speak—device agnostic. Meaning, chatter hops on and off digital and analog networks with scant respect for demographics, political persuasion, or pecking order.

Fascination with human networks that are social first, and digital later, is leading scientists and anthropologists to look at our conversations through the lenses of mathematics, computer science, biology, political science, and economics. You can be sure that, even as you read this, a student somewhere is writing a dissertation on this topic. Indeed, finding out how and why we chat is a work in progress.

As I come to the end of this book, I couldn't stress more how important it is for us to think deeply and critically about our own 'social' habits. Do you feel the urge to respond to an email thread, even though it rudely interrupts your busy day? Why comment on a podcast? Why tag a photo on Facebook? Are we so hard-wired to join a conversation? We all have strong opinions on this.

As we have found out, organizations that used to *not* chat with their stakeholders, especially those locked into one-way, mass media, have begun to experiment with the big talk-back switch we like to call social media. For the *hoi polloi,* it is the operating system of our brand new republic.

BONUS MATERIAL

Case Study 1 — Adapting

IT TAKES A VILLAGE (AND A SMART PHONE)

A short distance from the busy town of Kurunegala in Sri Lanka, once a citadel of kings, is the tiny hamlet of Alegoda. The place is accessible only by mud roads. It is home to small arts and crafts workshops out of which artisans turn out handmade coir brushes and utility items out of polished coconut shells. Some of these products find their way to five-star hotels and urban homes in Sri Lanka's capital, Colombo. It's therefore hard to imagine a group more far removed from social media than the small artisans of Alegoda. But that's exactly the challenge for Isura Silva, an engineer.

Isura, a program director at Sarvodaya Fusion, a technology arm of a grassroots organization, is happy to admit that he is an accidental social-media user. He has spent a lot of his time trying to crack the code as to what kind of social-media engagement might be valuable to this community. "Social media is powerful, but I find it is valuable in spite of being unable to manage it," he says. He has seen its ability to hop across typical barriers. Social-media networking is no different from a social relationship we have face-to-face, he says. "The only thing that should matter in both cases—our analog and the digital relationships—is that you should love interaction, talking to people and respecting each other's viewpoints."

Integrating social media into this community had to be thoughtful. Alegoda is far from any wireless network and the nearest Internet café or community center with a computer is 10 miles away. Even if there was computer access, the community would not use it. His Fusion team believed that growth in a community ought to be organic. "We didn't want to force a technology (or a program involving technology) on a village." The people in the village had begun to express an interest in education, and wondered how they might digitize information about the coir products they were manufacturing. They instinctively understood supply and demand, that if no one heard about their awesome product, no one would want to buy it; they did not want to be a small business forever.

So Fusion talked to them about smart phones, to test their interest. These smart devices (Google Nexus phones) gave them access to the Internet via a mobile signal. Someone showed them what Facebook was all about, and another created a simple Facebook page. They had heard about blogging through another pilot program.

Before long, a craftsman in the community used the smart phone to photograph coir products and upload pictures to their Facebook page. Then, a lucky break. Someone working for a global supplier of textiles, tea, construction material, and coir-based goods spotted the products. A conversation started with the company, Hayleys. It agreed to buy one million items a month. One million!

What did it take to get to this point? A device? A connection to a business network? A serendipitous conversation? It's easy to say 'all of the above.' But there is one thing we tend to overlook: the yearning to tell one's story, and the community's passion to participate in a conversation—even a conversation with outsiders.

One way to think about technology adoption is to treat it like a handful of seeds. Left to germinate—out of sight, at their own pace—ideas will begin to sprout. This is one of the most misunderstood aspects of social media, for the simple reason that managers who base their expectations on experience with traditional media expect instant results: click-throughs, likes, and rapid ROIs.

What are the must-haves in building a community? Silva has three suggestions. They are not a one-size-fits-all solution, but could be adapted to suit the need.

PRACTICE INSIDE-OUT THINKING. Managers typically impose an outside-in mindset, because it always feels safe to use a strategy that has been adopted elsewhere. Inside-out thinking flips the switch. Once you identify a problem or need, real creativity comes

Learning about smart phone usage at a 'Nenesala' (a knowledge center) in a rural community in Sri Lanka.

when you allow community input at the planning phase prior to execution. "Inside-out thinking means putting faith in the participants, as much as you have in your consultants or technology," says Silva.

BE PREPARED TO ADAPT. Very often, the thing that you set out to accomplish changes once a product or service is launched. In the world of technology, the term 'pivoting' is used to explain this readiness to shift gears. Managers used to consider a mid-course change of direction as a flaw in the strategy. But in an environment where organic change is expected, this is part of the plan. Discovery is sometimes more important than consistency.

PUT PEOPLE BEFORE TECHNOLOGY. We tend to fall in love with our shiny new objects too fast. But before these tools emerged, people (not devices) did the heavy lifting in communities. Humans, not clicks, spread ideas. Gossip was the world's favorite hyperlink in a pre-Internet world, one in which people told each other stories. Today, organizations get hoodwinked into tool obsession. The tool might catalyze a movement, but the movement needs human beings as its operating system. When pressed to explain how much technology really matters in community building, Silva invokes Steve Jobs: "We should stand at the intersection of technology and humanity."

Case Study 2 — Listening

YOU SPOKE. WE LISTENED

It's one thing to embed digital media as a listening strategy. But it's another thing to have to change an operational decision based on what your customers tell you (yell at you, sometimes!) through those channels. Many of the companies I speak to use digital media—email, surveys, and newsletters—more than social media to solicit feedback. This seems manageable, since no one needs to be tasked with checking every online feed for negative feedback.

But like it or not, with a social media presence of not, organizations are being forced to hear from their customers. Major brands such as HSBC, Nestle, and Motrin, to name a few, have had their ears bent by people whom they would have never paid attention to before.

The makers of Maker's Mark, a popular bourbon in the U.S., experienced this in early 2013, when it decided to adjust its whiskey strength in anticipation of a supply problem. The brand had been facing unforeseen demand and had therefore decided to decrease its alcohol volume to 84-proof, from 90-proof (or 45 percent alcohol). No big deal, it thought. It was an operational decision that it was going ahead with to make sure it met market needs.

Maker's Mark had done its homework. Consumer research had showed that there was no difference in the taste. The company, however, thought it would be upfront with its customers, even though it felt people might have never noticed. In other words, it was being transparent.

What followed, however, was a transparency backlash. (Around this time Arizona State University faced a similar backlash. It had changed the costume of its mascot, Sparky, but got so much pushback, that it had to abandon the move.) Maker's Mark heard from its customers in no uncertain terms on Twitter and Facebook, of course—the posting channels that just happen to also be the unstructured, cacophonous listening posts. Customers thought that changing the proof meant they would be getting a more 'watered down' whiskey. Said one customer, dredging up another famous brand formula-change debacle:

"Hey, @MakersMark, raise prices if you must, but don't mess with success! Ever heard of New Coke?"

The bourbon maker was unprepared for this, yet it realized that it had to take all this chatter and back-channel conversations seriously. Just like Boeing, and just like many other organizations that will sooner or later hear from their stakeholders, it recanted. In full public glare.

What's most telling is that Maker's Mark defined it as a listening experience. The chairman's apology letter was titled "Your spoke. We listened." Below is the letter to its customers. Note the penultimate line, implying that from now on it would be huge on listening.

YOU SPOKE. WE LISTENED

Dear Friends,

Since we announced our decision last week to reduce the alcohol content (ABV) of Maker's Mark in response to supply constraints, we have heard many concerns and questions from our ambassadors and brand fans. We're humbled by your overwhelming response and passion for Maker's Mark. While we thought we were doing what's right, this is your brand—and you told us in large numbers to change our decision.

You spoke. We listened. And we're sincerely sorry we let you down.

So effective immediately, we are reversing our decision to lower the ABV of Maker's Mark, and resuming production at 45% alcohol by volume (90 proof). Just like we've made it since the very beginning.

The unanticipated dramatic growth rate of Maker's Mark is a good problem to have, and we appreciate some of you telling us you'd even put up with occasional shortages. We promise we'll deal with them as best we can, as we work to expand capacity at the distillery.

Your trust, loyalty and passion are what's most important. We realize we can't lose sight of that. Thanks for your honesty and for reminding us what makes Maker's Mark, and its fans, so special.

We'll set about getting back to bottling the handcrafted bourbon that our father/grandfather, Bill Samuels, Sr. created. Same recipe. Same production process. Same product.

As always, we will continue to let you know first about developments at the distillery. In the meantime please keep telling us what's on your mind and come down and visit us at the distillery. It means a lot to us.

Sincerely
Rob Samuels, Chief Operating Officer - rob@makersmark.com
Bill Samuels, Jr. Chairman Emeritus - bill@makersmark.com

Case Study 3 — Engaging

A CASE FOR A REAL-TIME, 'MACHINE READABLE' DEMOCRACY

Indrajit Samarajiva lives one part of his life immersed in social media, but that is not to say he is a completely digital chap. He doesn't obsess about how many Twitter followers he has, but is optimistic that Asians, now tethered to digital tools, will play a more active role in how their community functions.

He speaks of how people in the rural areas yearn to contribute—not just consume content. He scoffs at those who ask 'is social media important?' It's like asking 'is writing important?' or 'is art important?' he says. His passion, however, isn't about 'checking in' to earn badges, or about blogging—which he does a lot. One of Samarajiva's several startups, Kottu.org, is a news blog that aggregates more than a thousand local blogs on cricket, music and politics.

Samarajiva's abiding interest is democracy in the digital age. "Modern democracy is based on paper technology and hasn't been upgraded for 300 years," he laments. "It's based on representatives, but when you look at how democracy works, it is essentially based on meetings and paper. Not very engaging!" Few leaders are wont to pursue real-time democracy so that their citizens can be heard and participate directly.

What's wrong with meetings and paper? Lawmaking and elections require meetings and paper.

"Look at it this way: You physically send people to a certain place (parliament, or city council) to represent you. You give out paper ballots, but you do this only every four years. And then you physically write legislation, which you need lawyers to write and read.

So what's the solution?

"It is quite possible to have a more 'machine-readable democracy,' one in which we are voting on a more daily basis. A system that would capture our voices and ideas in real-time, and which also captures and processes anonymous background data on a statistical level.

Some sort of an always-on digital stream for governance?

"What if there was some algorithm that shows a politician what's happening in the country, that enables policymakers to make better decisions on our behalf?

What kind of 'machines' are you anticipating?

"Look, I'm a fairly connected person, but I don't have any contact with my MP (Member of Parliament). Political representation is not working. Business and culture has moved up to a higher technology. Politics needs to follow that model. This does not mean that the old way of doing politics will not go away. As you can see from Mohamed Morsi in Egypt, and the use of Internet fundraising in the U.S. to buy TV ads, old school politicking still dominates."

Could you expand on the 'machines' idea?

The point is not machines per se but being machine readable. Anybody can read a bunch of blogs but since blogs use RSS (Real Simple Syndica-

tion, an XML tagging technology) machines can read them. That means we can sort and process thousands of blogs on Kottu, taking in user input (how much they share and tweet them) to show what's important.

And where would we citizens come in?
On a practical level, you could file concerns like customer service tickets, socially network with people in your neighborhood to raise issues and—more passively—have government respond to things like transport and infrastructure concerns automatically.

Where do you see real-time democracy going?
"On the simplest level, if information is put online it can gather more support and lead to action faster. We could set up social media-powered ward-level meetings. For governance, we need data; good data. We could have young people 'embedded' in meetings, feeding the information from the meetings into a digital system. This data could then, in real-time, pop up on a dashboard in a Town Hall, telling citizens that here are these issues in Maradana, these are the issues in Mattakuliya."

Samarajiva is onto something, and he senses it. There is a growing interest in 'Big Data' as a basis for better governance. This broader, more integrated use of social media is more than how it is being used today for candidates' PR work or the party's get-out-the-vote campaigns. This is about citizens taking charge of their lives and their country, as is expected in most republics.

That is quite a vision for a 30-year old. Samarajiva anticipates our skepticism: real-time democracy does sound like a buzz phrase.

"It's not like a crazy idea," he says. "It will happen at some point."

ACKNOWLEDGEMENTS

A book, like a story, is a work in progress. There are many events that led to this, and there were many people who walked with me along this journey. This includes editors, students, colleagues, friends—indeed 'upper-case' friends and the Facebook type—and family who have been so generous with their time.

I am greatly indebted to two magazine editors who gave me a shot at exploring some of the topics covered in this book: Natasha Nicholson, publisher of *Communication World* magazine, who gave me the opportunity to talk to a global community of business professionals; Hiran Hewavisenti, editor and publisher of *LMD*, a premier business magazine in Sri Lanka, who invited me to be its marketing and technology columnist within a year of its launch in 1994.

There have been hundreds of people I have had the opportunity to interview over the years. I am truly thankful for their time, particularly those whose insights have informed the chapters of this book: David Traver Adolphus, Jason Baer, Rohit Bhargava, Josh Bernoff, Bill Brandt, Alberto Cairo, Ken Colburn, Bill Calder, David Cohn, C.C. Chapman, Priscilla Grim, Sanjana Hattotuwa, Shel Holtz, Neville Hobson, Linda Hoshaw, Rohan Jayaweera, Mitch Joel, Vadim Kaushek, Doug Kaye, Jason Kintzler, Jason Lankow, Vadim Lavrusik,

Springfield Lewis, Jessica McCann, Bo Mueller-Moore, Dan Nelson, Dr. Michael Netzley, Donna Papacosta, Emanuel Rosen, Dhanushka Samarakone, Indi Samarajiva, Isura Silva, Michael Lee Stallard, Matt Thompson, Dan York, Linda VandeVrede, Shannon Whitley, Marc Wright and Johann Xavier. Russell Miranda went to the heart of the idea with his cover illustration that suggests our world is one giant speech bubble. There are others, too numerous to mention who have opened doors, fact-checked, provided feedback, and helped shape the book's outcome. To all of you, and Martin Coffee, thanks!

A special thanks to three big influences: Derrick Mains invited me to co-host a weekly radio show, *Your Triple Bottom Line*, in 2010. Our conversations before an invisible audience, which often included discussions about the intersection of social media and business, planted a seed for the overarching theme of this book. Professor Jude Fernando (no relation) goaded me on, believing there was a book inside me waiting to get out. The book would not have looked this way if not for Venu Mathukumalli who did an awesome job of shepherding this project from a stack of paper to a clean format with such creativity and patience!

And last, but not least, I am grateful to my family, especially my wonderful wife Tanu, and my children Aaron and Nadia who stood by me with encouragement. And how could I ever thank my mum and late dad, who instilled in me the power of community.

ANGELO FERNANDO
Gilbert, Arizona. USA
April 2013

NOTES

PREFACE—Zip It Up!
1. In case you're wondering, yes, I had been tempted to tell them to go jump a lake, since I had not intended to damage their brand.
2. Henry Jenkins, *Convergence Culture, Where Old and New Media Collide* NYU Press, 2008. p. 134.
3. George Lucas originally sued anyone who mashed-up his *Star Wars* movies, and was known as 'Lucas The Litigator' for his attempts to clamp down on illegal mash-ups—but eventually gave in, recognizing that fans feel they 'own' the franchise. More about how he relented, in a story by Drew Grant, "George Lucas loses Stormtrooper helmet battle." *Salon.* July 27, 2011. http://www.salon.com/2011/07/27/george_lucas_stormtroopers/
4. The Unilever commercial for the Dove brand, titled "Self Esteem," was part of a 'Campaign for Real Beauty.' It was a brilliant 75-minute story about supporting women's inner beauty. It went on to win two Cannes Grand Prix awards in 2006. A parody of it, however, soon appeared, mocking Unilever's double standard, promoting overtly sexist stereotyping via another of its brands, Axe: http://www.youtube.com/watch?v=7-kSZsvBY-A
5. Harry Potter fan pages and unauthorized sequels to the movies have irked both J. K. Rowling and Warner Brothers. Among them was a Bollywood movie, *Hari Puttar: A Comedy of Terrors*, and a "Captain Underpants" book (!) titled *Hairy Potty and the Underwear of Justice*.
6. In 2004, six years after my legal hiccup as an online publisher, I set up my own blog, appropriately called *Hoi Polloi Report*. It was where I have been writing about and commenting on the intersection of social media, business, and technology. Maintaining the blog has taught me a lot more than just blogging. It has made me see other points of intersection between PR and marketing, journalism and trust, and between offline communities and online ones. And yes, I also mine the complex territory of branding. No one has asked me to shut up—yet!
7. The idea of a Web 2.0 was first coined by Tim O'Reilly, of *O'Reilly Media* to describe a more collaborative Web experience. The Web, he suggested was not

a destination, but a 'platform,' on top of which applications would run. But that world too is maturing into a Web 3.0 experience.
8. Richard Macnamus, "Berners-Lee disses Web 2.0." http://ReadWriteWeb.com. August 26, 2006.

INTRODUCTION—Why Don't We Chat?
1. The Methodist Hospital System introduced social media in 2009. Its management, particularly its legal team, had expressed reservations about a Facebook presence wondering if employees might abuse their access by spending work time on personal Facebook accounts, or share private patient information, etc. Would it have a negative impact on the hospital system? They found that social media gave the organization a unique way to communicate with its community and provide an opportunity for consumers to become more actively involved in their own health. Denny Angelle and Clare L. Rose, "Conversations with the Community: The Methodist Hospital System's Experience with Social Media." *Frontiers of Health Services Management, 28*(2).
2. "The New Conversation: Taking Social Media from Talk to Action." Harvard Business Review. Analysis Service Report, 2010.
3. "Tribalization of Business Survey," a study by Deloitte LLP's Technology, Media & Telecommunications Practice, Beeline Labs, and the Society of New Communications Research, 2011.
4. Academia is no different. Knowledge is often trapped in jargon-infested papers that few could decipher. "The principal occupation of the academic community is to invent dialects sufficiently hermetic to prevent knowledge from passing between territories," observed John Ralston Saul in *The Doubter's Companion: A Dictionary of Aggressive Common Sense*. Free Press, 2002.

CHAPTER 1—Talk On the Street
1. Wael Ghonim, *Revolution 2.0*. Houghton Mifflin Harcourt, 2012. Ghonim, a Google marketing executive in Egypt, arguably triggered the revolution on the streets of Cairo in January 2011 by creating a Facebook page.
2. The new 12th edition of the *Concise Oxford English Dictionary* (its centenary edition) contains some 400 new entries, which include *cyberbullying, sexting, slow food,* and *textspeak*.
3. Words such as piffle ('to talk or act feebly'), trifle and potty ('trivial, small') must have seemed vulgar then. Angus Stevenson, editor of the 12th edition, writing on the Oxford University Press blog, explains that the goal has been to be progressive and up to date. "Defining our language for 100 years." (http://blog.oup.com/2011/08/concise).
4. Eric Raymond, *The Cathedral and the Bazaar*. Snowball Publishing, July 2010. Raymond describes the Linux community that grew around Linus Torvalds' invention of the radical, open source operating system, as having many conflicting agendas, out of which something cohesive emerged.
5. 58 million regular users log on exclusively through a phone or tablet, "Facebook mobile audience jumps in 2011." *Silicon Valley Mercury News*, http://www.mercurynews.com 7 March, 2012. On a related note, mobile phone use outstripped

NOTES

use of landlines in the U.K. in September 2011.

6. Twitter put this in perspective on its blog, saying "every day, the world writes the equivalent of a 10 million-page book in tweets or 8,163 copies of Leo Tolstoy's *War and Peace*. Reading this much text would take more than 31 years."
7. Suzahn E., "An Occupier's Note." *Tidal*, a publication of Occupied Media, Issue 1, December 2011.
8. Alongside this, is another phenomenon known as Fon. It is a global organization that enables what amounts to a crowd-sourced Wi-Fi network. Once you sign up, you agree to share "a little bit of your WiFi at home" with fellow travelers. Members of this organization have built a 'network of five million hot spots available to each other, worldwide.'
9. Michael Arrington, "Yelp Stats Show iPhone App Usage Staggeringly Deeper Than Website." *TechCrunch*. June 3, 2010.
10. In one month, half a million calls made to local businesses came from a Yelp iPhone application. That is equal to one call every five seconds. *TechCrunch, ibid.*
11. The movement, under the umbrella of Global Days of Action against Capitalism was best known for its action against the World Trade Organization (WTO) in Seattle in 1999, and subsequent campaigns against multinational institutions in Prague, Quebec, Genoa, Barcelona, and Porto Alegre.
12. Paul D. Armond, "Black flag over Seattle." *Albion Monitor 72*, March 2000. www.monitor.net/monitor/seattlewto/index.html
13. C.W. Anderson, Paper on Journalistic Symmetry: "Principles of Journalistic Symmetry: Building News Networks Before and After the 'Publication' of News." College of Staten Island, New York (CUNY).
14. "Ruckus' decision to utilize a text messaging service as a supplement to their planned comms-facilitation activities (sic) came late in the game—a mere two weeks before the RNC. While we had some knowledge of the service offering by TxtMob, it was decided that analternate, (sic) redundant, and complentary (sic) system wouldn't be a bad idea." A longer discussion thread could be found here: http://www.scribd.com/doc/5403691/RNC04-in-160-Character-Bytes (Accessed on March 10, 2012).
15. Howard Rheingold, *Smart Mobs: The Power of the Mobile Many*. Basic Books, 2002. p. 158.
16. Rick Stengel, "Person of the Year: The Protester." *Time. Dec 2011 – Jan 2, 2012.*
17. Activists in Barcelona, for instance "argued that future campaigns should be organized along network lines, combining horizontal coordination around common objectives with maximum diversity and autonomy."
18. This update came, naturally, via a tweet, from Twitter on October 12, 2011.
19. A foundation called the Freedom Network Foundation devised a Freedom Tower using two modems and six radio antennas for WiFi to make sure the Occupy movement's New York activists are connected. Sarah Kessler, "How Occupy Wall Street Is Building Its Own Internet." *Mashable*. Nov 14, 2011. http://mashable.com/2011/11/14/how-occupy-wall-street-is-building-its-own-internet-video (Accessed on June 25, 2012).
20. Sarah Van Gelder, Introduction. *This Changes Everything*. Berrett-Koehler Publisher, Nov 2011.

21. In its fundraising effort at Kickstarter.com, the Occupy movement made the point that "Occupy Wall Street Media is not the 'official' media of the occupation— there is no official media!" It was supposed to be the product of an inclusive group of voices, not an exclusive group.
22. Find the paper online at http://www.indig-nacion.org.
23. Priscilla Grimm. Interview with Author, April 2012.

CHAPTER 2—Just Chatting
1. Not the founding father John Jay! This is creative director John C. Jay, of Weiden+Kennedy, Portland, Oregon. The quote if from his "10 lessons for young designers." American Institute of Graphic Arts http://www.aiga.org/design-journeys-john-jay. Jay now leads the agency's newly minted indie creative shop known as W+K Garage.
2. Joseph Jaffe, *Join The Conversation*. Wiley, October 2007. In his book about the power of engaging audiences, Jaffe makes the case that consumers who are both medium and message are chatting among themselves; it behooves marketers to lean forward and listen in and engage in dialogue.
3. David Shahel, Ph.D. and Kaveri Subrahmanyam, Ph.D., "'Any Girls Want to Chat Press 911': Partner Selection in Monitored and Unmonitored Teen Chat Rooms." *Cyberpsychology & Behavior, 10*(3), 2007.
4. Emanuel Rosen gives us six reasons why we talk. Because we are programmed to do so; to connect to make sense of our world; to reduce risk cost and uncertainty; because it makes economic sense to relieve tension. "Why We Talk." *The Anatomy of Buzz*. Doubleday, 2000.
5. The Fireside Chats were 27 speeches, beginning March 12, 1933. Roosevelt had used radio before as governor of New York, to talk directly to citizens. He didn't call it a fireside chat initially. The title was given by a CBS executive, and Roosevelt later referred to these as 'chats,' recognizing that radio was a very intimate medium and connected him to the people in a very real way.
6. "His paternal, colloquial broadcasting style helped soothe a troubled nation's fears," notes Geoffrey Storm, of Utica College, Utica, New York http://www.historycooperative.org/journals/nyh/88.2/storm.html
7. "You are, I believe, the most enlightened, and best informed people in all the world at this moment. You are subjected to no censorship of news..." Roosevelt said in one chat on September 3, 1939, about the war in Europe.
8. Second "Fireside Chat," May 7, 1933. By: Arthur M. Schlesinger Jr., Fred L. Israel, David J. Frent. *The Election of 1932 & the Administration of Franklin D. Roosevelt*. Mason Crest, 2002. For a deep dive into hubs and networks, check out Albert-Lasszlo Barabasi, *Linked*. Plume, 2003. The author notes how Roosevelt, unknown to his audience, was one of the biggest 'hubs' of his era; his appointment book contained some 22,000 names.
9. Meebo rooms, created to let people chat about and share music, video, and websites, were discontinued in October 2011.
10. Second Life is still around, though. In 2008, it won a Technology & Engineering Emmy Award for advancing the development of online sites with user-generated content. Ralph Koster, game designer and author of *A Theory of Fun for Game*

Design had this to say of how relationships in Second Life give rise to new conversations in RL. "Virtual social bonds evolve from the fictional towards real social bonds. If you have good community ties, they will be out-of-character ties, not in-character ties. In other words, friendships will migrate right out of your world into email, real-life gatherings, etc." See: Wagner James Au, "When Second Life Starts Feeling Like a 3D Chatroom, Do You Start Using Second Life Less?" nwn.blogs.com. See also Chris Abraham, "Twitter Is What Second Life Wasn't: Light, Cheap and Open." http://www.adage.com, 26 June, 2009.

11. Roman Krznaric, "Are you hooked on gadgets? Then it's time you went on a digital diet." *The Independent*. January 1, 2012.
12. Derrick Mains, who spends most of his waking hours in social media channels, was a natural in this 'old media' format, a great listener and someone who could chat intelligently on almost any topic.
13. See how the Australian government is using digital channels to engage its publics at the Government 2.0 Taskforce. http://gov2.net.au/. Lindsay Tanner, minister for finance and deregulation, talks of dialogue and consultation, and how this Web 2.0 approach is about "encouraging online engagement with the aim of drawing in the information, knowledge, perspectives, resources and even, where possible, the active collaboration of anyone wishing to contribute to public life."
14. As of February 14, 2013, the channel had received 16,507 submissions, 7,524 questions.

CHAPTER 3—Community as a Fire-pit

1. Tyler Fonda, strategy director of agency named Gotham. Quoted in Danielle Sacks, "Can you hear me now?" *Fast Company*. February 2013.
2. Bonar K. Bulger, at http://www.quora.com, May 25, 2011.
3. Jacqui Taylor and J. MacDonald, "The Effects of Asynchronous Computer-Mediated Group Interaction on Group Processes." *Social Science Computer Review*. 2002.
4. "Communication technology and theory: Research into the interpersonal and social interface." http://www.gravity7.com/articles_arguments.html#ixzz1psBwT1RM
5. Pat Elliott. Interview with Author.
6. Frank Moss, *The Sorcerer and their Apprentices*. Crown Business, June 2011.
7. The Pharmacovigilance and Risk Benefit Management group is looking for ways to share knowledge about drug safety surveillance.
8. The MIT team set up an international LAM Registry, which is a companion community space for clinical researchers from around the world. They did this because patient information tends to be buried in silos separating even those who ought to be sharing knowledge and talking to each other.
9. Wikipedia entry, http://en.wikipedia.org/wiki/Community_of_practice. Accessed on July 20, 2012.
10. The communities within 'Avon Connects' include those for Business Development, Family Zone, A Stronger You, Product Buzz, Avon Opportunities, Money Talk, Helping Others, Fit And Fabulous, The Café, and Help Center.
11. Hemoglobin A1C is a 'marker' that gives patients an idea of how well they are

performing with long-term blood sugar control. The application was jointly developed by Children's Hospital Boston and TuDiabetes.org.
12. "Tribalization of Business Survey," a study by Deloitte LLP's Technology, Media & Telecommunications practice, Beeline Labs and the Society of New Communications Research.
13. Richard Millington, "Online Community Manifesto." Millington is the founder of FeverBee Ltd, a U.K.-based an online community consultancy.
14. Deloitte Study, *ibid*.
15. Richard Millington, *ibid*.

CHAPTER 4 — News-speak 3.0
1. David Ogilvy sent this internal memo to employees of his advertising agency, Ogilvy & Mather on September 7, 1982. He titled his memo "How to Write." From *The Unpublished David Ogilvy: A Selection of His Writings from the Files of His Partners*. Ogilvy Group, 1986.
2. Marc Wright, Interview with Author.
3. Andreas Weigend, Chief Scientist for Amazon. http://www.youtube.com/watch?v=sdzUPdcWScg&feature=player_embedded
4. Kevin Gibbons, "How To Write a Successful Corporate Newsletter." *Econsultancy.com*. August 12, 2010.
5. Joe Manna. Interview with Author. March 2011.

CHAPTER 5 — Speaking Out of Turn
1. The fairness doctrine ran parallel to Section 315 of the Communications Act of 1937 which required stations to offer "equal opportunity" to all legally qualified political candidates for any office if they had allowed any person running in that office to use the station. Museum of Broadcast Communications, www.museum.tv
2. 'Fair and Balanced' has been the trademarked tagline of Fox News in the U.S. However there is plenty of dispute about its bias. Al Franken, a comedian and now senator, wrote a book about it in 2003 (*Lies and the Lying Liars Who Tell Them: A Fair and Balanced Look at the Right*.) More recently, a Pew Research Center study found that Fox News was more biased than MSNBC. The bottom line is that both do not exactly subscribe to the Fairness Doctrine.
3. *Unspeak: How Words Become Weapons, How Weapons Become a Message, and How That Message Becomes Reality*. Grove Press, April 2006.
4. *The Cluetrain Manifesto*. Perseus Books, 2000.
5. Clay Shirky, *Cognitive Surplus*. Penguin, 2010.
6. Sam Diaz, "Internet brand-jacking: What can be learned from Exxon Mobil?" ZDNet. August 7, 2008.
7. U.S. Agency for International Development was created through the Marshall Plan for the reconstruction of Europe after World War II in 1950. It sought to engage in technically-based international economic development. President John F. Kennedy signed the Foreign Assistance Act into law in 1961 and USAID was created by executive order.

NOTES

8. "The role of media in Democracy: A Strategic Approach." Office of Democracy and Governance Bureau for Democracy, Conflict, and Humanitarian Assistance. USAID Washington, DC, June 1999.
9. Veteran journalist, and member of the White House Press Corps, Helen Thomas, voiced her concerns about citizen journalism in December 2007 in *The Huffington Post*. "I do think it is kind of sad when everybody who owns a laptop thinks they're a journalist and doesn't understand the ethics. We do have to have some sense of what's right and wrong in this job. Of how far we can go. We don't make accusations without absolute proof. We're not prosecutors. We don't assume."
10. Dan Gillmor, *Mediactive*. Lulu.com. December 2010.
11. The First Amendment to the U.S. Constitution, adopted in December 1791, states that "Congress shall make no law respecting an establishment of religion, or prohibiting the free exercise thereof; or abridging the freedom of speech, or of the press; or the right of the people peaceably to assemble, and to petition the Government for a redress of grievances."
12. Jeff Jarvis, *What Would Google Do?* Harper Business, January 2009.
13. "Public More Critical of Press, But Goodwill Persists." Pew Research Center for the People & the Press, June 2005.
14. Dan Gillmor, *Mediactive. ibid.* Gillmor says that the media is being used by "liars, dissemblers and opinion launderers" who rely on lazy, credulous journalists to carry their stories. The future of the new ecosystem of media and journalism is up to us, as there is no longer a "them," he says.
15. Dan Gillmor, in an interview with the Author for "Eye Poppong Podcasts." Arizona State University. October 2008.
16. Gillmor, *Mediactive. ibid.*
17. Jay Rosen, "Bloggers Vs Journalists. It's a Psychological Thing." Presentation at South By Southwest conference, 2011. http://sxsw.com/node/7372
18. Internews has media partners that help citizens produce content in 73 languages, from Acehnese to Zaghawa. It has spearheaded journalism programs that encourage reporting on health, human rights, digital technology, and governance. Its directors are represented by people from the Corporation for Public Broadcasting, World Affairs Council, the World Economic Forum, and ESPN, among others. Find out more at www.internews.org
19. Craig Lambert, "Air Afghanistan." *Harvard Magazine*. March-April, 2011. http://harvardmagazine.com/2011/03/air-afghanistan
20. Global Voices uses Lingua Editors who work with teams of volunteers (translators) to make Global Voices heard. The idea is to make non-English speaking bloggers more available in other languages. Find out more at http://globalvoicesonline.org
21. Witness, an international organization promoting storytelling by citizens, is big on video. The idea is that video storytelling will be able to "pressure those in power or with power to act." Just like Global Voices and Internews, just like Ground Views, it is into using new media and technology for advocacy.
22. Sanjana Hattotuwa, interview with Author. March 2013.

CHAPTER 6—Less Noise, More Curation
1. T.S. Eliot. "The Rock," 1934.

NOTES

2. In keeping with the definition of an echochamber, it involves a hollow space surrounded with hard, reflective material. The farther away from the speaker, the louder the echo that is produced.
3. The number of videos uploaded to YouTube continues to increase. In mid-May 2011, on YouTube's 4th anniversary, it recorded 48 hours of video are now uploaded per minute, accounting for 3 billion views a day. http://youtube-global.blogspot.com/2011/05/thanks-youtube-community-for-two-big.html
4. Leisa Reichelt, "Ambient Intimacy." http://www.disambiguity.com, March 1, 2007. In this blog post, Reichelt describes her experience with Twitter as Ambient intimacy. It transcends the 'meaning' of what's being said, she says. "Flickr lets me see what friends are eating for lunch, how they've redecorated their bedroom, their latest haircut. Twitter tells me when they're hungry, what technology is currently frustrating them, who they're having drinks with tonight."
5. Stanford Smith, "Is it time to ambush the Twitter re-tweet button." http://SocialMediaToday.com, December 24, 2011.
6. A similar problem faces bloggers who like to be given the same respect as journalists. The latter are obliged to work within the boundaries of journalism ethics. Bloggers can't pick which of these ethical behaviors they want and which to reject.
7. Adam Shlachter, "Getting Consumers to 'Touch and Feel Your Brand' Across Media." *Emarketer.com*. March 9, 2012.
8. Shel Holtz, *Communication World* magazine, Jan-Feb 2012.
9. Also check sites such as Populrs, Vivisimo, SecondBrain, and FriendFeed.
10. This point is made by Anne Handley of MarketingProfs. Also, Luigi Canali De Rossi, aka Robin Good, an independent media publisher elaborates on this very well: http://digg.com/newsbar/topnews/aggregation_is_not_curation_real_time_news_part_2
11. SEO, for those not familiar with it, is the activity known as 'search engine optimization' or making sure keywords used by customers bring up relevant results that eventually lead to a sale.
12. One site, Bootmyserps.com, says that "We guarantee the Client a minimum of 30 days of first page ranking on Google.com for the target URL and the corresponding keyword. This does not mean that the target URL will lose its position after 30 days. This only means that our guarantee is valid for 30 days." No authentic search engine optimization company guarantees rankings, and when they do it ought to be a big red flag.

CHAPTER 7—Human Transponders

1. WOMMA, the Word-of-Mouth Marketing Association, has about 350 members from agencies such as Edelman and Ogilvy to marketers such as Yum Brands, and even non-profits such as Mothers Against Drunk Driving.
2. *The Anatomy of Buzz*, Doubleday Business, October 17, 2000.
3. Slideshare, an online slide hosting service has 60 million monthly visitors, making it one of the 200 most visited websites in the world. It is sometimes referred to as the YouTube for slideshows, and accepts slides in PowerPoint, PDF, Open Office, or Keynote formats. www.slideshare.com

4. The "weak ties" phenomenon is based on a study by Mark Granovetter who surveyed people in professional, technical and managerial positions in Newton, Massachusetts. Granovetter, who studied networks about forty years before the advent of social networks, was surprised to find that more people found jobs through people outside their immediate network. He called this the "strength of the weak ties." Granovetter concludes that weak ties, which are typically denounced, are indispensable.
5. Chris Brogan went to the crux of the problem: "What seems to be at the heart of the controversy on Twitter (no finer teakettle has there ever been), is whether my involvement with a marketing campaign for Kmart somehow erodes my credibility as a social media business strategist." He cites other companies using brand spokespersons. Seagate has Robert Scoble, and Dell uses multiple voices at its Digital Nomads site. http://www.chrisbrogan.com/advertising-and-trust/
6. A Tremor campaign is one where consumer-to-consumer conversations are initiated, and its results are measured. The name, Tremor, was chosen for the ability to initiate the unexpected and start conversations. "The disruptive message serves as a discussion trigger" for its advocacy through half a million highly connected moms, it says.
7. *Oxford English Dictionary* defines a sock puppet as "a false online identity, typically created by a person or group in order to promote their own opinions or views."

CHAPTER 8—Citizen Mo

1. Joey Flynn, product designer on Facebook Timeline. In *Fast Company*, April 2013.
2. Joel Rubin, Andrew Blankstein and Scott Gold, "Twenty years after the beating of Rodney King, the LAPD is a changed operation." Articles.LATimes.com, March 3, 2011.
3. Stephen Franklin, a Knight International Journalism Fellow in Egypt. Quoted in Eugene L. Meyer, "By the People. The Rise of Citizen Journalism." A report to the Center for International Media Assistance. Dec. 2010.
4. For a good discussion of the struggle between Pros and Ams, listen to a BBC report here. http://bbc.in/LMD0711
5. Muhammad Mustafa Kaplan, quoted in a video on http://www.democracynow.org. March 17, 2011. Kaplan observes: "I consider myself now as a revolutionist. Now I don't—I forgot my job, completely. Actually, in the beginning of the revolution, nobody knew what to do. So I have some ideas, and the other people have some ideas. We built and we made this center, and I joined. And I continue my volunteering with them. So I quit my job now, for the time being."
6. Jay Rosen, "From 'write us a post' to 'fill out this form:' Progress in pro-am journalism." http://pressthink.org June 7, 2011.
7. Read Sanjana Hattotuwa's longer discussion at "Internet and Web based citizen Journalism in Sri Lanka," at http://ict4peace.wordpress.com

CHAPTER 9—Talk Like a Wikipedian

1. Phoebe Ayers, Charles Mathews, and Ben Yates, *How Wikipedia Works*. No Starch Press, 2008. The authors note that unlike earlier encyclopedias, which were comprehensive guides to defined subject areas, Wikipedia is a collection of both

NOTES

specialist and generalist knowledge.
2. WELL is the acronym for "Whole Earth 'Lectronic Link." It was the earliest network that promoted social participation. Members were contributors of a different way, in maintenance of conversations or conversation threads, known as 'conferences.' According to a Wikipedia entry on WELL, these conversations were "supervised by conference hosts who guide conversations and may enforce conference rules on civility and/or appropriateness. Initially all hosts were selected by staff members."
3. Michael Netzley, interview with author. May 2011. Netzley, who is assistant professor of corporate communications, teaches writing, case analysis, group processes, and aspects of social media. He spends weeks allowing students to work privately (on blogs or wikis) before opening them up to the world. The idea, he says, is to help them develop confidence in private online environments, so that they bring higher level behaviors when they 'go public.' See also "Social Networks and a Desire to Save Face: A Case from Singapore", by Michael Netzley and A. Rath, Business Communication Quarterly 75
4. Robert E. Cummins, writing for *Inside Higher Ed*, noted that "students are often shocked when Wikipedians respond to their contributions with a critical eye. Sometimes those responses are polite, and sometimes not, but they are mostly accurate and engaging." http://www.insidehighered.com, March 12, 2009.
5. More about NOR here http://en.wikipedia.org/wiki/Wikipedia:No_original_research. Or use the short cut WP:NOR within Wikipedia.
6. *How Wikipedia Works, ibid.*
7. David Traver Adolphus. Interview with Author.
8. For more about the people behind the edits, see the BBC story, "Wikipedia: Meet the men and women who write the articles." www.bbc.co.uk/news/magazine-18833763. July 14, 2012.

CHAPTER 10—If These Press Releases Could Talk!
1. Andrea Seabrook, outgoing Congressional Correspondent for *National Public Radio* (NPR) in the U.S., speaking of her frustration with covering a 'broken' government. Interview on "All Things Considered." NPR. July 18, 2012.
2. Linda Vandevrede, *Press Releases Are Not a PR Strategy*. VandeVrede Public Relations, LLC, 2007.
3. Tom Foremski, in a blog post headlined, "Die! Press release! Die! Die! Die!" *Silicon Valley Watcher*. February 27, 2006. http://www.siliconvalleywatcher.com/mt/archives/2006/02/die_press_relea.php. Accessed on March 14, 2012.
4. Linda VandeVrede. Interview with Author. April 12, 2012.
5. SHIFT Communications, "The new social media press release." http://www.shiftcomm.com/social_media_press_release.html/ You could find the Social Media Release template here.
6. Steve Myers, "Kansas City Star columnist Steve Penn fired for plagiarism." http://www.poynter.org July 13, 2011.
7. Shannon Whitley, Interview with Author. February 17, 2011.
8. Jason Kintzler, Interview with Author. February 17, 2011.

NOTES

9. Mark Blevis, "Social media releases. Five harsh thoughts." MarkBlevis.com, February 26, 2010.
10. Dan Nelson. Interview with Author. March, 2011.

CHAPTER 11 — The Revolution Will Be Uploaded

1. Dan Gillmor, *We The Media: Grassroots Journalism by the People, for the People.* O'Reilly Media Inc., 2004.
2. President Ahmadinejad won by a landslide in 2009 though his opponent, Mahmoud Mousavi claimed the results were fraudulent. In the aftermath of the elections, wide-scale protests took place, many were arrested and killed.
3. The BBC admitted that with international journalists forced to stay in their hotel rooms in Iran, amateur journalists' reports were all that major news organizations could rely on.
4. Andrew LaVallee, "Web Users in Iran Reach Overseas for Proxies." Digits, The Wall Street Journal blog. June 15, 2009. A proxy server is a simple bit of software that you run on your computer. It effectively lets you share your computer with anonymous strangers as a 'repeater' for content that they aren't allowed to fetch themselves. Open Web proxies are valuable commodities in places where it's forbidden, and possibly dangerous, to surf the Internet.
5. "The Iranian Election on Twitter. The First Eighteen Days." The Web Ecology project. http://www.webecologyproject.org, June 26, 2009.
6. "U.S. State Department speaks to Twitter over Iran." Reuters. June 16, 2009.
7. http://www.iranhumanrights.org/2012/02/malekpour-sister
8. The George Polk award, to a non-journalist, was hailed by most mainstream media outlets, putting behind the one-time animosity between professionals and amateurs.
9. James Cowey, "The Proxy Fight for Iranian Democracy." *Renesys* blog. June 22, 2009.
10. Read more about this experience in a post titled "Check point" at the *Inside Iraq* blog, June 27, 2009. http://washingtonbureau.typepad.com/iraq/
11. Dan Gillmor, *ibid.*
12. Read more here: http://www.guardian.co.uk/world/2011/jun/17/saudi-arabia-women-drivers-protest
13. There was already a Facebook page created for Khaled Mohamed Said, who had apparently been beaten to death by the Egyptian secret police. Ghonim who was also the admin for the Facebook page for Mohammed ElBaradei, a Nobel Prize winner, who was a promising opponent to Hosni Mubarak, created another, thinking the former was using too strong language and sounded vengeful.
14. Kurt Anderson, "The Protester." Time. December 26 2011 – January 2, 2012.

CHAPTER 12 — Voices On

1. Steven Johnson. *Future Perfect: The case for progress in a networked age.* Riverhead Books, 2012.
2. The full story is reported here: http://www.associatedcontent.com/article/7860086/

comedian_gilbert_gottfried_fired_by.html
3. The full story is reported here: http://www.theage.com.au/world/britains-new-mi6-chief-caught-in-facebook-scandal-20090705-d95k.html
4. Robert Scoble and Shel Israel, *Naked Conversations*. John Wiley and Sons, 2006.
5. According to the Gallup study, in 'world-class' organizations, the ratio of engaged to actively disengaged employees is more than nine to one (9.57:1). In 'average' organizations, that ratio of engaged to actively disengaged employees is almost one to two (1.83:1). "Employee Engagement: What's Your Engagement Ratio" 2008, 2010, Gallup Consulting.
6. Josh Bernoff, *Empowered: Unleash Your Employees, Energize Your Customers, and Transform Your Business*. Harvard Business Press, September 2010.
7. Michael Lee Stallard is the primary author of *Fired Up or Burned Out: How to Reignite Your Team's Passion, Creativity and Productivity* (Thomas Nelson, 2007). He is presently researching how voice plays a role in innovation at organizations including the NASA Johnson Space Center. Interview with Author, April 24, 2013.

CHAPTER 13—Bathed in Buzz

1. Nancy Blatt, Director of Public Information for the Water Environment Federation, in John C. Stauber and Sheldon Rampton, "Let them eat sludge." www.prwatch.org
2. "Colonel Gaddafi ordered Lockerbie bombing." *BBC News*. February 23, 2011.
3. "Evidence grows of Blair's links with Gaddafi." *The Independent*. September 18, 2011.
4. "Patton Boggs in Middle of Sri Lanka's Battle for World Public Opinion." *Law.com*. October 2009.
5. The letter to agencies, from Ali Darwish, Mission for Peace, Ministry of Information. "Exclusive: Full Text of Gaddafi Email to PR Firms." *The Algemeiner*. July 31, 2011.
6. Joel B. Pollack, "Qadaffi declares PR war on United States, UN." www.breitbart.com. August 6, 2011.
7. As Consular general in Toronto, Canada in 2010, Bandula Jayasekera, a former journalist, engaged the media in a way that was somewhat creative since diplomats are not exactly known to do their own PR. Jayasekera's term was subsequently shortened, but many Sri Lankan-Canadians think he pushed the envelope by not being a victim of the media.

CHAPTER 14—Link Love

1. Jeff Jarvis, talking about the relationship between the content economy and the link economy. "The imperatives of the link economy." Blog post on July 20, 2008.
2. Jeff Jarvis has been an advocate and defender of the link economy. See more about it here on his blog: http://www.buzzmachine.com/2009/08/14/on-the-link-economy. His latest book is *Public Parts: How Sharing in the Digital Age Improves the Way We Work and Live* Simon & Schuster, September, 2011.
3. The Associated Press has contested news aggregation first in 2008, when it sued the Drudge Report, and again in 2009, and 2012. http://www.ap.org/pages/about/

pressreleases/pr_021412a.html. More recently the AP began softening its stance on links and backs links, even going so far as to permit short URLs such as bit.ly. See story on Neimanlab.org "AP will link back to newspapers who get scoops." July 20, 2011.

4. Anthony de Rosa of *Reuters* makes a good point that the old guard of media professionals and digital natives might be ready to shake hands on this standoff. For its part, *Reuters*, an old guard media company, does believe in the link economy, and its president has given it his blessing. http://blogs.reuters.com/mediafile/2009/08/04/why-i-believe-in-the-link-economy/

5. David Weinberger, *Everything is Miscellaneous*. Times Books, May 2007.

6. FactCheck.org and Poligraft let you check on an organization. FactCheck.org monitors the factual accuracy of statements made by major U.S. political players in their television ads, debates, speeches, interviews and news releases. Influence Explorer, a search engine from the Sunlight Foundation, will let anyone sift through organizations connected to stories in US politics, with data easily called up on campaign finance, lobbying, earmarks, and federal spending.

7. SMARTU, stands for Social Media And Responsibility Training University.

8. Sharon McIntosh, in a podcast interview with "For Immediate Release." February 23, 2012.

9. Matt Thompson. Interview with Author.

10. Matt Thompson, "Five concrete steps to improving the news." September 1, 2009 http://newsless.org/2009/09/five-concrete-steps-to-improving-the-news/

11. *Esquire* noted this about the use of Augmented Reality, a "brave new and interesting technology" for a print publication: "We are presently intertwined in an AR environment...It's about the artistry of technology."

CHAPTER 15—Amateurs With Microphones

1. Benjamin Franklin, describing a preacher named Mr. Whitefield whom he had met in London. Franklin had been at the back of a crowd listening to the speaker, realizing how far his voice carried. His calculation that this voice radiated 30,000 feet was in sync, he says, with "newspaper accounts of his having preached to twenty-five thousand people in the fields." Benjamin Franklin, *Autobiography*. Dover Publications, 1996.

2. The 'anti-globalization' movement has been also called the 'alter-globalization' or 'anti-corporation' movement. Activists opposed unregulated political power exercised through established global institutions such as the World Trade Center, the World Bank, and the International Monetary Fund. They accused corporations of seeking profits at the expense of jobs, and stood for fair trade and human rights.

3. *The Urban Dictionary* was founded in 1999. Just as in *Wikipedia*, a user submits word entries and content is moderated by volunteers. Words often represent slang, and ethnic or cultural words. Therefore in its policies, the company warns that "The Website is not suitable for all audiences. Its content is frequently presented in a coarse and direct manner that some may find offensive."

4. Richard Kim, writing for *The Nation* made this observation: "But the greatest hidden virtue of the human mic has been the quality that almost every observer

has reflexively lamented: it is slow. I mean incredibly, agonizingly, astonishingly slow; it can take over an hour for the General Assembly just to get through a nightly refresher course on group protocols before starting in on announcements, which precede debate about anything new, like whether or not the occupation should make a list of demands and if so, what those demands should be. Imagine collectively debating and writing the Port Huron Statement, by consensus, three to five words at a time." http://www.thenation.com/blog/163767/we-are-all-human-microphones-now

5. Hendrik Hertzberg, "A Walk in the Park." *The New Yorker.* October 17, 2011. http://www.newyorker.com

6. The event is not some underground event as it might seem. EMI Music, Red Bull, and *The Guardian* are sponsors. Hackers at the event develop tweaks for music sites, Facebook, and Twitter.

7. This is "thin-skinned democracy" at work, according to Tony Curzon Price, writing for OpenDemmocracy.org. "Every meeting I saw, from small teach-ins on how to facilitate a group to the General Assembly in the park, was characterised by an almost obsessive attention to being inclusive, open and accountable. Consensus was sought everywhere; self-criticism and *mea culpa's* worn with pride as a public virtue; interventions were conducted on the basis of 'progressive stack', where anyone could ask to be put on the list of speakers, but participants were asked to always remember to 'step up, step back'—to give priority to anyone who had a background of not having their views heard or taken seriously."

8. Sarah Van Gelder, *This Changes Everything: Occupy Wall Street and the 99% Movement.* Berrett-Koehler Publishers, 2011.

9. Politicians have a lot to learn from this process. They think they invite crowd participation in, say, Town Halls, but it is a highly controlled process. Politicians do pass the microphone—the physical microphone—to the audience. But the microphone 'belongs' to the speaker. Senator John McCain of Arizona, in his presidential bid in 2009, passed his wireless microphone to a woman in the audience who told him, "I can't trust Obama. I have read about him and he's not, he's not uh—he's an Arab." According to news reports McCain 'retook the microphone' and refuted her claim.

10. For more on how this inversion of logic works, read Conor Tomás Reed's essay, in *Tidal*, a journal dedicated to Occupy theory: "Step 1: Occupy Universities. Step 1: Transform Them." December 2011, Issue 1, http://occupytheory.org

11. Instructions posted on Movements.org http://www.movements.org/how-to/entry/how-to-use-communicate-anonymously-with-vibe1

CHAPTER 16—Crowd-sourcing Ideas (Managers Not Required)

1. Find out more about the Harvard Catalyst crowd-sourcing project at http://catalyst.harvard.edu

2. "Majority of American Workers Not Engaged in Their Jobs." Gallup. 28 October, 2011. http://www.gallup.com/poll/150383/majority-american-workers-not-engaged-jobs.aspx

3. The DARPA challenge was called the "Experimental crowd-derived combat-support vehicle xc2v-design-challenge." The challenge was opened to anyone

NOTES

to "conceptualize a vehicle body design for two different missions—Combat Reconnaissance and Combat Delivery & Evacuation. Moreover, it had to be designed and prototyped in 80 percent less time. Garcia's design, 'Flypmode,' won the challenge. More information on the challenge, here: http://challenge.gov/DoD/129-experimental-crowd-derived-combat-support-vehicle-xc2v-design-challenge. Accessed on 12 March, 2012.

4. Aneesh Chopra, speaking at FedTalks, on "10 'Wins' Delivered on Open Innovation." http://fedscoop.com/events/fedtalks2011/ Also at Educause Now, conference 10 Nov, 2011. "There are hidden pockets of innovation throughout this country. There are Victor Garcias in every neighborhood. This is what open government is all about," noted Chopra.

5. For more information on this, visit http://www.slideshare.net/GasPedal/blogwell-new-york-social-media-case-study-walmart-presented-by-lisa-thurber

6. A good discussion of Innovation Tournaments could be found here: http://bigidea.med.upenn.edu/how-it-works

7. James Surewiecki, *The Wisdom of the Crowds*. Anchor, August 2005.

8. Frank Moss, *The Sorcerer's Apprentice*. Crown Business, 2011.

9. More idea-sharing, crowd sourcing sites could be found at www.openinnovators.net/list-open-innovation-crowdsourcing-examples

10. Frank Moss, *ibid*.

11. The story, "The great drain robbery,' broke in the *Sun* tabloid in October 2008. The newspaper investigated and found the practice was consistent, saying the amount of water lost would fill an Olympic pool every 83 minutes.

CHAPTER 17—Texting Under the Influence

1. Bill Gates in an email conversation with Jonathan Letham, at www.pen.org

2. Find out more about the service at http://www.tigertext.com/recall-texts

3. "TigerText Disposes Of 'Sender's Remorse' With New Privacy And Control Features For SMS." *TechCrunch*. June 15, 2011.

CHAPTER 18—OMG! The State Department's On Facebook!

1. Massimo Calabresi, "Hillary Clinton and the rise of smart power." *Time*. November 7, 2011.

2. Harold Lasswell, (1902 – 1978) a political scientist who studied the meaning of political symbols, showed that communication involved control analysis, content analysis, media analysis, audience analysis, and effect analysis.

3. Edward L. Bernays (1891 – 1995) was considered the 'father of public relations, and sometimes, the 'father of spin.' A nephew of Sigmund Freud, Bernays was associated with the Woodrow Wilson government in promoting America's war efforts during World War I.

4. Details of this program are available at the Department of Defense website. http://www.dod.mil/pubs/foi/operation_and_plans/MilitaryAnalysts. *The New York Times* uncovered this in a story on April 20, 2008: "Behind TV Analysts, Pentagon's hidden hand."

5. Sean McCormack, in one of the first posts (September 25, 2007) noted that the

team would attempt to try and break through the jargon and talk about how the State Department operates around the world. He added in a PPS that "We're new at this. It looks like we broke our own rule and used State jargon in our blog title. 'Dipnote' refers to a diplomatic note."
6. The Iraq war is a case in point. In October 2001, deep in the bowels of its offices, a highly secretive group of planners would meet with experts from the Pentagon and the CIA on what was called the "Future of Iraq Project."
7. Hillary Clinton, *ibid.*
8. Speech at Washington University. February 15, 2011. "Internet Rights and Wrongs: Choices and Challenges in a Networked World." http://www.state.gov/secretary/rm/2011/02/156619.htm
9. Find it at http://www.cato.org/pub_display.php?pub_id=6654
10. See "Wal-Mart vs. the Blogosphere." *Business Week.* http://www.businessweek.com/bwdaily/dnflash/content/oct2006/db20061018_445917.htm
11. For a good definition of this go to http://www.sourcewatch.org/index.php/Astroturf
12. Find a Foreign Service document about this, archived by George Washington University, at http://www.gwu.edu/~nsarchiv/NSAEBB/NSAEBB78/propaganda%20016.pdf
13. Check the initiative called Digital Town Hall of the Americas http://townhall.america.gov/. Consider too, Exchanges Connect, an intellectual network of those in the educational and cultural sphere is clearly identified as a program by the State Department.

CHAPTER 19—Low-hanging Fruitcake

1. David Meerman Scott and Brian Halligan *Marketing Lessons from the Grateful Dead.* Wiley, 2010.
2. Brian Fugere, Chelsea Hardaway, Jon Warshawsky, *Why Business People Speak Like Idiots: A Bullfighter's Guide.* Free Press, 2005.
3. The name of the real company was substituted with X-company to protect the victim.
4. Brian Williams, speaking about having to tell a story about a disaster such as Hurricane Katrina and its human tragedy in New Orleans. Interview with Charlie Rose. November 20, 2006. http://www.charlierose.com/view/interview/121
5. Christopher Peterson, "Goal Setting: Don't Pick the Low-Hanging Fruit." *Psychology Today.* September 6, 2011. He cites a friend, a fruit picker. "In the case of fruit, if it is hanging low, it may be bruised or damaged by bugs or varmints. It is also less likely to be ripe. Experienced fruit pickers always start at the top of a tree, where the fruit is more ready to eat because of greater exposure to the sun. And because a picker places fruit in a bag slung over his or her shoulder, the bag gets heavier as the job progresses, and starting at the top puts gravity on the side of the picker."
6. http://www.pcr-online.biz/news/36514/Panasonic-unveil-mission-critical-Toughbook-tablet
7. Starbucks began a podcast in 2006 called "Coffee College," with topics such as fair trade, home brewing, and coffee composting. It seemed too scripted, and

dull. It quickly ran out of course material, so to speak.
8. David Weinberger, *The Cluetrain Manifesto*. Perseus Books, 2000.
9. Jonathan Schwartz, quoted in Robert Scoble & Shel Israel, *Naked Conversations*. John Wiley & Sons Inc., 2006.
10. William Safire, Nixon's speech writer, coined the phrase 'nattering nabobs of negativism,' used by Spiro Agnew. Later, Safire called his former boss a 'lizard-lidded paranoid' for mistrusting him and authorizing wiretaps of his phone.
11. Larry King, *How To Talk To Anyone, Anytime, Anywhere*. Crown Publishers, 1994.
12. Dom Crincoli believes that while traditional newsletters have lost their charm, online versions provide robust interactivity and honesty. At Ragan.com, April 14, 2011.
13. The calendar was published by The Rogers Group, a research and creative services outfit.
14. Enron created off-the-books divisions with names such as Chewco, Death Star, and Jedi. One of these outfits (Chewco's) "ownership structure was a mystery to most Enron employees, including many who dealt with Chewco on behalf of Enron." Source: http://fl1.findlaw.com/news.findlaw.com/wsj/docs/enron/sicreport/chapter2.pdf
15. George Orwell, *Politics and the English language*. http://orwell.ru/library/essays/politics/english/e_polit
16. David Meerman Scott's *Gobbledegook Manifesto* could be found at http://www.davidmeermanscott.com/documents/3703Gobbledygook.pdf

CHAPTER 21 — Talking Like Humans
1. Ira Glass, "Radiolab. An Appreciation." Transform.org. November 8, 2011. Ira Glass is host of "This American Life," a weekly radio show from American Public Radio.
2. The genesis of the idea for David Cohn, who had been involved with Newassignment.net, came while working as a research assistant to author Jeff Howe, for the book, *Crowdsourcing: Why the Power of the Crowd Is Driving the Future of Business*. He found out how micro-philanthropy worked via the Web, and how sites such as Kiva and DonorsChoose worked by being highly targeted. Cohn has written for *Wired*, *The New York Times*, and *Columbia Journalism Review*.
3. Lindsey Hoshaw. Interview with Author.
4. The call to have UNESCO name a pile of trash as a state came from Italian architect Maria Cristina Finucci, via a Facebook page. "As an artist, borrowing the techniques of advertising communication, I have created a state to raise awareness," noted Finucci. Quoted in "Welcome to Garbage Patch State, Where Plastic Rules." http://www.unesco.org/new/en/venice/about-this-office/single-view/news/the_garbage_patch_territory_turns_into_a_new_state/
5. Jay Rosen, "Boggers vs. Journalists." *ibid*.
6. Clark Hoyt, "One Newspaper, Many Checkbooks." *The New York Times*. July 18, 2009. http://www.nytimes.com/2009/07/19/opinion/19pubed.html?_r=1
7. The funding was initially thought to be $6,000, and that was the goal put up at Spot.Us. Later Hoshaw found that she needed an additional $4,000, but the

NOTES

website was designed in a way that the financial goal could not be changed. She then pitched the idea via Facebook Causes, and collected the additional funds.

8. Ira Glass, *ibid.*
9. From David Cohn's comments left on my blog post ("Civic journalism is coming. get used to it") July 14, 2009. www.hoipolloireport.com
10. For more on this read Jay Rosen at http://archive.pressthink.org/2006/08/15/ear_ntw.html
11. Steve Rubel, *Insights on the Future of Media*, Vol. 1, January 2012. In this free eBook, Rubel talks how HuffPo has a traffic and trends team that looks out for trending topics on social networks and search engines and writes stories about those topics.
12. Global Editors network, http://www.globaleditorsnetwork.org/2011/david-cohn-hyperlocal-journalism-berkeley/
13. "The latest news headline. Your news counts." Pew Research Center's Project for Excellence in Journalism. September 12, 2007. http://www.journalism.org/node/7493
14. David Cohn, interview with Author. April 2012. Cohn recently co-founded Circa. Circa is news experience born on (and for) the mobile device. It is a way to generate news by not writing 'articles' but collating what he calls 'atomic units' of stories themselves: the facts, the quotes and images. These become the mobile version of 'living stories' (referred to in Chapter 14), because they are undated with stories fresh data all the time.
15. Ta Nehasi Coates, "On the Media," a weekly radio show hosted by Bob Garfield and Brooke Gladstone on *National Public Radio*.
16. A blog, while capturing people's voices in a crisis like the tsunami, pales in significance when compared to the massive data-gathering effort that citizens spearheaded. Within two days (28 Dec, 2004) a disaster-response group of individuals from universities, local and international software companies and the country's Telco, began writing software that included a missing persons registry. The organization would later become Sahana, an open-source disaster management system. It has been used by the governments of Sri Lanka, Pakistan (2005), the Philippines (2006), and Indonesia (2006).

CHAPTER 22 — Your Podcasting Voice

1. Cynthia Zhai, www.connectingtosuccess.com
2. Oddly enough, the word 'loophole' comes from the small, narrow opening in a medieval castle or turret to let air and light in. Another definition of a loophole, however, is the opening through which archers shot at attacking armies!
3. Tee Morris, Chuck Tomasi, Evo Terra, Kreg Steppe, *Podcasting for Dummies*. Wiley Press, 2005.
4. Mark Smith, Interview with Author. March 22, 2013. At the time of writing, iPadio is being used by podcasters in 180 countries.
5. Full disclosure. I met Tony Sant in London in 1987 when we both went through BBC training in radio production. This was years before digital recorders, but Sant was a master of holding conversations on radio.
6. Arizona State University has many divisions that have published a plethora of

podcasts on iTunes, at http://itunes.asu.edu

7. Mitch Joel, a Canadian-based communications consultant, author, and head of a digital marketing agency, Twistimage, blends blogging and podcasting into one seamless conversation. Find his podcasts at http://www.twistimage.com/podcast
8. BlogTalkRadio has 16,000 active hosts. Both services let you seamlessly integrate a conversation with other social media publishing channels.
9. Podcasting Resources: Software: Garage Band (for the Mac) or Audacity; Music: http://www.musicalley.com; Voice Overs: mediamusicnow.co.uk/podcast_production; Tools: Garage Band (Macs) and Audacity (Windows); Hosting: www.libsyn.com, iTunes.com, BlogTalkRadio.com; Great Resources: Association for Downloadable Media: www.downloadablemedia.org; *How To Do Everything With Podcasting*, by Shel Holtz and Neville Hobson, McGraw-Hill Osborne Media, 2007; *Podcasting for Dummies*, by Tee Morris, Chuck Tomasi, Evo Terra, Kreg Steppe. Wiley Press, 2005; *Podcasting Bible*, by Mitch Ratcliff and Steve Mack, Wiley, 2007.

CHAPTER 23—Rethinking Digital Storytelling

1. Nicholas Carr, *The Shallows: What the Internet Is Doing to Our Brains*. W. W. Norton & Company, June 7, 2010.
2. Matt Thompson, Interview with Author. February 2010.
3. Vadim Lavrusik, "Five key building blocks to incorporate as we're rethinking the structure of stories." He asks: So "How can we hack today's story into something that reflects the needs of today's news consumers and publishers, integrates the vast amounts of content and data being created online, and generally leverages the opportunities the Web has created?" Nieman Labs, July 2011 http://www.niemanlab.org/2011/07/vadim-lavrusik-five-key-building-blocks-to-incorporate-as-were-rethinking-the-structure-of-stories/
4. Vadim Lavrusik, Interview with Author. August 16, 2011.
5. Bill Calder, Interview with Shel Holtz, on "For Immediate Release" a weekly podcast about PR and technology. June 29, 2011.
6. Bill Calder, Interview with Author. August, 2011.
7. Chris Perry, "Do Organizations Need a Chief Content Officer?" *Forbes*. October 27, 2011.
8. Pew Research Center, State of the News Media Report, 2011. The study states that "Among the major sectors, only newspapers suffered continued revenue declines last year—an unmistakable sign that the structural economic problems facing newspapers are more severe than those of other media. When the final tallies are in, we estimate 1,000 to 1,500 more newsroom jobs will have been lost." http://pewresearch.org/pubs/1924/state-of-the-news-media-2011
9. ProPublica (www.propublica.org) is a newsroom built around issues and stories with a 'moral force' producing journalism "that shines a light on exploitation of the weak by the strong."

CHAPTER 24—Can You Hear Me...Now?

1. Maggie Jackson, *Distracted*. Prometheus Books, October 2009.
2. You could read the letter from Boeing, here: http://www.johnwinsor.com/.a/6a00

NOTES

3. Interview with Dr. Cyndi Laurin, on a radio show I co-hosted called "Your Triple Bottom Line."
4. More about the Boeing letter could be found at John Windsor's blog post, of April 26, 2010 at http://www.johnwinsor.com
5. John Windsor's blog post, updated readers on the developments. "Harry and Boeing: The Update." http://www.johnwinsor.com May 4, 2010.
6. Todd Blecher, quoted by Stephanie Clifford, "Boeing's Social-Media Lesson." *The New York Times*. May 3, 2010.
7. Avinash Kaushek's blog, *Occam's Razor* (www.kaushik.net) is a wonderful resource. He has two best-selling books, *Web Analytics 2.0*, and *Web Analytics: An Hour A Day*. Proceeds from both books are donated to The Smile Train, Doctors Without Borders, and Ekal Vidyalaya.
8. "Malcolm Brandt," like most employees in many organizations, is not authorized to speak to reporters or disclose work-related conditions. Interview with Author. November, 2011.
9. The video that got the Comcast's attention could be viewed here: http://youtu.be/CvVp7b5gzqU [accessed on March 14, 2012].
10. Jason Baer and Amber Naslund. *The Now Revolution*, John Wiley & Sons, 2011.
11. "United Breaks Guitars," a music video by Dave Carroll includes rich detail about his complaint, and the refusal of United Airlines to listen to him. It was uploaded on July 6, 2009, and now has a Wikipedia entry that documents the event even further.
12. 'United Song 2' by Dave Carroll was uploaded on August 17, 2010. It was soon followed by 'United Song 3.' To rub it in further, at the end of the music video, 'United Song 2,' after the credits roll, there is an aerial view of the scene as the musicians exit the scene. The guitar remains on the grass, and after 10 seconds, from the bottom left of the screen a white van, with United markings enters, and proceeds to drive over the guitar, crushing it. View the video here: http://www.youtube.com/watch?v=h-UoERHaSQg&feature=relmfu
13. The program was a huge success for Verizon Wireless. Net customers grew 10% to 32.5 million in 2002 vs. 2001 and 15% more to 37.5 million in 2003. Customer turnover, a major expense referred to as "churn" in the business, is at 1.8%, down from more than 2.5% in 2000, according to technology tracking firm The Yankee Group. *USA Today*, Feb 23, 2004.
14. "Verizon disconnects 'Can You Hear Me Now?' guy." *Reuters.com*, April 14, 2011. Marcarelli's initial five-year contract forbade him from talking about his job or from taking any other acting gigs.
15. Paul Gillin, *The New Influencers: A Marketer's Guide to the New Social Media*. Linden Publishing, 2007.
16. I simultaneously blogged about it, and within a few hours, another company representative, Brandon Disney commented on the blog with a response. "If we failed to deliver on that, then I will make sure we make it right. Feel free to contact me via email with the best way to reach you and we'll get to the bottom of things." See entire post here: www.hoipolloireport.com, on 5 Jan, 2011.
17. Listen to his genuine apology and offer to make up for the poor service. I posted

this audio clip on my blog. http://hoipolloi.files.wordpress.com/2011/01/robert_datadoctors_your3bl_edits.mp3

AFTERWORD—What for the Talking?
1. Katy Steinmetz, "Single people are all thumbs." *Time*, August 27, 2012.

Angelo Fernando has worked in business communication for the past 25 years. Throughout his career he's written about the big shifts he's experienced in the industry: Leaving top-down advertising he worked in bottom-up marketing communications; trained in broadcasting in the late eighties, he turned to podcasting, and co-hosted a live radio-show. A technology columnist for print media, he began blogging in 2004. An award-winning writer, and contributing editor to a business magazine, Angelo is now an elementary school teacher and robotics coach. He lives with his wife and two children in Gilbert, Arizona.

Made in the USA
Charleston, SC
05 May 2013